W9-AAZ-939

HEALED & SET FREE BIBLE STUDY

Tammy Brown

"Stories of real people, real hurts, real healing, and a real SAVIOR"

What Readers are Saying...

"I wanted to write to let you know that I am pleased to lead women through the **Healed and Set Free Bible** study.

My husband, Pastor Kurt and I have looked at a great deal of similar studies, and this is the best one we've come across!

For 3 reasons:

1. Tammy's personal triumph is an incredible story of Christ's transforming power. Because she was willing to share something so personal, others can know that she relates to them and their hurts. Tammy's desire to glorify Him through it is admirable.

2. It's biblical! Modern psychology has told so many that they behave a certain way because of their circumstances. So many women I talk with believe the lie that their past controls them; they believe they are doomed to a hopeless life as a response to past events. But love hopes all things "day by day and choice by choice." Healed and Set Free study gives tremendous hope through Christ and His love and His enduring, eternal word.

3. **Healed and Set Free** covers a multitude of issues using the same 4 powerful tools.

As I read Tammy's story I wept at God's marvelous healing power and I praise Him for her obedience to produce this material."

Pastors wife , Ohio

"PRAISE GOD! God is really using **Healed & Set Free** to bring women into a closer fellowship with Jesus. I am a volunteer counselor for a non-profit group in Sacramento, WEAVE (Women Escaping a Violent Environment). I thought this study would be good for me to give to victims of domestic violence. I felt I should complete the study before I started recommending it to others. Well, to make a long story short, I needed to be "Healed and Set Free" from a history of beatings from my first husband, as well as promiscuity, alcohol abuse, rape, abortion, and divorce (all before the age of 20 - I'm 38 now). I knew I had been through a lot in my life, but I didn't know I needed to give all those past hurts and the anger to the Lord. When I did, I was able to live, really live, for the first time in my Christian life.

"I heard the Lord call to my heart to start a study. I spoke with my pastor, and he said to go for it! I did, and now there is a study on Tuesday evenings at our church. Last night 3 of the ladies revealed they gave their hurts and anger to the Lord and are beginning to walk in victory, they who have been Christians most of their lives."

Set Free to Really Live The Christian Life, California

> *"To give you a future and a hope..."*
> *Jeremiah 29:11*

What Readers are Saying...

"The **Healed & Set Free Bible Study** has turned out to be a wonderful blessing for all of us participating. Satan kept whispering lies in my ears. He tried to tell me that I could not lead other women through this study. I began praying for God's help and it is WONDERFUL. God is doing a work in my life as well as the ladies in this group study. I am personally able to put pieces of my life back together that had been fragmented. All of God's principles are put together in a way that we are all able to apply them to our own unique situations. We have grown in love for each other, and can't wait to meet each week to get into **Healed & Set Free**. God is so good and He is so faithful to move us forward and heal our hearts when they are crippled."

         My Crippled Heart Has Been Healed ~ Cheryl, Minnesota

---

"As I was taking the **Healed & Set Free Bible Study**, I was continually reminded in each chapter that I needed to SEE what was really going on in my heart and get real with the hurts that still lingered. As I completed the Bible study homework, God began to show me that my heart had a junk drawer where I kept all my pain over the years. Most homes have a junk drawer, a drawer to throw odds and ends such as screwdrivers, pencils, pens, and all the items you don't know where to put. I didn't realize that I had been keeping a junk drawer in my heart ever since my stepfather had sexually abused me at a very young age. Throughout my life, I learned to put broken trusts, painful memories, and hurts that still lingered into the junk drawer of my heart. My heart became filled with unforgiveness, bitterness, and wrongs that others had committed against me. After being a Christian for over 20 years, I was now being faced with the contents of my hearts junk drawer. I needed to clean out the drawer. **Healed & Set Free** gave me the tools to clean out the junk drawer in my heart. I now have a heart that has been **Healed & Set Free**, and I know how to keep it that way. I lead other women through this **Healed & Set Free Bible Study**, to comfort them with God's truth and love."

         I Received the Tools I Needed to Become Healed & Set Free ~ Debbie, Idaho

---

"Watching the Lord heal and comfort my mother's heart made me wonder if he could do the same for me. I had just rededicated my life to Christ. However, I still hung onto my "justified pain and anger". I was hurting so bad my heart had been lied to by so many guys so many times. I lived in fear of getting close to someone because to me, getting close meant getting hurt and walked over. I was sick of hurting and not trusting anyone. I wanted to be freed from my past but I didn't know how.

"So I signed up to be "**Healed & Set Free**". I thought signing up and going to the study would be enough to heal my heart. It wasn't! I needed to actively choose to apply the tools and the word to my own life. When I realized I couldn't do it on my own, I needed to truly let Jesus heal me after I applied the things I learned in the study to my heart, that is when I became totally aware of God's awesome power. Being healed was an awesome experience. The Lord rescued me from MYSELF. HE was preparing my heart to love again. I was amazed.

"He is continually working in my life. Being healed doesn't promise me I'll never hurt or fall down again. It does, however, cause me to see how much I truly need a Savior to save me from falling."

         Teen Girl, Idaho

HEALED & SET FREE

...from lingering hurts

Tammy Brown

Calvary Chapel churches are an international non-denominational fellowship of believers in Jesus Christ. Our mission is to reach, disciple, and equip people to know Jesus Christ and to make Him known through successive generations.

Healed and Set Free is a ministry of Calvary Chapel of Idaho Falls, Idaho.

Healed and Set Free is a Bible study written to help people in bondage to painful hurts that still linger, by teaching Biblical truths to apply to their lives so Jesus Christ can set them free.

© Copyright 2000, © Copyright 1998 by Tammy Brown

All rights reserved. No part of this Bible study may be reproduced in any form without written permission from Calvary Chapel of Idaho Falls.

All scripture quotations, unless otherwise indicated, are taken from the *New King James Version*, © Copyright 1982 by Thomas Nelson, Inc. Used by permission. All rights reserved.

Brown, Tammy
      Healed and Set Free: A Bible Study/ by Tammy Brown
      Cover title: **Healed and Set Free**

ISBN LOG NUMBER
0-9704770-0-7

Formatting and graphic designs, Printcraft Press, Idaho Falls, Idaho

Printed in the United States of America

The spirit of man will sustain him in sickness, but who can bear a borken spirit?

Proverbs 18:14

The Lord is near to those who have a broken heart and saves such as have a contrite spirit.

Psalms 34:18

TO ORDER THE HEALED AND SET FREE
BIBLE STUDY WORKBOOK

or

LEADER'S GUIDE
Call 208-524-4747

or

Write to:
Calvary Chapel of Idaho Falls
P.O. Box 52243, Idaho Falls, ID 83405

To Rick with love eternal

Contents

You shall know the truth, and the truth shall make you free. John 8: 32

A Warm Thank You To:

First to my great Savior Christ Jesus:

My eternal thankfulness for Your Truth, Your Word, and Your Healing power. Which have opened the shackles so we may be Healed and Set Free.

And to my Family:

To my husband Rick -
I am grateful for your prayers, godly wisdom, patience and encouragement. I couldn't have done this without your support. I love you Sweetness.

Caleb and Jessica -
Two children who have taken my heart hostage. My love and thanks for all your hugs and smiles of love.

To my Parents Ron & Lara Davis-
I am so blessed to have your constant source of encouragement and love.

And to my church family at Calvary Chapel:

A pastor's wife could not ask for a more supportive and responsive flock of committed believers.

Gordon and Roxanne Boyle -
for your undivided heart toward Christ and your love for our family.

Denise Landis -
for your typing and encouragement .

Jonnie Landis , Frosty Wilson, Cheryl Lewis, Steve James, Debbie and Ray Fury. -
for your joyful hearts to edit this work.

David Elder -
for your servants heart and professional work on the final touches of the formatting and graphics.

Why Healed & Set Free Was Written

Healed & Set Free was formed out of a God-given desire to see people freed from the shackles of a painful past. I would like to update you on how **Healed and Set Free** began. Shortly after our women's retreat in 1998 two precious Christian women approached me with serious deep-rooted problems and hurts. One of these ladies shared her story of repeated sexual abuse by her three brothers and her fear of pregnancy as a result of her abuse at the age of twelve and the battle she faced daily with bulimia. The other shared that she was in great bondage to anorexia, an all too common eating disorder. As we prayed and cried together my heart was broken for both of them. I knew full well exactly what kind of pain these women were going through. It was shortly there-after that the Lord strengthened and guided me to develop the Bible study Healed and Set Free. I wanted to comfort these women and others like them with the comfort I had received from the Lord after my own healing process from my painful past. As a victim of childhood sexual abuse, date rape, and bulimia the Lord was faithful to move me forward and to heal my broken heart. This Bible study is designed to help women, teens, and couples move forward through our healer, Christ Jesus.

We know it is Satan's ministry to keep people in shackles. One by one, as each person gets real with God, His love and truth opens those painful shackles.

We all live in a fallen world where sin abounds and hurts and pains from others can affect our lives if we let them. Satan continually tries to accuse and discourage us. However, God gives us exactly what we need in order to grow and move toward Him and move away from the destruction Satan desires to do in our lives.

Dedicated To :

Derra, Debbie, Frosty, Cheryl, Pam, Gina, Maurette, Vickie, Val, Shawna, Jacqi, Leah, Jeanette, Ami, Denise, Jody, Shawna, Sue, Gina, Sheila, Teresa, Erika, Tammy, Janae, Jenny, Suzie, Pam, Kasey, Cheryl, Tracey, Susan, Jonnie, Becky, Renee, Suzie, Katherine.

And to all

Who have stepped out in courage to open their hearts up to the true Healer and let Him set them free from their shackles of anger, shame, heartbreak and tears.

Suggestions For Individual Study

The *Healed and Set Free Bible study* is "user friendly" It has been designed so that any one can use it regardless of whether or not they can get around in their bible or if they don't even own a bible. We don't want this to be an issue that would stop any one from completing this study. All of the Bible verses are typed right in the study so no one will have to put their study on a shelf because they couldn't get around in their Bible. A Bible scholar or an unsaved person can feel the freedom to complete this study and receive a fresh beginning.

1. Begin each study with prayer. Ask God to help you understand the passage and to apply it to your life.

2. Develop daily quiet times with the Lord. Read and reread the passage (s). You must know what the passage says before you can understand what it means and how it applies to you.

3. This study has been structured so there are daily questions with space provided for your answers. There may be questions where the Lord prompts you to write more than available space allows. It will be very beneficial for you to keep a spiral notebook handy. You may want to jot down your thoughts, insights and prayers, asked or answered. This Bible study has proven most fruitful when the individual completes the daily questions and Bible study.

Quiet time with God is not just one more chore that you can't manage.

Just come to Him one day at a time to offer Him whatever is troubling your heart.

My devotional time is not a gift I give to God.
My devotional time is a gift God gives to me.

Suggestions For Group Study

1. Come to the study prepared. Careful preparation will greatly enrich your time in-group discussion.

2. The group meets once a week, with the members having answered their questions beforehand.

3. The group discussion leader will not be lecturing but will encourage people to keep focused on the study and on how God is working in their lives and what they have learned in the passage. The leader will encourage discussion from all who are ready to share. Think through and pray about your answers and insights before sharing with your group.

4. Some will feel comfortable sharing their history while others will prefer to keep details private. Some will feel comfortable praying out loud while others won't. This study is to encourage you to feel comfortable sharing your true self, your hurts, your sins, and your fears with God. You will never be forced into sharing with your group, although when you share from the insights God has given you, your whole group will benefit.

5. Stick to the passage being studied. Base your answers on the verses being discussed.

6. Try to be sensitive to the other members of the group. Listen attentively when they speak, and encourage whenever you can.

7. Be careful not to dominate the discussion. It's important that you participate! But allow others to have equal time.

8. As you begin this study of God's Word, you will be given many opportunities to see God's healing in progress in your own life and in the lives of others. We will be obedient to God's word as we encourage and comfort one another, and cry and rejoice together in this journey to be Healed and Set Free.

9. If you are the discussion leader, you will find additional suggestions and helpful ideas in the **Healed and Set Free** Leader's guide that can be ordered through Calvary Chapel of Idaho Falls (208) 524-4747

✿ AGAPE LOVE:

The commitment I make to each individual in our group will be in the spirit of God's love that says, "Nothing you say or do will make me stop loving you."

> *No one has seen God at any time. If we love one another, God abides in us, and His love has been perfected in us. 1 John 4:12*

> *But above all these things put on love, which is the bond of perfection. And let the peace of God rule in your hearts, to which also you were called in one body; and be thankful. Colossians 3:14-15*

✿ PRAYER:

I will pray for each member of our group consistently.

> *Likewise the Spirit also helps in our weaknesses. For we do not know what we should pray for as we ought, but the Spirit Himself makes intercession for us with groanings which cannot be uttered. Romans 8:26*

✿ CONFIDENTIALITY:

I understand other points in this covenant are only possible in the security of a relationship of trust.

> I will make the commitment to our group to share NOTHING outside our group that has been shared inside our group, including the names of those in our group, not even with my spouse or best friend.

> *A talebearer reveals secrets, But he who is of a faithful spirit conceals a matter. Where there is no counsel, the people fall; But in the multitude of counselors there is safety. Proverbs 11:13-14*

✿ OPENNESS:

I understand I cannot know you and you cannot know me unless we tell each other who we are. I will make the commitment to tell you who I am, in my strengths and in my weaknesses.

> *Confess your trespasses to one another, and pray for one another, that you may be healed. The effective, fervent prayer of a righteous man avails much. James 5:16*

✿ SENSITIVITY:

I will ask God to make me sensitive to the needs of each person in our group. I will make the commitment to consciously LISTEN to each person each time they speak, whether in words, actions or attitudes.

> *Let nothing be done through selfish ambition or conceit, but in lowliness of mind let each esteem others better than himself. Let each of you look out not only for his own interests, but also for the interests of others. Philippians 2:3-4*

☞ HONESTY:

I understand speaking the truth in love is both positive and constructive unto bodily growth. I will allow God to use me in our group's growth process by telling you when I agree and when I disagree.

> *But, speaking the truth in love, may grow up in all things into Him who is the head; Christ; Ephesians 4:15*

☞ ACCOUNTABILITY:

It is my conviction that God has placed me in our group for building up the Body of Christ. From time to time it will be necessary for me to seek the mind of the Lord through the counsel and advice of those in our group. I will accept the responsibility for their counsel and advice and report to them what I have done with their collective wisdom.

> *Where there is no counsel, the people fall; But in the multitude of counselors there is safety. Proverbs 11:14*

Signature and Date _____

- **Do you have a true desire to get real with God?**

  Yes or No

- **Have you decided you can no longer live the way you've been living?**

  Yes or No

- **Are you ready to have hope win out over despair?**

  Yes or No

- **Have you lost your perspective: In your marriage, with your children or in other relationships?**

  Yes or No

- **Are you ready to make the time each day to spend in the Healed and Set Free Bible study?**

  Yes or No

"First as a child, then as a new Christian, then later as a Pastor's wife, I tried to forget the pain that was too deep for words, but the emotional memories kept me in shackles..."

*T*he private overwhelming memories of repeated sexual abuse in my early childhood, then later being date raped as a teenage virgin, and my later struggles with bulimia caused me to suffer in silence. I felt like a big zero, and my life seemed to be in tatters. Little by little, my lingering hurts began to possess me, affecting my outlook on life, my marriage, my approach to parenting, and my ministry as a Pastor's wife. I had become a prisoner to the unacceptable hurts, that lingered in my heart, causing my family to also be in shackles. The Bible say in Proverbs 14: 1, Every wise woman builds her house, but the foolish pulls it down with her hands. Suddenly, I was thrown onto a path of reality. I had to face the fact that I was a self-destructive woman going nowhere in life. I had to "get real" with who I was and who I was becoming. Satan's evil desire was to keep me in those painful shackles from paralyzing shame, out of control anger, and deep seeded bitterness that had hardened my heart and gotten in the way of my future and the happiness God had planned for me.

I had doubts of ever experiencing real freedom from the emotional turmoil I had lived with for over 20 years. I then learned that God's open arms had been there the entire time ready to heal and set me free. I embraced those open arms and trusted Him with my pain too deep for words. It was not until I opened my hidden heart and decided to "get real" with God where the hurts still lingered and stopped giving a false performance to God that I learned life-changing TOOLS.

**"For the first time,
I'm Healed & Set Free
to live, really live
the abundant life..."**

God has been faithful to move me forward by showing me four simple yet powerful TOOLS to unlock the shackles from the shame, anger and hollow feelings that unacceptable hurts bring. They are {SEE, GIVE, FORGIVE, FORGET, and BE SET FREE} Christ Jesus, my Savior taught me that He is the only one that heals the brokenhearted. It's not ourselves or ungodly counsel. The Bible says, He heals the brokenhearted and binds up their wounds. His love and truth has set me completely free from the shackles that once enslaved my soul to the unacceptable hurts left over in my heart. Satan works through hurt, guilt and fear, to steal, kill and destroy lives. Christ has come to offer us the abundant life. To get out of the shackles we have to WANT to get out of the shackles, as well as to have the True Healer release us from them. Invite Him into the dark room where you hide your pain. Pray and ask Christ to show you the hidden hurts that need to be healed.

Set free in Christ,

Tammy Brown

Thinking about the PAST

will never change the PAST, But you can change your FUTURE

and Be SET FREE from your PAST hurts that linger in your heart.

About the
Author

*T*ammy is the wife of senior Pastor Rick Brown and a homemaker. She and her husband, Rick, are parents of two children, Caleb and Jessica. They live in Idaho Falls, Idaho. The Lord led the Browns to establish two Calvary Chapel churches in eastern Idaho, as well as a Christian school, Calvary Christian Academy. In the summer of 1998, God led Tammy to write *Healed and Set Free* so that she might comfort hurting people with the comfort she has received from God, learning to forgive the unacceptable. She has a God-given desire to see others set free from the heartaches and hurts from the past through God's truth and love. Tammy's private story of God's healing in her life is told throughout **Healed and Set Free**, along with the painful stories shared by many women who have completed **Healed and Set Free** Bible Study.

Healed and Set Free

A Pure white dove, You were learning to fly.
Crippled in flight, You were left to die.

No bandage or brace could heal the wound.
As you looked ahead, You felt you were doomed.

It is said God knows when even a sparrow falls.
He knew you were hurt, He answered your calls.
The bondage was removed and you now are free.

For a moment I thought you no longer needed me.
By grace God showed me, She's not saying good-bye.
She's spreading her wings and learning to fly.

So spread your wings and fly my dove.
We've truly been blessed with
God's Pure Love.

Written by Dean Jay,
dedicated to his wife Tracey

Chapter 1

Getting Real With God
Where I Need Healing

*All things are naked and
open to the eyes of Him to
whom we must give
account.*

Hebrews 4:13

Getting Started...

Dear friend,

Okay, I know what you're thinking. "I'll just skip these first few pages with all this reading and get right to the questions." Well, hold on. Just wait. This reading is preparation for what you are about to learn in this Bible study.

This is not a fast food restaurant. Run in, quickly place the order, inhale our food and run out to the next event.

Reading this Bible study is like hanging out with a best girl friend. (No, you will never take a Bible study out to a garage sale but when you read a Bible study, you do spend time alone and give it your undivided attention.) I hope you're not the type that's a fair weather friend. The type who reads to the second chapter of a book or Bible study, and then dumps it. If you are, you probably won't get much out of this one. As with a meaningful friendship, reading this Bible study requires a certain level of commitment - a commitment to think, get real with God, be honest with yourself, and actively apply the healing tools to your life.

Do you find yourself saying, "I want to be an example for Christ, I want my words and my actions to match." But how, on earth, do I do that when my heart is filled with lingering pain I can't seem to get past, no matter how hard I try?" "Does anyone else out there struggle with hurts from the past????"

First things first dear friend, you need to know you're not the only one that has struggled with lingering hurts. You see, for a LONG, LONG time I was convinced I was the ONLY one suffering in silence. Okay, now I know Satan had one up on me. Ahhh, the joke was on me. Now its time to EXPOSE those lies. This is no joke or game when we are in shackles to hurt. Not one person is able to escape hurts in this fallen world we live in. It doesn't matter if your smart, poor, middle class, or rich, you have a wall full of awards or no awards, you are raised in a Brady bunch home, or raised with an ex-convict as a stepfather. Hurt has touched all of our lives in one form or another.

The bad news is hurts can cripple, damage and paralyze our mind and soul, creating a person we don't want to be.

Lingering hurts such as:

- Sexual abuse
- Physical abuse
- Shame
- Divorce
- Verbal abuse
- Rape
- Betrayed by someone you trusted
- Guilt
- Rejection - by a family member or brother or sister in Christ
- Cruel words hurled to cut deep into your heart

Now that we know the bad news let's get to the good news. We don't have to continue to live an empty, hopeless, hurting life. We can live a victorious life in Christ, even after unacceptable hurts. Oh really, how do we do that when the hurt is so deep? One incredible reason: we have a *LOVING, POWERFUL GOD* that is faithful to move us forward and HEAL our hearts when we are crippled. Okay, now God will be faithful to do His part, but we do have some personal responsibility. Responsibility? Yes responsibility. The Tools to Freedom will only *"SET YOU FREE"* when you apply them to your heart (rather than everyone around you). *He heals the brokenhearted and binds up their wounds. Psalms 147:3.*

Okay Girl, are you ready to learn four tools that will refresh your soul, bring healing to a crippled heart, and renew your mind in the word of God? It's awesome to know the truth, because the truth is what will set us free. *Therefore, if the Son makes you free, you shall be free indeed. John 8:32-36*

You and I will step by step learn about: **SEE, GIVE, FORGIVE, FORGET** so we **BECOME SET FREE.** Getting real with God is the first step you need to take as you learn to use the tools to become **Healed and Set Free.** It is a process that does not happen overnight. So don't get down or discouraged. This may be a painful journey, but the journey will give you freedom if you don't give up.

God's Invitation to come to Him

Come to Me *all you who labor and are heavy laden and I will give you rest. Take my yoke upon you and learn from Me, for I am gentle and lowly in heart and you will find rest for your souls. For My yoke is easy and My burden is light." Matthew 11:28-30*

Tools To Become Set Free

- **Tool #1 "SEE ":** Learn how I must **SEE** the truth about what is in my heart, so I'm not defiled.

  Looking carefully lest anyone fall short of the grace of God; lest any root of bitterness springing up cause trouble, and by this many become defiled. Hebrew 12:15.

- **Tool #2 "GIVE":** Learn how I must **GIVE** the sin in repentance, knowing Christ is waiting to take it. (I must be sorry enough to change and choose to go God's way over my own way.)

  For godly sorrow produces repentance leading to salvation, not to be regretted; but the sorrow of the world produces death. 2 Corinthians 7:10

- **Tool #3 "FORGIVE":** Learn how I must **FORGIVE**, as I am forgiven by Christ. (Forgiving those that hurt, bruised, wronged, hurt, rejected, betrayed, or harmed me whether unintentionally or deliberately.) Ask God to Forgive you for holding unforgiveness and know that He will.

  Bearing with one another, and forgiving one another, if anyone has a complaint against another; even as Christ forgave you, so you also must do. Colossians 3:13

- **Tool #4 "FORGET":** Learn how I must **FORGET** by remembering to no longer dwell on the hurt. (Not dwelling on painful reminders, such as phrases, smells, places, songs, and comments, <u>putting my mind on the higher calling Christ Jesus</u> has for me.)

  Brethren, I do not count myself to have apprehended; but one thing I do, forgetting those things which are behind and reaching forward to those things which are ahead. Philippians 3:13.

BECOME SET FREE: Learn how Christ will open the shackles from my past hurts showing me the truth so I can become a cleansed vessel that is Healed and Set Free.

You shall know the truth, and the truth shall make you free. Therefore, if the Son makes you free, you shall be free indeed. John 8:32-36.

> (*Christ Jesus, help me* **SEE** *what wounds need the Healer to set me Free.*) *The Lord is near to those who have a BROKEN HEART and saves such as have a contrite spirit. Psalms 34:18*

What comes first, SEE or FORGET? *(When the hurt is so deep)*

Notice that the first tool is **SEE**. It is not **FORGET**. Many times we just want to jump ahead to FORGET because the hurt is so painful that we want to push it away from our hearts and minds, erasing it from our lives. But it does not work in that order. For example, you cannot bake a cake without first taking the time and steps to measure and mix up the ingredients. It is then that you are ready to put the cake batter in a pan and bake your cake. If you decided to skip the first steps and jump ahead because you don't have the time or the ingredients, you will end up with an "EMPTY, BURNED" pan. If we try to FORGET our pain before we first take the time and steps to SEE what is left over in our hearts, we will come up "EMPTY and BURNED" without ever being Healed and Set Free.

Satan wants to keep you in Shackles

Some of us have been shackled down with burdens of guilt, shame, bitterness, fear, and discouragement since childhood. We are tired of trying to stand, let alone walk under such a heavy load. One thing you need to know is hurt doesn't just go away by itself. God is right there ready to heal your broken heart. If we all put on a smile and pretend nothing bothers us, we are lying to God and ourselves. This allows Satan to keep us in shackles to those lingering hurts. You must **SEE** what is affecting you today from your past so you can **BE SET FREE.** Examine your heart, examine your way of thinking and compare it to God's way of thinking. Only the truth will set you free. AMEN!

AUTHOR'S REFLECTION
Why Couldn't I Forget The Defiling Memories?

Every night for years I would watch the dark, chilling shadows creep past my window from the lights of passing cars. I would lay there and wonder if he was coming to get me, to hurt me one more time or even kill me. As I lay in bed at the age of seven, scared to fall asleep I would watch the shadows on my window and want so desperately to run to my parent's room. I would plan over and over in my mind how I would tell my Mom how my uncle would take me to his secret, dark places when she would drop me off to play with my cousins. The haunting words from my uncle would flood my mind, "I will kill your parents if they ever find out." Then the shameful words," If your parents ever find out what a dirty little girl you are they will be so ashamed of you." I had been silenced in shame, fear and torment. Each time my old, overweight and slightly bald uncle would come near me I would run as fast as I could from him screaming in silence.

But somehow he managed to have me once again on the cold, dark, dirty garage floor with walls covered in pornography as he engaged in sexual acts that would continue to haunt me and emotionally cripple me for the next twenty years.

Childhood is a time of special innocence. Not yet acquiring adult defense mechanisms, children respond to their world with delightful honesty and trusting those around them. My journey of childhood trust and innocence abruptly came to and end at the tender age of seven, when I learned the meaning of fear, shame, hate, and suffering in silence with a shattered, fragmented heart. From that moment, I tried to Forget time and time again those emotional defiling memories. I continued on this path to put this behind me, first as a child, then as a new Christian, and later as a Pastor's wife. I tried to FORGET the pain too deep for words, but the emotional memories kept me in the shackles of shame, anger and deep seeded bitterness that grew over the years.

The over-whelming memories of repeated sexual abuse in my childhood by my uncle and his sons and then later being date raped as a teenage virgin kept me a prisoner to my past. This affected my marriage and my outlook on life, hardening my heart and getting in the way of the future and the happiness God had planned for me. I had to face that I was a self-destructive woman going nowhere in life. I had to "get real" with who I was and who I was becoming. I believed the day I gave my life to Christ would be the day my heartache and all that troubled my mind would just INSTANTLY vanish. I loved Christ with all my heart. *Why* was all the pain still filling my mind? *Why* was all the hate still in my heart? *Why* couldn't I FORGET? *Why* couldn't I put this behind me?

As I looked around at other Christians no one seemed to have any problems with lingering hurts from their past. I became even more isolated and confused. I thought I was the only one who would always have all these memories troubling my mind. I thought that I would continue to live in this state of anger, shame and phoniness, pretending like it didn't bother me, but in fact I continued to suffer in silence.

I could no longer walk under such a heavy load. For the first time, I learned that my problem was that I was trying to **FORGET**. I've learned, I needed God to help me **SEE** what had defiled my heart and mind. What was REALLY left over in my heart towards those that had violated me from the past and those that had wronged me along the way. I needed to open my heart to the truth in order to be Healed and Set Free. I've experienced true healing and freedom from His love and truth and you can too. *"Come to Me, all you who labor and are heavy laden, and I will give you rest." Matthew 11:28.* Jesus is saying, come to Me and I will give your soul rest and freedom from the painful burdens we try to carry. We can learn to lay them at His feet.

> **It's Satan's evil desire to keep anyone he can in painful shackles caused from unacceptable hurts that still linger causing many to suffer in silence.**

Getting Real with God

It's time to get real with God. Be honest with God about your resentment, your bitterness, your jealousy, your hatred, your fears and your shame. He already knows about it. He has seen it all. You cannot give a false performance for God. You may act like everything is okay. You may even give a sterling performance to the world, but the rough, rocky, painful road that you walk cannot be hidden from God. He knows about the pain, the shame and the guilt, because He has already carried it all. There's no reason for you to carry it any longer … Is there?

God is truth and only the truth can set you free.

What hurts do you still have?

You can either embrace the truth and let go of the burdens you carry, or carry your burdens and reject the truth and the freedom it brings.

Will hope win out over Despair? The choice is yours.

Would You Like to KNOW GOD and Receive LIFE EVERLASTING?

In order to GET REAL with GOD you need to receive Christ into your heart as your Savoir

God's Invitation to come to Him

Follow after Christ Jesus. From the cross He was saying I love you, I love you, I love you. I love you enough to die for all your sins and take care of you. God loves you and created you to know Him personally now and save you're soul from death. After your lifeless body is in the coffin with weeds growing up around the headstone, other people's lives get so busy they don't even bother to stop by.

Remember, it really does not matter. Why? Because Jesus Christ will have your soul forever. He will take care of it throughout eternity with unfailing love in heaven. But you are the only one that can make that decision to follow Christ. If you desire to find your life in Christ today, just pray the life-changing prayer that follows to SEE your need for a Savior.

How to Receive Christ and Have Everlasting Life

a. Admit you are a sinner in need of a Savior.

b. Be willing to repent by turning from your sins.

c. Believe that Jesus Christ died for you on the cross and rose from the grave.

d. Through prayer, invite Jesus Christ to come in and control your life through the Holy Spirit, receiving Him as your Lord and Savior.

What to Pray:

Dear Lord Jesus,

I know I am a sinner and need Your forgiveness. I want to turn from my sins. I believe You died for my sins. I now invite You to come into my heart and life. I want to trust and follow You as my Lord and Savior.

In Jesus' name, Amen.

Welcome to God's family. You now belong to Him.

This is just the beginning of a wonderful new life in Christ. To deepen this relationship you should:

- Read your Bible every day to know Christ better.
- Talk to God in prayer every day.
- Tell others about Christ.
- Worship, fellowship and serve with other Christians in a church where Christ is reached.
- God has a plan and purpose for every believer. Open your arms of God's love and truth to others.

Questions/Answers about Everlasting Life

🌹**Question:** In whom must you believe to avoid perishing and have eternal life?

Answer: *That whoever believes in Him (Christ Jesus) should not perish but have eternal life. John 3:1*

🌹**Question:** Why was Christ offered?

Answer: *So Christ was offered once to bear the sins of many. To those who eagerly wait for Him He will appear a second time, apart from sin, for salvation. Hebrew 9:28*

🌹**Question:** Why did God give His only begotten Son?

Answer: *"For God so loved the world that He gave His only begotten Son, that whoever believes in Him should not perish but have everlasting life." John 3:16*

🌹**Question:** What is the way to eternity in heaven? What is the truth?

Answer: *Jesus said to him, "I am the way, the truth, and the life. No one comes to the Father except through Me." John 14:6*

🌹**Question:** What does God promise that you will lose if you follow anything other than Jesus Christ, who was sacrificed for your sins?

Answer: *"For whoever desires to save his life will lose it, but whoever loses his life for My sake will find it. For what profit is it to a man if he gains the whole world, and loses his own soul? Or what will a man give in exchange for his soul?" Matthew 16:25-26*

> *Bow your heart before Christ in prayer before answering the questions. Ask Christ Jesus to help you **SEE** what wounds need the Healer to set you Free.*

1. Write down the ways Satan has come to **STEAL**, **KILL** and **DESTROY** in your life.

   The Thief does not come Except to Steal, and to Kill, and to Destroy. *John 10:10.*

    a. What has been STOLEN? _____

    b. What has been KILLED? _____

    c. What has been DESTROYED? _____

It's Satan's evil desire to keep anyone he can in painful shackles caused from unacceptable hurts that still linger causing many to suffer in silence. God's love is BIGGER than all of our hurts and fears.

The Results of the Ways Satan has Come to STEAL, KILL and DESTROY in Tammy Brown's Life.

*The Thief does not come Except to **Steal**, and to **Kill**, and to **Destroy**. John 10:10.*

    a. Tammy's innocence had been STOLEN as a child.

    b. Tammy's dreams of being a virgin bride had been KILLED as a teenager.

    c. Then Tammy's Spirit was being DESTROYED with shame, resentment, unforgiveness, and wanting to get even. As a result she suffered in silence for over 20 years.

SEE, GIVE, FORGIVE, FORGET, BE SET FREE

Come to Me all you who labor and are heavy laden, and I will give you rest. Take my yoke upon you and learn from Me, for I am gentle and lowly in heart and you will find rest for your souls. For My yoke is easy and My burden is light. Matthew 11:28-30

DAY 2

God, give me a heart to SEE the truth about what has me in shackles today, keeping me in bondage to my past. *The spirit of a man will sustain him in*

God Heals the Brokenhearted

He heals the brokenhearted and binds up their wounds. Psalms 147:3.

1. *Healed* Means ~ mend, get better, put right, restore, cure, cause to heal or be healed; Are you ready to open up All of your heart to the only one that can Heal your heart? Do you desire to be *Healed and Set Free?*

2. Lets take a look at *Hebrews 12:12, Therefore* **strengthen the hands which hangs down,** *and the feeble knees, and make straight paths for your feet, so that what is* **lame** *may not be* **dislocated, but rather be healed.**

3. Look up the word **lame** in the dictionary and write it out.

4. Write down the ways the unacceptable hurts that linger cause your heart and mind to be *lame?*

_____

_____

_____

_____

_____

_____

_____

_____

_____

_____

_____

_____

_____

_____

_____

_____

_____

Set Free at Last

I came to the **Healed and Set Free** Bible study with pretty dim hopes of ever changing the bitter woman I had become inside. During our first session I confessed that I was not the type of person to open up and dig out all the hurt and ugliness within my heart. Not to mention forgive myself for all the sins that followed from lack of self-control! Little did I know, that confession alone was a true step in opening my heart, it was pure honesty!

As a victim of child abuse I carried a heavy burden around; if my own parents did not love me or want me then who else possibly would? I felt like beaten, damaged and used goods! I carried these feelings into my marriage and it affected my relationship with my husband and children. I was a "high maintenance" wife and mother with anger splashing out from seemingly nowhere and burning everyone around me! During this study I got on my knees and for the first time in my life I begged the Lord to help me SEE what was in my heart and heal it so I could live the rest of my life in peace, not in shackles!

A mind-transforming miracle happened to me during this precious Bible study. I learned that Jesus Christ loved me and always has! For once in my life I looked beyond my own self-absorbed world of fear and bitterness and gave these feelings of inadequacy to the unfailing love of Christ. I learned that I did not have to live as a victim of a horrible crime forever but that with Christ's love and God's truth I could now live as an enlightened survivor, truly Healed and Set Free.

By God's truth my whole mind set has changed. I could never go back to those shackles again! It's as if the dark cloud that hung over my head my whole life was completely evaporated by the power of God's light and truth! I have learned how to forgive!

To all of those beautiful sisters of mine who have suffered the loss of innocence, I want to say to you, do not fear letting go of your shame, guilt or anger: fear is of the enemy! Christ died for all sins including yours and he is waiting for you to come to him, for he is pure love and wouldn't you just love to walk in his pure love? I do.

Thank You, Tammy, for allowing the Lord to use you in such a wonderful way, you are truly a vessel unto Him.

An enlightened survivor ~ Cheryl, Idaho

> *(God, Help me be honest with what's in my heart.)*
>
> *You shall know the truth, and the truth shall make you free. John 8:32*

Thinking about the past will never change the past. But you can change your future and **BE SET FREE** from your past.

Learn the truth and **SEE** what has you in shackles today, keeping you in bondage to your past. Hurt does not go away by itself. If you are denying the hurt. It will find ways to express itself forming roots of bitterness, hurting many that stand in its way, and continuing to affect your life. It's time to get real with God about what is left over in our heart because of unacceptable past hurts.

You can attempt to bury your heartache and put on a smile and say everything is just fine. But on the inside your heart will still be filled with fear, shame, resentment, guilt, unforgiveness, self-centered desires, jealousy, and uncontrolled anger. (It puts you right under the black cloud of depression.)

Emotional scars can affect other areas of your life: your marriage, your children, your friendships, and your school or job performance. You may turn to the harmful behaviors of drug and alcohol abuse, deep depression, suicidal tendencies, eating disorders, outbursts of anger, and rebellion. You attempt to ease your pain, but you fail to heal your heart.

First Healing tool of Truth ~ To Remember

 1. **SEE:** Learn how **I must SEE** the truth about what is in my heart, **so I'm not defiled.**

*Looking carefully lest anyone fall short of the grace of God; lest any root of bitterness springing up cause trouble, and by this <u>many become</u> **<u>defiled</u>**; Hebrew 12:15*

Look up the word **_defiled_** in the dictionary and write it out.

SEE: Learn how **I must SEE** the truth about what is in my heart, **so I'm not _defiled._** *Looking carefully lest anyone fall short of the grace of God; lest any root of bitterness springing up cause trouble, and by this <u>many become</u> **<u>defiled</u>**; Hebrew 12:15*

DAY 3

> *(Christ Jesus, help me* **SEE** *what could be defiling my heart)*
>
> *Looking carefully lest anyone fall short of the grace of God; lest any root of bitterness springing up cause trouble, and by this many become defiled; Hebrews 12:15*

Personal Questions

The questions in this section are based on the experiences of people who have had painful hurts. In reading through these questions, be aware of any emotional or physical responses you may have and record them. Answering these questions honestly will put you in touch with areas of your life that have been affected by your emotional past-issues like sexual abuse, rape, pre-marital pregnancy, abortion, divorce, loss of a job, and painful memories of feeling like a lamb being lead to the slaughter.

1. Which of the following describe what is in your mind, heart and life from hurts that linger? Circle those that apply. *(God, help me be honest with You and myself.)*

   - I am angry. I hate them for hurting me!
   - It was wrong!
   - I am justified to hold hate in my heart because of what they did to me.
   - I am overwhelmed with emotion just thinking about what happened to me.
   - I am so tired of the emotions that are consuming my life. I need God to lead me to His truth, to purify my heart.

2. Which of the following describe what has been creeping out of your heart from hurts that linger? Circle those that apply. *(God, help me* **SEE** *what could be defiling my heart.)*

Fear	Anxiety
Hurt	Insecurities
Negative thoughts	Comparing myself to others
Defensiveness	Bitterness
Need to control	Desire to get even
Resentment	Guilt
Doubt	Self-pity
Pride	Feeling dirty

3. Do you find yourself struggling to turn off the feelings connected to your emotional past, perhaps telling yourself over and over to forget it or try to sweep it under the rug?

> *(God, help me examine my heart.)*
>
> *Let us search out and examine our ways, and turn back to the Lord; let us lift our hearts and hands to God in heaven. Lamentations 3:40-41*

4. Do you find that you react physically by tightening your stomach muscles, clenching your jaw, or holding your breath when molestation, rape, abortion, divorce, church split, or the name of the one who hurt you is mentioned in public? Do tears of emotion overcome you or does anger fill your heart? If so, what happened?

5. Do physical reminders like smells, phrases, places, songs, etc. affect you? Recognize its Satan's way to keep you in shackles to the past hurts.

6. Do you feel uncomfortable trusting others? If so, why?

7. Do you feel resentful and unforgiving toward anyone for his or her involvement in your painful memories? This may include parents or step-parents, children or step-children, past romantic interests, spouse or ex-spouse, brothers, sisters, extended family members, friends or ex-friends, or bosses or co-workers.

Fill in the blanks

SEE: Learn how **I must SEE** the truth about what is in my heart, **so I'm not *defiled*.**

_____ _____ *lest anyone fall short of the grace of God; lest any_____ of bitterness springing up cause _____, and by this many become **defiled**; Hebrew 12:15*

Day 4

> *(Christ Jesus, help me SEE what wound needs the Healer to set me Free.)*
> *He heals the brokenhearted and binds up their wounds. Psalms 147:3*

1. Do you find yourself out of control with your emotions concerning anger or sorrow? If so, explain.

2. Do you find yourself avoiding relationships or becoming more dependent in them?

3. Do you have memories from past sexual acts committed against you or by you that are causing difficulty with intimacy in your marriage? If so, what happened.

4. Do you find sexual intimacy to be a burden to you in your marriage?

5. Have you begun to use drugs or alcohol, or indulged yourself with uncontrolled buying sprees, or over compulsive eating or starving yourself?

6. Have you had suicidal thoughts?

7. Have you experienced any flashbacks relating to your memories of the past? If so, what continues to reacquire?

8. Have you felt a vague sort of emptiness leading to a deep sense of loss for a spouse, a child, your virginity, a trust, a position, etc.?

9. When talking about your hurt are you overcome with shame, sorrow, anger, or guilt?

10. Are you compelled to conceal your pain and suffering from the past from certain people in your life, or are you compelled to tell many people about your experience?

11. If you have children now, do you smother them with your love or overprotect them? Are you unable to bond with the child or children you have now?

12. Did you stop growing emotionally after your experience? Do you see repeating patterns such as outbursts of anger or depression in your behavior? Explain.

13. Do you struggle with eating disorders such as overeating, starving yourself, or overeating and then vomiting the food up?

14. Do you tend to look at your life in terms of before and after the painful memories?

15. Did the painful event(s) bring you closer to God or turn you away from Him? Explain.

16. Are the memories more painful than the actual experience? If so, how?

17. Read Luke 18: 9-14. *Also He spoke this parable to some who trusted in themselves that they were righteous, and despised others: "Two men went up to the temple to pray, one a Pharisee and the other a tax collector. The Pharisee stood and prayed thus with himself, 'God, I thank You that I am not like other men-extortioners, unjust, adulterers, or even as this tax collector. I fast twice a week; I give tithes of all that I possess. 'And the Tax collector, standing afar off, would not so much as raise his eyes to heaven, but beat his breast, saying, 'God, be merciful to me a sinner!' I tell you, this man went down to his house justified rather than the other; for everyone who exalts himself will be humbled, and he who humbles himself will be exalted." Luke 18:9-14*
Do you **SEE** the need for God to be merciful to you? If so, why do you need God's mercy?

Fill in the blanks

SEE: Learn how **I must SEE** the truth about what is in my heart, **so I'm not _defiled_**.

_____ _____ *lest anyone fall short of the grace of God; lest any* _____ *of bitterness springing up cause* _____*, and by this __many become **defiled**__; Hebrew 12:15*

Day 5

After finishing this questionnaire, you may be aware of other areas of your life that have been affected. Use the space provided on this page to write down what continues to flood your mind about the hurts that still linger. Do not stop the tears or the pain. Let God show you your heart. It is time to get real with God. It is time to **SEE.** Allow Him into the dark secret rooms of your heart. God is not looking for performance, just the truth. God is serious about His love for you. Let's be people who are serious about being honest with the living God.

Open your heart and let the Healer in.
Write down what continues to flood your mind about the hurts that still linger.

"Stories of real people, real hurts, real healing, and a real SAVIOR"

I Didn't Realize Anger & Hurt, Sorrow & Shame Didn't Just "Go Away"

Living with an alcoholic, verbally abusive father, I learned early not to show hurt - out of self-defense and pride. My mom's way, and in turn ours, of dealing with negative feelings was to "go to our separate corners, and get over it". Then we were to come out as if nothing had happened. When my mom discovered that my brother, sister, and I were being sexually molested by my grandfather since we had been very small she "dealt" with it the same way; we never talked about it, And everything went on as if nothing unusual had happened. I thought that was normal; it became my way of dealing with things. My Christian teaching - don't be angry; forgive and forget- matched my own warped and reinforced my mother's training. So as I grew up and went through Bible College and into ministry, I continued to DENY my hurt, anger, shame, sorrow, and any negative feeling. I would LOSE myself in books and TV until "it" didn't bother me anymore. I didn't realize anger and hurt, sorrow and shame didn't just "go away". I became so disconnected from my feelings, I really felt nothing about those hurtful situations of my past or my present for that matter; I really thought I had "dealt" with it in a godly, Christian way.

I didn't realize it came out in other ways. I'd struggled with uncontrolled, over the top, anger for years with my children and husband. The anger and rage would come out of nowhere, I'd been praying for years for God to HELP me with my anger and show me its root cause. Then, God directed me to lead this Bible study. (I thought I didn't need it because I had "dealt" with my past already!) PRAISE THE LORD! I SAW what was in my heart - ugly roots of anger and wrath, hurt and shame, sin and sorrow. My past had been ruling my present; I had been blind and deceived. But through this Bible study, the truth has set me free! I am Healed and Set Free! Praise the Lord! To first **SEE**, GIVE, then to **FORGIVE**, and **FORGET**.

Thank you for your ministry.

🌹 The truth has set me free ~ Eileen, Philadelphia

SEE, GIVE, FORGIVE, FORGET, BE SET FREE

How to Pray

🌸 **Question:**   What do I pray for?

Answer: *Some of the many issues to pray for include: being thankful, being sorry for sinning or asking God to help us share Christ with others, being afraid, uncertain or discouraged.*

It is hard to get into the habit of talking with God everyday. Maybe you could start by picking a special time everyday. Think about the things you want to say. The most important thing is to have a personal relationship with God through talking and listening to the Lord daily about those issue that are on your heart and in your life. You can talk to God like you talk to your dad, spouse, or friend.

🌸 **Question:**   Should I close my eyes to pray?   Should I pray on my knees? Should I only pray alone or only in a group? Can I pray driving down the road?

Answer: *All of the above are ways to pray. God is concerned about your prayer, not your body position or location.*

You can talk to God anywhere, anytime. He's always right there with you. The key is to talk to God daily in order to keep your relationship close. He loves you and is always waiting with joy in His heart to hear from you.

The Lord is near to all that call upon Him, to all that call upon Him in truth. Psalm 145:18

🌸 **Question:**   Can I tell God anything?

Answer: *Yes. You can tell Him anything because He already knows everything. You need to be transparent before Him.*

There is not one thing you could say to Him that would make Him stop loving you.
You can tell Him when you are sad or grumpy.
You can thank Him when everything's going your way.
You can ask him to provide for your every need.
You can tell Him when you have no love in your heart for someone.
As you pray ask God to show you His truth and His will for you.

All things are naked and open to the eyes of Him to whom we must give account Hebrews 4:13

Another helpful way to get started Praying is to brake down the word **ACTS** into a prayer list.

Adoration   Having a heart of Adoration toward Christ Jesus, our Savior and God, our great creator and Father.

Confession   Having a heart to Confess your sins before Christ in repentance.

Thankfulness   Having a heart of Thankfulness for all the many blessing God brings into your life.

Supplication   Having a heart to ask God to help you with your needs: Spiritually, Physically, Emotionally, or Financially.

The Empty Chair

A man's daughter had asked the local pastor to come and pray with her father. When the pastor arrived, he found the man lying in bed with his head propped up on two pillows and an empty chair beside his bed. The priest assumed that the old fellow had been informed of his visit. "I guess you were expecting me," he said.

"No, who are you?"

"I'm the new associate at your local church," the pastor replied. "When I saw the empty chair, I figured you knew I was going to show up." "Oh yeah, the chair," said the bedridden man. "Would you mind closing the door?"

Puzzled, the pastor shut the door. "I've never told anyone this, not even my daughter," said the man. "But all of my life I have never known how to pray. At church I used to hear the pastor talk about prayer, but it always went right over my head." "I abandoned any attempt at prayer," the old man continued, "until one day about four years ago my best friend said to me, 'Joe, prayer is just a simple matter of having a conversation with Jesus.

Here's what I suggest. Sit down on a chair, place an empty chair in front of you, and in faith see Jesus on the chair. It's not spooky because he promised, 'I'll be with you always.' Then just speak to him and listen in the same way you're doing with me right now."

"So, I tried it and I've liked it so much that I do it a couple of hours every day. I'm careful, though. If my daughter saw me talking to an empty chair, she'd either have a nervous breakdown or send me off to the funny farm."

The pastor was deeply moved by the story and encouraged the old guy to continue on the journey. Then he prayed with him, and returned to the church.

Two nights later the daughter called to tell the pastor that her daddy had died that afternoon.

"Did he seem to die in peace?" he asked.

"Yes, when I left the house around two o'clock, he called me over to his bedside, told me one of his corny jokes, and kissed me on the cheek. When I got back from the store an hour later, I found him dead. But there was something strange, In fact, beyond strange—kinda weird. Apparently, just before Daddy died, he leaned over and rested his head on a chair beside the bed."

- author unknown

🧝 Prayer Requests 🧝

Knowing
God's Heart

He heals the broken hearted
and binds up their wounds.
Psalm 147:3

There are four main tools we will weave into the very fiber of our hearts day by day: **SEE, GIVE, FORGIVE, FORGET,** and **BE SET FREE**. Thinking about the past will never change the past. But you can change your future and Be Set FREE from your past. As you deal with your past and present hurts, you can either embrace the truth and let go of the burdens you carry, or carry your burdens and reject the truth and the freedom it brings. The choice is yours. Getting real with God is the first step you need to always take as you face deep, dark hurts that have chipped away at your peace for 1 year, 10 years, 20 years, and some 50 years. God's love is bigger then all of our hurts and fears. You will have many blessings in front of you as God's truth unfolds in your heart and Sets you Free.

Let's Day By Day Go over the Four Steps to Keep Our Hearts Clean

Tools To Become Set Free

- **Tool #1 "SEE":** I must **SEE** the truth about what is in my heart, so I'm not defiled.

    Looking carefully lest anyone fall short of the grace of God; lest any root of bitterness springing up cause trouble, and by this many become defiled. Hebrew 12:15.

- **Tool #2 "GIVE":** I must **GIVE** the sin in repentance, knowing Christ is waiting to take it. (I must be sorry enough to change and choose to go God's way over my own way.)

    For godly sorrow produces repentance leading to salvation, not to be regretted; but the sorrow of the world produces death. 2 Corinthians 7:10

- **Tool #3 "FORGIVE":** I must **FORGIVE**, as I am forgiven by Christ. (Forgiving those that hurt, bruised, wronged, hurt, rejected, betrayed or harmed me whether unintentionally or deliberately.) Ask God to Forgive you for holding unforgiveness and know that He will.

    Bearing with one another, and forgiving one another, if anyone has a complaint against another; even as Christ forgave you, so you also must do. Colossians 3:13

- **Tool #4 "FORGET":** I must **FORGET** by remembering to no longer dwell on the hurt.

    Brethren, I do not count myself to have apprehended; but one thing I do, forgetting those things which are behind and reaching forward to those things which are ahead. Philippians 3:13.

BECOME SET FREE: Christ will open the shackles from my past hurts showing me the truth so I can become a cleansed vessel that is Healed and Set Free.

You shall know the truth, and the truth shall make you free. Therefore, if the Son makes you free, you shall be free indeed. John 8:32-36.

SATAN IS DEFEATED AND THE SHACKLES ARE GONE AND YOU ARE FREE!

Week 2, Day 1

> *Bow your heart before the Lord in prayer before completing today's Bible study.*
> *Ask Him to draw near to you.*

God's Heart to Counsel

God invites us to get close to Him. Knowing God's heart encourages us to be like Him, to bring our needs to Him, to love and trust Him and to respond to Him, in joyful obedience. We must lay our will down and desire to apply His Word (the truth) to our lives, one day at a time and choice by choice, as we trust that He is all-knowing, the Provider, the Counselor, the Healer, the Prince of Peace. God is LOVE.

How does a woman draw near to God's heart? What can we do to put ourselves in a position where God can grow each of us into a woman that's Healed and Set Free?

#1 Develop the habit of drawing near to God--- Only through routine, regular exposure to God's Word can you and I draw the nutrition needed to grow a heart of faith. Yet I know firsthand how hard it is to develop the habit of drawing near to God and how easy it is to skip and miss. For some reason, I tend to think I'll spend some time with God later, I'll get around to it in a little while, or I'll miss just this one-day but catch up with God tomorrow!

I've learned, however, that my good intentions don't go very far. It's easy for me to start the day planning to have devotional time a little later, *after* I've done a few things around the house, made the bed, tidied up the living room, reminded Caleb and Jessica to make their bed's and brush their teeth, made some phone calls, wiped down the kitchen counter and oh, I almost forgot to feed the little lamb and water the horses. Suddenly I'm off and running and somehow I never get the time for the most *important relationship* in my life – my relationship with God! That's why I have to be firm with myself and aim for scheduled time with God whether I feel like it or not. The only "wrong" time for having your time alone with God would be no time! So pick a time that matches your lifestyle. A dear friend taking the Healed and Set Free Bible study had hers every morning after dropping the children off at school over at the green belt "a river" that runs through Idaho Falls. Some nursing mothers have their time while their children are asleep. I set aside 7:00 a.m. every morning for my devotions and Bible study.

Read Deuteronomy 7:6-7 "For you are a holy people to the LORD your God; the LORD your God has chosen you to be a people for Himself, a special treasure above all the peoples on the face of the earth. The LORD did not set His love on you nor choose you because you were more in number than any other people, for you were the least of all peoples; but because the LORD loves you...

1. Who choose you? Look to Deuteronomy 7:6-7

2. Why are you a special treasure above all the people on the face of the earth?

3. Do you trust God with your painful hurts?

Read Psalm 1:1-2 Blessed is the man who walks not in the counsel of the ungodly, or stands in the path of sinners, nor sits in the seat of the scornful; but his delight is in the law of the Lord, and in His law he meditates day and night.

4. Are you to seek ungodly counsel from those in your life that do not follow after God's counsel? Why or why not?

5. Does ungodly counsel remove the shackles and set you free?

Read Psalm 1:6 For the Lord knows the way of the righteous, but the way of the ungodly shall perish.

6. What happens to the ungodly ways of counsel?

7. Where are you most often prompted to make a choice between dwelling in God's counsel or lingering in the ungodly counsel of a friend, spouse, or your own thinking?

Read Proverbs 1:5 A wise man will hear and increase learning, and a man of understanding will attain wise counsel.

8. Where is wise counsel found?

9. What happens when you apply God's wisdom to your life?

10. In John, chapter 5 Jesus asks, "Do you want to be made well?"

Before you personally move on in this journey, you need to know the answer to the question Jesus has asked you. Search your heart—**your** heart—not your dad or mom, step-father or step-mother, your boyfriend, or the heart of the person that hurt you. You must make a stand in your own heart that you want to be made well from the hurts that still linger. This is critical.

11. Do you desire to be **Healed & Set Free**? If so, How big is your desire? Be specific.

---

*Therefore **strengthen the hands which hangs down,** and the feeble knees, and make straight paths for your feet, so that what is **lame** may not be **dislocated, but rather be healed**. Hebrews 12:12*

Week 2, Day 2

Bow your heart before the Lord in prayer before completing today's Bible study. Ask God to prepare and soften your heart to listen to His still, small voice.

God's Heart to Heal

Read Psalm 107:19-20 Then they cried out to the Lord in their trouble, and He saved them out of their distresses. He sent His word and healed them, and delivered them from their destruction.

1. What are some of the ways God promises to heal you?

2. Fill in the blanks as you see how much God loves you.

Then they _____ _____ _____ _____ _____ in their trouble, and He _____ _____ out of their distresses. He sent _____ _____ and _____ _____, and delivered them from their _____. Psalm 107:19-20

3. On a separate sheet of paper. Name those hurts that cause trouble and distress in your mind and heart. Tell God all about it.

Read Exodus 15:26 And there He tested them, and said, "If you diligently heed the voice of the Lord your God and do what is right in His sight, give ear to His commandments and keep all His statutes, I will put none of the diseases on you which I have brought on the Egyptians. For I am the Lord who heals you."

4. Do you believe God can be your personal healer with the issues that trouble your heart?

5. Do you desire to learn how to **SEE** the truth about what is left over in your heart?

6. Write down what has already been revealed to you.

Read Exodus 15:26 "If you diligently heed the voice of the Lord your God and do what is right in His sight, give ear to His commandments and keep all His statues, I will put none of the diseases on you which I have brought on the Egyptians. For I am the Lord who heals you."

7. Under what conditions would the Israelites be healed?

8. We are reminded in the book of Exodus chapter 15 that Moses threw a piece of wood into the waters at Marah to turn the bitter waters sweet. The cross of Christ can turn your bitter life experiences into something sweet for Him. Pray and confess what bitter waters need to be healed. Write down your prayer.

Read James 5:13-16 " Is anyone among you suffering? Let him pray. Is anyone cheerful? Let him sing psalms. Is anyone among you sick? Let him call for the elders of the church, and let them pray over him, anointing him with oil in the name of the Lord. And the prayer of faith will save the sick, and the Lord will raise him up. And if he has committed sins, he will be forgiven. Confess your trespasses to one another, and pray for one another, that you may be healed. The effective, fervent prayer of a righteous man avails much.

9. After meditating on James 5:13-16, what steps do you need to take to be obedient to God's words in your healing? Write down that which applies to you.

10. In the midst of the storm of heartache you need to apply the message from James to this healing time. Remember, Christ needs to be the center of every conversation concerning your hurt in order to heal. The memories, heartache, anger and resentment can be pushed deep down in your heart, and once you begin to talk about it or look at it you may be overwhelmed with grief. But also know that once it is out, it feels so good. As your memories begin to consume your mind, pray for God's help to begin to heal. Pray and ask God to help you find one close, godly, Christian friend who is a good listener who will pray with you. Name this person.

_____.

11. The next step is to talk to your friend about the issues surrounding your hurt and let your friend know you are going through the Healed and Set Free Bible study.

Read Isaiah 53:4-5 "Surely He has borne our griefs and carried our sorrows; yet we esteemed Him stricken, smitten by God, and afflicted. But He was wounded for our transgressions, He was bruised for our iniquities; the chastisement for our peace was upon Him, and by His stripes we are healed.

12. All of the unacceptable, dark, gross sin that has happened in your life has been laid on Him, Christ Jesus. In your own words write down what is flooding your heart toward Christ after understanding the depths he went through in order for you to receive healing to your soul.

_____

_____

_____

_____

_____

_____

_____

_____

_____

_____

_____

_____

_____

_____

Read 1 John 2:1 My little children, these things I write to you, so that you may not sin. And if anyone sins, we have an Advocate with the Father, Jesus Christ the righteous.

13. Who is your Advocate when you sin?

14. Define righteousness using a dictionary.

Read Matthew 9:9-13

15. Considering the definition of righteousness and Matthew 9:9-13, why do you think Jesus said He did not come into this world for the righteous?

Read Matthew 9:12 When Jesus heard that, He said to them, "Those who are well have no need of a physician, but those who are sick."

16. The heart that is sick with pain, resentment, bitterness, unforgiveness, fear, past failures, self-absorption, guilt or pride needs Christ's great physical healing touch. Take some quiet time and search your heart. Invite Jesus Christ into the dark, private, painful room of your heart. Get real with God, with what is in your heart. Write down the areas of your life that are in need of Christ Jesus, The Great Physician's touch according to Matthew 9:12.

    1.

    2.

    3.

    4.

    5.

    6.

    7.

    8.

    9.

    10.

Read Lamentations 3:40-41 Let us search out and examine our ways, and turn back to the Lord; let us lift our hearts and hands to God in heaven.

17. Writing down what is in your heart concerning your hurts, what does Christ call us to do with those things in our hearts?

Many people genuinely desire to overcome hurts that stem from past experiences, to let go of their resentment or pain, to be free from the deep hurts. God wants to replace the pain with His healing power. God uses our failures. He knows we will fail and make bad choices with incorrect thinking. God uses these things in our lives as we learn the truth of God's will from His word.

18. Do you know in your heart of hearts that God loves you? Explain.

Realize that God Loves You

This is real love. It is not that we loved, God, but that he loved us... 1 John 4:10

Love is a powerful emotion, perhaps the strongest of human emotions. People will go to great lengths to express love, and they will do almost anything to get love. So if love is in such demand, why does it seem in such short supply?

The problem with human love is that it's usually self-centered. Much of the so-called love we feel could be summarized by the phrase, " What's in it for me?" We may think we love someone, but in reality we may simply love what he or she does for us.

In a book I recently read the Author quotes C. S. Lewis as he identified four different kinds of love, all but one of which are basically self-centered. First, there's *affection*, which is the kind of love we can have for something other than people, such as a dog, or a home, or a car. Then there *friendship*, a valuable love in the sense that it's the basis of most human relationships. And there's *erotic* love, which is beautiful between a husband and wife but a mess outside of married love. All of these are wonderful and necessary loves, but each of them depends on the object of our affection for complete fulfillment.

The only love that is completely other-centered is called *agape love*. This is love of the highest order. It's what Lewis called "Divine Gift-Love." When we love with *agape love* we desire the best for the people we love. We are even able to love those who are unlovable.

We are capable of *agape love* only to the extent that we give the details of our lives over to God and allow Him to work in us. But even before that can happen, we must realize that God loves us, and that He can only love us with this kind of love. God's love is never self-centered, and God's love is always sacrificial. While we were enemies of God, He loved us. When we ran from God, He loved us. And He loved us so much that He sacrificed the Son He loved most, so that we could experience eternal life.

Love is the essence of God. Love is what motivates Him to do what He does for us - down to the last detail- even when we don't love Him in return. Knowing that should give tremendous meaning to our lives.

🌹 Whenever you feel insignificant, remember how important you are to God.

🌹 We love God because we know who He is. God loves us despite who we are.

🌹 Be teachable every day.

🌹 Love yourself as the unique individual God created you to be- nothing more, nothing less.

🌹 Unconditional love comes only from our Heavenly Father

🌹 God does not help us because we deserve it; He helps us because He loves us.

🌹 Find your self-worth in God's unconditional love for you, not your accomplishments.

🌹 The love of God has no limits.

🌹 The reason we can love God is because He loved us first.

🌹 God's unconditional love for us should motivate us to love others unconditionally.

🌹 Never confuse love with lust.

🌹 Love isn't an option. We are commanded by God to love others.

🌹 Loving God is the greatest thing you can do.

"Stories of real people, real hurts, real healing, and a real SAVIOR"

From Tears of Sorrow To
Tears of Freedom ∿∿∿∿∿∿∿∿∿∿∿∿∿∿∿∿∿∿

Dear Lord,

As your hand guides me, may I share the truth of your love, mercies and joy with anyone who is seeking to be healed by your mighty power.

There were dark corners of my life where words were not allowed, deep hurts, incest, and betrayals. At first it was just a dark dirty memory of the sins that were put upon me, never to be spoken of. From that sin or memory, which I call the trunk, a tree grew. A few branches at first and then through the years it developed into an enormous sinful tree of sexual immorality, abortion, theft, lying, manipulation, judging, condemning, pride, self absorption, self pity, and deep roots of bitterness.

Sweet Jesus, knowing all, you never left me behind; you drew me in like a fish on the line. You put a hunger in my heart and nothing would fill it. So bit by bit I started to know your truths. I began to cry in sorrow years ago. I thought they were tears of poor me, but now as I'm growing in knowledge I realize they were tears that were setting me free. (2 Corinthians 7:10)

You Lord, showed me that I was lacking something vital, it was total faith in you. I know why we are here, it is to further Your kingdom. I know why we have suffering, it is to draw nearer to you, but I would always hold on to the question, "Why did it all start in the first place?" As I was asking you, you said because " GOD IS LOVE" and you created us for you to love on. Finally I understood Your love for me. Thank you, Lord.

As I began to SEE each one of my memories or the branches of my trees I would explore each branch of that memory eagerly to find what was hiding. As I did this Lord, yes, you revealed deep hurts were there, but I knew I could forgive the weaknesses of others because that is Your desire. The real agony and pain of my memories were actually my own sins that I needed to ask forgiveness for.

Oh Lord, I can SEE (looking Closely). I can GIVE (knowing You are waiting to take it). I can FORGIVE (As I am forgiven for Your mercies sake. Psalms 6:4). I can FORGET (until You, Lord, want to use my memories for your glory).

Now my trees are no longer dead, dark and broken, but have buds of love, forgiveness and mercies sprouting up everywhere.

Your truths are simple, Sweet Jesus, and may we all know Satan doesn't want us to see how easy being FREE is.

🌹 Renewed child of God - T.J.

SEE, GIVE, FORGIVE, FORGET, BE SET FREE

Week 2, Day 3

> *Bow your heart before the Lord in prayer before completing today's Bible study. Ask Him to reveal what areas in your heart need to be examined.*

God's Heart to SEE

> *And there is no creature hidden from His sight, but all things are naked and open to the eyes of Him to whom we must give account. Hebrews 4:13*

Read Psalms 10:14,17 "But You have seen, for You observe trouble and grief, to repay it by Your hand. The helpless commits himself to You; You are the helper of the fatherless. Lord, You have heard the desire of the humble; You will prepare their heart; You will cause Your ear to hear.

1. What do the Psalms reveal about what God sees and hears? What are the ways He responds to what He sees and hears?

2. Why is it so important to humble yourself before God according to the above scripture?

3. What thoughts are constantly bombarding you-thoughts about the betrayal, sexual abuse, rape, guilt, past failures, shame, abortion, eating disorder, pre-marital pregnancy, your personal painful memories? You need to **SEE** and examine your heart-get real with God! No false performance for God. Pray and let God show you the reason you rehash the heartache. Write these reasons down.

4. Do you desire to do evil to another person? Explain, being totally honest so you can **SEE** what God already sees in your heart.

Learning God's Truth

🌱 He _____ the brokenhearted and _____ up their wounds. _____ ____ : __

AUTHOR'S REFLECTION
Trapped in a Horrifying Nightmare

When I was a 15-year-old virgin, I had hopes and dreams that one day I would marry as a virgin bride. The groom would be a wonderful, handsome man that I would love and cherish for the rest of my life. My future was exciting. I felt wonder and anticipation when I thought about the special man who would come into my life.

This dream of mine came crashing down in one night. I went on a casual date with a friend from school that I liked as a friend, and I trusted as a friend. On this date the nightmare began. He raped me, and all my dreams of being a virgin bride were ended by this cruel and selfish act.

The rape started a root of bitterness and rebellion in my heart. My future was confused. He threatened to tell everyone that we had slept together, destroying my reputation. I had promised myself that sex was for marriage and now that was shattered. I was confused, angry, and filled with hate toward this guy. My life fell into a spiral of depression.

It didn't end there; he held it over my head. He knew I didn't want the reputation of sleeping around, so he used my fear to trap me into a relationship with him. The nightmare continued day after day. He physically abused me, and he threatened me with what he would do if I ever left him.

He played mind games and continued to force himself on me sexually. I was going through that first rape experience over and over again. I couldn't believe he had bullied his way into my life and was controlling me with fear. I was really afraid of him. I hated him!

He talked to me about marriage and having kids together. For the only time in my life, I thought about killing myself. The thought of marrying this guy that I hated and despised, spending the rest of my life with him, overwhelmed me. Never, never, never would I marry him. I hated him!

Trapped in silence for that entire year, I lost 15-20 pounds. I was depressed and stressed out from this horrifying nightmare. I never told anyone what I was going through-not my best friend, not my parents, not anyone. Why didn't I break the silence? Because I was so ashamed of my life. I was trying to bury the sick, shameful past of being sexually abused by my uncle as a child. Now I was trying to do the same thing with the deep-seated bitterness from this betrayal. I tried to live a halfway normal life, but I felt like a big zero.

Then, through a number of difficult circumstances, this sick relationship ended as quickly as it had started. My best friend saw all the bruises on my arms and asked what had happened. I finally told her how I was being hit and shoved around. She told some of our friends, Rick Brown and Shawn about the way I was being mistreated. Rick, who was not yet a Christian, went to have a talk with him. One thing led to another and Rick ended up beating him to a pulp. Right then the nightmare ended. I was released from prison and the control this guy had over my life. He never messed with me again. I never heard if he ever went through with all his threats. He probably thought he'd better keep his mouth shut, or Rick would be looking for him.

continuation of AUTHOR'S REFLECTION

The painful, abusive relationship continued to have its effect on me over the years. The terror may have ended physically, but not emotionally. I wanted to numb the pain. I began to party hard and became rebellious towards my parents. I was angry and critical and I didn't trust anyone.

I kept the pain of the rape and sexual abuse locked up tight. I never told anyone until after I married my high school sweetheart, Rick Brown. After we both became Christians, I finally broke down and told him about the shameful rape. I came clean with my hidden past.

Justified Wrongs

I felt <u>justified</u> in my thoughts of hatred toward this guy who had controlled my life, raped, and abused me. I was overwhelmed with resentment and bitterness toward him. I was unforgiving, unmerciful and desired to do evil. I felt driven to get even with him. I kept a long list of all the wrongs he had done to me. I was consumed with hatred for him. I justified my own anger and hatred. By the world's standards I was justified in hating that guy.

In my heart the list of wrongs done to me by him continued to grow longer and longer. He became a close friend of my parents. My parents had no idea what he had done to me because the only person I told was my husband. So now this guy was invited to family birthdays. He would show up at my parent's home and give them pictures of his family, which they would display. Each time I went to my parent's home I would walk in and feel slapped in the face by a picture that was given to my parent's by the guy that raped me, controlled me, and abused me. My hatred and bitterness was growing. My loving parents, with no knowledge of the hatred I held in my heart toward this guy, would even talk about getting our kids together to play with each other. In my mind I would think, "Over my dead body!" I would smile to hide my true heart. My mind and spirit were sick with hatred. It was ruining my happiness and it was not pleasing to the Lord. I knew I had to stop mulling this over in my mind and stop keeping a record of wrongs. Then one day, in the silence of my own mind, I got real with God. No more just putting on a smile and acting like everything was all right. It wasn't.

I was Blocking God out of My Life

After meditation on two important scriptures (Romans 1:21-22 and Hebrews 12:15) I learned that one of the most important steps I had to take was to look into my own heart and be willing to **SEE** what was in it. I saw sins of roots of bitterness, unforgiveness and futile thoughts of getting even. <u>I had been blocking God out of my life</u> in the very moments I needed him most!

I was a Christian woman, a pastor's wife and a child of God, but I was thinking like the world as it is described in Romans 1:21-22.

- *Although they knew God, they did not glorify Him as God, nor were thankful, but became **futile in their thoughts,** and their **foolish hearts were darkened**. Professing to be wise, they became fools. Romans 1:21-22*

- *Looking carefully lest anyone fall short of the grace of God; lest any **root of bitterness** springing up cause trouble, and by this **many become defiled**; Hebrews 12:15*

Like Romans 1:21-22 describes, my heart had been darkened. God shined His spotlight on my self-centered heart. I was foolish in my heart. I had never realized how my bitterness, hatred, resentment and unforgiveness had covered over my heart and had prevented God's love from coming forth. Totally broken and repentant, I GAVE it to God and asked for His forgiveness. After this, I genuinely forgave the guy who raped me. When I became an open vessel, I not only received God's love, but I also received God's thoughts. Having the mind of Christ, I was then able to **SEE** things more clearly from God's perspective.

- As Jesus hung on the cross He said, *"**Father, forgive them for they know not what they do.**" Luke 23:34*

Are there any areas from your painful experiences that you think are unrighteous? These could include holding record of wrong, resentment, bitterness, judgement, hatred or jealously. Confess them now and ask for God's forgiveness. What does God promise to do according to 1 John 1:9? This is the Christian bar of soap.

My Foolish Heart

In reading the following scripture I saw my thoughts had become unprofitable, unsuccessful and futile. As I sat down and prayed for God to show me what I could be thankful for, I was forever transformed.

- *Although they knew God, they did not glorify Him as God, **nor were thankful**, but became futile in their thoughts, and their foolish hearts were darkened. Professing to be wise, they became fools. Romans 1:21-22*

It is never right to rape someone. But God did help me to **SEE** there were things to be thankful for, even in my year of terror brought about by the date-rape experience. I wrote out a list of 10 things that God showed me.

- *Finally, brethren, whatever things are **true**, whatever things are **noble**, whatever things are **just**, whatever things are **pure**, whatever things are **lovely**, whatever things are of **good report**, if there is any **virtue** and if there is anything **praiseworthy** - __meditate on these things__. Philippians 4:8*

THANKFUL FOR

*(practical, **praiseworthy** things I meditated on)*

1. I am thankful the abuse stopped.

2. I am thankful I did not get pregnant.

3. I am thankful I did not get a disease.

4. I am thankful I was not trapped into marrying that guy.

5. I am thankful the silence is broken.

6. I am thankful I could find the strength from God to tell my husband the painful truth.

7. I am thankful Christ gave me spiritual eyes to **SEE** the truth about the sin of unforgiveness.

8. I am thankful I learned to forgive and press toward the higher calling in Christ Jesus.

9. I am thankful I can comfort others who hurt with the comfort I have received through the healing power of Christ.

10. I am thankful through Christ and by His stripes, I have been **Healed and Set Free**.

The Old is gone, the New has come, Tammy Brown

Although they knew God, they did not glorify Him as God, nor were thankful, but became futile in their thoughts, and their foolish hearts were darkened. Professing to be wise, they became fools. Romans 1:21-22

Have your thoughts become unprofitable, unsuccessful and futile. Ask God to show you 10 things for which you can be thankful. What is true today that you can see more clearly about your future? Don't let your heart become foolish and darkened by the past hurt.

Lord,

*I pray, help me move past the futile thoughts and help me keep my heart from being foolish and darkened by the hurts. Help me **SEE** what I can be thankful for. In Jesus' name,*

I'M THANKFUL FOR:

...whatever things are true, whatever things are noble, whatever things are just, whatever things are pure, whatever things are lovely, whatever things are of good report, if there is any virtue and if there is anything praiseworthy-meditate on these things. Philippians 4:8

1.

2.

3.

4.

5.

6.

7.

8.

9.

10.

Learning God's Truth

__ heals the _____ and binds up their _____. *Psalm 147:3*

AUTHOR'S REFLECTION
God Wasn't Finished ∿∿∿∿∿∿∿∿∿∿∿∿∿∿∿
With Me Yet

One area of my life that was affected by my past was my marriage. Especially with submission to my husband. I can remember reading the Bible's description about our roles as husbands and wives.

Wives submit to your own husband, as to the Lord. Ephesians 5:22

I cringed at the thought of ever giving anyone total control over my life. Never would I be another person's doormat. I balked at this submission bit for years. It was not fair and I was scared. My perspective was wrong because of the terror I had gone through. Then I realized that my husband hadn't asked to be the head or leader over our home. That responsibility was placed on him by the Almighty God, and that is God's plan for the husband. One day husbands will stand accountable for what they did with that leadership in their home. This realization was the turning point in my thoughts toward submission. No, I'm not a doormat. That's not God's plan either. In a Biblical sense, submission means yielding my own will to the will of my husband as unto the Lord. When I am willing to lay down my own will and submit my life to God by letting my husband lead, then I am embracing God's will for my life.

If we confess our sins, He is faithful and just to forgive us our sins and to cleanse us from all unrighteousness. 1 John 1:9

The Fact of Submission

Author Elizabeth George describes her insights on "submission", as she points out the assignment she's on from God to submit to her husband. "When it comes to marriage, God arranged for the sake of *order* that the husband lead and the wife follow. For marriage to run smoothly," God has said, "The head of every man is Christ, the head of woman is man, and the head of Christ is God (1 Corinthians 11:3)."

Now don't be alarmed. The husband's headship doesn't mean we wives can't offer wise input (Proverbs 31:26) or ask questions for clarification during the decision making process. But the husband's headship does mean that he is responsible for the final decision. Author Elisabeth Elliot describes her father's headship in her childhood home. "Head of the house" did not mean that our father barked out orders, threw his weight around, and demanded submission from his wife. It simply meant that he was the one finally responsible. In the end, the husband is accountable to God for his leadership decisions and we are accountable to God for how we submit to that leadership. Our husband answers to God for leading and we answer to Him for following. Now I ask you, which responsibility would you rather have?

Submission is a wife's choice. She decides whether or not to subject herself to her husband. No one can do it for her, and no one can make her do it. Her husband can't make her submit, her Pastor can't make her submit, nor can a Christian counselor. She alone must decide to submit to her husband.

Do you know the main reason why we wives don't submit to our husbands? Its *fear*. We are afraid of what will happen if our husbands do things their way instead of our way. Once again it became clear to me that my submission has nothing to do with my husband and everything to do with God! God has instituted submission, commanded submission, and given me the faith in Him to be able to submit----and He is honored when I do! My obedience to my husband testifies to all who are watching that God's Word and His way are right. This call to submit is indeed a high calling!

Dedicate you heart to honoring your husband ~~~ Change requires a decision, and that's definitely the case with submission.

Remember to respect ~~~ Submission flows from the basic heart attitude of respect. God states, let the wife see that she respects her husband. (Ephesians 5:33) God isn't telling us to feel respect, but to show respect, to act with respect. A good way to measure our respect for our husband is to answer the question, "Am I treating my husband as I would treat Christ Himself?"

Respond to your husband's words and actions positively ~~~ Old ways die hard. We can snort, buck, kick, and fight with our husbands about everything. I struggle with how fast he's driving, his method of disciplining the children versus mine, how he should handle his ministry, how we should handle the money, what we should buy for the living room. On and on our struggles can go.

Phase one: *Say nothing!*

Have you ever been in the presence of a woman who doesn't respect her husband? She nags at him, picks him apart, and disagrees with him in public. She corrects him, struggling with him over every little thing ("No, Scott, it wasn't eight years ago; it was seven years ago.) Or she cuts him off, interrupts, or worse, finishes his sentences for him. Clearly, saying nothing is a great improvement over that kind of behavior.

Phase two: *Respond with a single positive word. Start to respond with one positive word.*

One godly Christian woman chose the word "Sure" I chose the word "Okay" and that's with melody in my voice. And I began to use this positive response and say, "Okay!" on the small things.

After reading a true story about a gal that chose the word "Sure", let me tell you something that happened in her family as a result. Her husband loved to go to Price Club, a crowded and noisy discount ware house, and many times he would announce after dinner, "Hey, lets all go to Price Club!" Well, she with three children, one of them a baby at the time, could have presented a watertight case against dragging the entire family out to Price Club on a school night after dark but she didn't. She also never challenged her husband as the leader in front of her little family. Instead, she just smiled, responded " Sure!" and got everyone into the car for another trip to Price Club. Many years later as, one by one her family members shared around the Thanksgiving dinner table about their favorite thing to do as a family, all three of her grown up children said, "Going to Price Club as a family." *Family unity, fun, and memories came because of her sweet heart-- and word -- of submission.*

NOTE: Every new testament passage about the husband and wife relationship either begins or ends with a command for mutual submission.

1. JESUS IS HEAD OF THE CHURCH.

2. HUSBAND IS HEAD OF THE WIFE AS CHRIST IS HEAD OF THE CHURCH AND DIED FOR HER.

3. WIFE SUBMIT TO THE HUSBAND AS AN ACT OF SUBMISSION TO THE LORD.

GOD'S COMMANDMENTS FOR MARRIAGE:

Ephesians 5:21-25

- ⚘ Submit to one another out of reverence for Christ.
- ⚘ Wives, submit to your husbands as to the Lord.
- ⚘ For the husband is the head of the wife as Christ is the head of the church, his body, of which he is the Savior.
- ⚘ Now as the church submits to Christ, so also wives should submit to their husbands in everything. Husbands, love your wives, just as Christ loved the church and gave himself up for her

---

GOD COMMANDS US TO ESTEEM OUR HUSBANDS:

There is scripture after scripture calling us to respect and help our husbands win!

"Your desire will be for your husband," Genesis 3:16

Genesis 2:18 : "It is not good for man to be alone. I will make a helper suitable for him. Suitable for him doesn't say: doormat, slave or insignificant other. The Hebrew word for helper = someone who enables a person otherwise incapable.

Take a lesson from Tamara, a dear friend of mine who e-mailed me from her home in San Jose where she and her husband minister. She said, "I'm asking myself these days what can I do for this marriage, NOT.... What can I get out of this marriage." Let me tell you how blessed her marriage is because of it. She desires to be a servant like Jesus and she says this also includes the "S" word, "Submission". The Bible also makes it clear as to when we are to submit! *Now as the church submits to Christ, so also wives should submit to their husbands in everything. Ephesians 5:24 (NIV)*

Tamara points out to women, "we are on an assignment from God to submit to our husbands, okay, you are hesitating! You're sitting there going.... Forget this! For me, the only thing that held me back from submitting was fear! I thought my way was sure. I was *afraid* that the kids wouldn't be properly disciplined if Jeff did it or that he would ask me to do something I maybe didn't particularly like to do."

"It's your decision to submit. Submission is totally your choice! No one can make this decision but you! Today you must come face to face with God's plan for marriage from His Word or beware of the world infesting and destroying your marriage. I had to face this by force of the gracious Lord's Hand (not as much fun as when you choose to submit out of obedience!) I was horribly sick in bed for 3 years and had no choice but to allow my husband to take the lead. What I came to learn is that my husband never demanded the headship and would have never demanded it. It had to be a free gift from me to him. At our 2000 New Year's party with a couple of dear couples, my best friend of 20 years said to me, "I've noticed such a difference in your marriage: you have stepped back and Jeff has blossomed! By coming underneath Jeff's authority, he has grown in the Lord, and your marriage is so much closer and intimate."

If we are trying to control our marriage in the flesh and in our own tactics: *strategies, manipulation, and intelligence,* we are looking for disaster. Our hearts become a desert because we don't get what we want.

We lose the joy and contentment of marriage because our focus is on what we want not on how we can trust in the Lord for our husbands. Today, may you make a choice to serve your husband, not because I've told you or Tamara has told you, but because the Lord encourages you to do so. You can make a free will choice to see the assignment from God to be a blessing to your Savior and to your husband. You will be amazed at the blessings that flow from heaven because of your heart of obedience!

So many marriages are not experiencing fulfillment in marriage. In fact, most marriages are failing, not thriving.

Why? *We aren't following God's perfect plan, perfect Word in the Bible.*

In Tamara's obedience to serve her husband she came up with a list of
"HUSBAND PLEASERS"

🌹 **Take interest in his work:** Know what he does. Ask questions, better you than a secretary who is interested in his day! This shows you are genuinely interested in him. Let him know how much you appreciate him working.

🌹 **When he walks in the door after work: Greet him with a big kiss and hug:** Hang up the phone! Don't unload your day's problems yet. If you sense he has had a tough day, bring him a coke and tell him to relax in his favorite chair until dinner.

🌹 **Plan romantic nights:** Lingerie is very important. You can buy it very cheap at Wal mart

    A. Husbands never complain if you buy sexy underwear.

    B. Candle light dinner.

🌹 **Compliment your husband: Song 5:10-16**
My lover is radiant and ruddy, outstanding among ten thousand. His head is purest gold; his hair is wavy and black as a raven. His eyes are like doves by the water streams, washed in milk, mounted like jewels. His cheeks are like beds of spice yielding perfume. His lips are like lilies dripping with myrrh. His arms are rods of gold set with chrysolite. His body is like polished ivory decorated with sapphires. His legs are pillars of marble set on bases of pure gold. His appearance is like Lebanon, choice as its cedars. His mouth is sweetness itself; he is altogether lovely. This is my lover, this my friend, O daughters of Jerusalem.

    A. Call him good looking (IN PUBLIC)

    B. Let him know how wonderful he is!

🌹 **Make him master of your home:**

    A. Look to him for advice especially in spiritual areas.

    B. Feed him his favorite meals.

    C. Fold his shirts and socks the way he likes.

    D. Iron ahead of time so he doesn't have to ask.

☞ **Regular sex life:** Scriptures have high view of sex within marriage. The Bible doesn't blush when it talks about sex. Do not deprive your husband of regular sexual relations: *1 Corinthians 7:5 Do not deprive each other except by mutual consent and for a time, so that you may devote yourselves to prayer. Then come together again so that Satan will not tempt you because of your lack of self-control.*

    A. If we do, we are giving Satan a foot in the door of our marriage. Pornography and affairs may result.

    B. Pray and seek the creator of sex, if having problems. (Avoid secular books and magazines, as they will leave you more frustrated.)

    C. Communicate with your husband on how to please each other. If you don't share with each other, how can either of you possibly know?

    D. Recommendation for 2 Christian books on sex. Intended For Pleasure and Restoring The Pleasure

☞ **Make your bedroom a special place:**
Proverbs 31:22 She makes coverings for her bed; she is clothed in fine linen and purple.

    A. Decorate your bedroom.

    B. Make it cozy and romantic. (Put many candles, spray the bed with perfume.)

    C. Keep your bedroom clean and uncluttered. (One woman said, "The worse thing we ever did was try to make our bedroom the "office/bedroom" we had to move the computer downstairs! Now it's just our "love nest".

Please don't go home and tell your husband what you read: ***show him!!!!***

Sometimes we're tempted to dismiss God's plan, saying, "My husband isn't walking with God, so I don't have to submit to him" or "My husband isn't a Christian, so I don't have to submit to him." The apostle Peter wrote the following words to help women in those exact situations, women with unbelieving and or disobedient husbands: *"Wives, be submissive to your own husbands, that even if any do not obey the Word, they, without a word from {their wives,} may be won by the conduct of their wives" (1 Peter 3:1).* In other words, our submission to our husband ,whether or not he is a Christian, whether or not he is obeying God, preaches a louder and more powerful sermon than our mouths ever could!

It's important to mention here the one exception to following your husband's advice, and that is if he asks you to violate some teaching from God's Word. If he's asking you to do something illegal or immoral, go to a trusted pastor and follow the counsel you receive there.

Once you've begun to respond positively to the small things, you'll quickly find it becoming easier and even natural to respond positively to larger and larger issues. For example: car purchases, job changes, and household moves.

1. What changes of heart do you desire God to work in you so you can submit willingly and even joyfully?

2. With some practice, "Okay" or "Sure" became an automatic response to my husband's request. Choose your own positive word of response and put it to use today.

Week 2, Day 4

> *Bow your heart before the Lord in prayer before completing today's Bible study. Ask Him to help you know Him better.*

God's Characteristics

Today, we will look at some of God's characteristics, and at knowing God as the Almighty God. He will encourage you to trust Him with the pain and sorrow you've experienced.

Drawing life from God's Word

One Christian author says, "If God is going to be first in our heart and the Ultimate Priority of our life, we must develop a root system anchored deep in Him. Just like a plant with its roots hidden underground, you and I, out of public view and alone with God, are to draw from Him all that we need to live the abundant life He has promised His children (1John 10:10). We must live our life near to God indeed, hidden in Him!"

But it's so easy for you and me to get this all backwards. It's easy to think that what counts in the Christian life is the time spent in public with people, people and more people! We seem to always be with people-people at work, people on campus, people in the dorms, people from the Bible studies, people we live with, people in discipleship settings or fellowship groups. But the truth is "the greater the proportion of our day – of our life-spent hidden in quiet, in reflection, in prayer, (in study,) in preparation – the greater will be the effectiveness, the impact, the power, of the part of your life that shows." As I heard one Christian leader say, "You cannot be with people all of the time and have a ministry to people. The impact of your ministry to people will be in direct proportion to the time you spend away from people and with God."

God is Never-Changing

1. Does God ever change according to Malachi 3:6 or Hebrews 13:8?

   - *For I am the Lord, I do not change; therefore you are not consumed, O sons of Jacob." Malachi 3:6*

   - *Jesus Christ is the same yesterday, today, and forever. Hebrews 13:8*

2. Fill in the following blanks with the characteristics of God that never change. What characteristics of God do you find comforting because they never change and never fail?

   The _____ of God never changes. Numbers 23:19

   His _____ never fail. Lamentations 3: 22-23

   His _____ never fails. Psalm 18:50

   The _____ of God never changes. 2 Peter 3:9

God is All-Powerful

Read Jeremiah 32:17 "Ah, Lord God! Behold, You have made the heavens and the earth by Your great power and outstretched arm. There is nothing too hard for You"

3. Describe God's power according to Jeremiah 32:17.

Read Psalm 77:13-15 "Your way, O God, is in the sanctuary; Who is so great a God as our God? You are the God who does wonders; You have declared Your strength among the peoples. You have with Your arm redeemed Your people, the sons of Jacob and Joseph"

4. What are some of the ways God displays His power?

Read Romans 1:16 "For I am not ashamed of the gospel of Christ, for it is the power of God to salvation for everyone who believes, for the Jew first and also for the Greek".

5. Is your heart ashamed of letting others at work, child's school, or home know that you are a Christian? Explain.

Read Acts 1:8 "But you shall receive power when the Holy Spirit has come upon you; and you shall be witnesses to Me in Jerusalem, and in all Judea and Samaria, and to the end of the earth."

6. How do you have access to the power of God?

7. What is one way God intends for you to use His power?

8. Are you a witness to those around you in your home, at your place of work, and School?

God is All-Knowing

Read John 3:19-20 "And this is the condemnation, that the light has come into the world, and men loved darkness rather than light, because their deeds were evil. For everyone practicing evil hates the light and does not come to the light, lest his deeds should be exposed"

9. Does God know everything? What are the ways you practice evil in your heart concerning you're past?

Read Psalm 44:20-21 "If we had forgotten the name of our God, or stretched out our hands to a foreign god, would not God search this out? For He knows the secrets of the heart.."
Read 1 Corinthians 4:5 "Therefore judge nothing before the time, until the Lord comes, who will both bring to light the hidden things of darkness and reveal the counsels of the hearts. Then each one's praise will come from God"

10. Which areas of your life does God know about?

Read Hebrews 4:13 "And there is no creature hidden from His sight, but all things are naked and open to the eyes of Him to whom we must give account."

Read Daniel 2:22 "He reveals deep and secret things; He knows what is in the darkness, and light dwells with Him"

11. What areas of your life do you think are hidden from God? Ask God to help you SEE what secret things from the past are in your heart. How's your heart?

Read 1 Chronicles 28:9 "As for you, my son Solomon, know the God of your father, and serve Him with a loyal heart and with a willing mind; for the Lord searches all hearts and understands all the intent of the thoughts. If you seek Him, He will be found by you; but if you forsake Him, He will cast you off forever."

12. If you believe that God knows everything, what is one way you can respond to this belief?

13. Rewrite 1 Chronicles 28:9

14. Do you desire to have God's ways in your life even if it does not feel comfortable?

15. What can you SEE more clearly about your own heart after examining and seeing God's heart?

God is Able to Protect

16. From Psalm 18:16-19, circle the words that imply that David felt God's protection.

I will love You, O Lord, my strength. The Lord is my rock and my fortress and my deliverer; my God, my strength, in whom I will trust; my shield and the horn of my salvation, my stronghold. I will call upon the Lord, who is worthy to be praised; so shall I be saved from my enemies. Psalm 18:1-3

He sent from above, He took me; He drew me out of any waters. He delivered me from my strong enemy, from those who hated me, for they were too strong for me. They confronted me in the day of my calamity, but the Lord was my support. He also brought me out into a broad place; He delivered me because He delighted in me. Psalm 18:16-19

17. What does God promise to protect you from if you seek Him?

Learning God's Truth
Fill in the blanks.

🕊 __ ____ ___ _____ ___ *binds up their* _____. _____ ___:__

- *You are my hiding place; You shall preserve me from trouble; You shall surround me with songs of deliverance. Psalm 32:7*

- *I sought the LORD, and He heard me, and delivered me from all my fears. Psalm 34:4*

- *But the Lord is faithful, who will establish you and guard you from the evil one. 2 Thessalonians 3:3*

18. How does God protect you?

Read John 10:27 "My sheep hear My voice, and I know them, and they follow Me."

19. What does God ask of you in order for Him to provide the protection you need?

The Lord Rescued Me ～～～～～～～～～～～～～～～
FROM MYSELF

Watching the Lord heal and comfort my mother's heart made me wonder if he could do the same to me.

I had just rededicated my life to Christ. However, I still hung onto my "justified pain and anger". I was hurting so bad because my heart had been lied to by so many guys so many times. I lived in fear of getting close to someone because, to me, getting close meant getting hurt and walked over. I was sick of hurting and not trusting anyone; I wanted to be freed from my past but I didn't know how.

So I signed up to be "Healed and Set Free." I thought signing up and going to the study would be enough to heal my heart. It wasn't!! I needed to actively choose to apply the tools and the Word to my own life. When I realized I couldn't do it on my own I needed to truly let Jesus heal me after I applied the things I learned in the study, to my heart. I became totally aware of God's awesome power. Being healed was an awesome experience. The Lord rescued me from MYSELF. HE was preparing my heart to love again. I was amazed.

He is continually working in my life. Being healed doesn't promise me I'll never hurt or fall down again. It does however cause me to see how much I truly need a Savior to save me from falling.

🌹 Jesus Healed me ~ Teen girl Renee

SEE, GIVE, FORGIVE, FORGET, BE SET FREE

Week 2, Day 5

> *Bow your heart before the Lord in prayer before completing today's Bible study. Ask Him to help you love Him with all your heart.*

God's Unfailing Love for You

It is so important to your healing to know and believe that God's heart is to love you. If you do not learn to love and be loved in the way God intended, and for the reason you were created in the first place, you have truly wasted your life. When you serve and obey the Lord's will, you will **BE SET FREE.**

- *He who does not love does not know God, for God is love. 1 John 4:8*

- *Love suffers long and is kind; love does not envy; love does not parade itself, is not puffed up; does not behave rudely, does not seek its own, is not provoked, thinks no evil; does not rejoice in iniquity, but rejoices in the truth; bears all things, believes all things, hopes all things, endures all things. Love never fails. But whether there are prophecies, they will fail; whether there are tongues, they will cease; whether there is knowledge, it will vanish away. 1 Corinthians 13:4-8.*

If you have parents who don't keep their promises and frequently change their minds, it can affect your ability to grab onto God's promises and believe they are for you. You must remember that God's love is greater than your parents' love, because God is the definition of love.

1. *Read 1 John 4:18-19 "There is no fear in love; but perfect love casts out fear, because fear involves torment. But he who fears has not been made perfect in **love**. We love Him because He first loved us"*

Fill in the blanks from 1 John 4:18-19:

> *There is no _____ in love.*

> *But perfect love casts out_____.*

> *Because _____ involves torment.*

> *But he who_____ has not been made perfect in _____.*

> *We _____ Him because He first _____ us.*

Read 1 John 4:7 " Beloved, let us love one another, for love is of God; and everyone who loves is born of God and knows God. He who does not love does not know God, for God is love. In this the love of God was manifested toward us, that God has sent His only begotten Son into the world, that we might live through Him."

2. In two sentences, describe God's love for you.

God's Promise to Never Leave You

Read Hebrews 13:5 "Let your conduct be without covetousness; be content with such things as you have. For He Himself has said, I will never leave you nor forsake you."

3. What does Hebrews 13:5 say about God being there for you?

4. Write our Hebrews 13:5

Read John 14:16-18"And I will pray the Father, and He will give you another Helper, that He may abide with you forever "the Spirit of truth, whom the world cannot receive, because it neither sees Him nor knows Him; but you know Him, for He dwells with you and will be in you. I will not leave you orphans; I will come to you."

5. What promises does God give you to hold onto during the times you feel alone, rejected and abandoned?

Read Deuteronomy 31:6 "Be strong and of good courage, do not fear nor be afraid of them; for the Lord your God, He is the One who goes with you. He will not leave you nor forsake you."

6. What is one thing you can do when you think God is not there for you?

The Father

God wants to be your Father. Are you comforted by that idea or does the word father bring feelings of hurt and bitterness? Accepting God Almighty, as your heavenly Father may be difficult if you have broken relationships with your authority figures here on earth. If your parents were not there for you for various reasons, such as divorce, death, or any type of addiction, you may have a hard time believing that there is a heavenly Father who cares and who is always there. Parents who have abused their children may damage their child's ability to believe that God the Father is their protector.

God's promises are for all His children. He keeps His promises. He promises to be a Father to you and He will never change His mind. Your Father, God longs for you to come to Him with all your needs. He wants to meet your need for love and acceptance.

7. How do these verses describe God?

- *For unto us a Child is born, unto us a Son is given; and the government will be upon His shoulder. And His name will be called Wonderful, Counselor, Mighty God, Everlasting Father, Prince of Peace. Isaiah 9:6*
- *Therefore, do not be like them. For your Father knows the things you have need of before you ask Him. In this manner, therefore, pray: Our Father in heaven, Hallowed be Your name. Matthew 6:8-9*

Learning God's Truth

Fill in the blanks.

___ heals the ______________ and binds up their __________. _____ 147:___

Read Psalm 68:5 "A father of the fatherless, a defender of widows, is God in His holy habitation."

8. To whom will God be a Father?

Read 1 John 2:23 "Whoever denies the Son does not have the Father either; he who acknowledges the Son has the Father also."

9. How could you deny the Son in your life?

Read Galations 3:26 "For you are all sons of God through faith in Christ Jesus."

10. Have you by faith received Christ into your heart? If so, when?

11. Have you told others about Christ? If so, give an example.

Read John 1:12 "But as many as received Him, to them He gave the right to become children of God, to those who believe in His name"

12. Who can be called children of God?

Read Romans 8:12-16 "Therefore, brethren, we are debtors; not to the flesh, to live according to the flesh. For if you live according to the flesh you will die; but if by the Spirit you put to death the deeds of the body, you will live. For as many as are led by the Spirit of God, these are sons of God. For you did not receive the spirit of bondage again to fear, but you received the Spirit of adoption by whom we cry out, "Abba, Father." The Spirit Himself bears witness with our spirit that we are children of God."

13. How are you able to call Him "Father"?

Learning God's Truth
Fill in the blanks.

___ *heals the* _____ *and binds up their* _____. _____ 147:___

*Read Galatians 5:19-21 "Now the works of the flesh are evident, which are: adultery, forni-
cation, uncleanness, lewdness, idolatry, sorcery, hatred, contentions, jealousies, outbursts
of wrath, selfish ambitions, dissensions, heresies, envy, murders, drunkenness, revelries,
and the like; of which I tell you beforehand, just as I also told you in time past, that those
who practice such things will not inherit the kingdom of God."*

14. What is the flesh? Write down each word and ask yourself if the flesh is at work in
    your life?

15. Do you desire to continue to walk in the flesh or apply *2 Corinthians 7:10* to your daily
    attitude and actions?

(**GIVE:**   Give the sinful burden to the Lord in repentance.) I must be sorry enough to
change and choose to go God's way over my own way.

*For godly sorrow produces repentance leading to salvation, not to be regretted; but the sor-
row of the world produces death.   2 Corinthians 7:10*

*Read Galatians 5:22-31 "But the fruit of the Spirit is love, joy, peace, longsuffering, kindness,
goodness, faithfulness, gentleness, self-control. Against such there is no law."*

16. What is the fruit of the Spirit? Write down each word and ask yourself if the fruit of
    the Spirit is at work in your life?

17. In what practical ways will you apply the fruit of the Spirit to your life?

Learning God's Truth
Fill in the blanks.

ॐ ___ heals the _____ and binds up their _____. _____ 147:___

The Father's Discipline

God is like a parent to you; consequently, He disciplines you. His discipline is wiser than your parents' discipline.

1. Using a dictionary, write out a definition of discipline.

Read Hebrews 12:5-11 " And you have forgotten the exhortation which speaks to you as to sons: My son, do not despise the chastening of the Lord, nor be discouraged when you are rebuked by Him; for whom the Lord loves He chastens, and scourges every son whom He receives. If you endure chastening, God deals with you as with sons; for what son is there whom a father does not chasten? But if you are without chastening, of which all have become partakers, then you are illegitimate and not sons. Furthermore, we have had human fathers who corrected us, and we paid them respect. Shall we not much more readily be in subjection to the Father of spirits and live? For they indeed for a few days chastened us as seemed best to them, but He for our profit, that we may be partakers of His holiness. Now no chastening seems to be joyful for the present, but painful; nevertheless, afterward it yields the peaceable fruit of righteousness to those who have been trained by it."

2. Describe the difference between the way God disciplines us and the way our earthly parents disciplines us.

Read Hebrews 12:6 "For whom the Lord loves He chastens, and scourges every son whom He receives."

3. Whom does God discipline?

4. For what does God discipline you personally?

5. Using a dictionary, write out the definition of sin or iniquity.

If anger, resentment, unforgiveness, hard heartedness, or disobedience takes over your heart and you choose to not deal with it and **SEE** it, your heart will grow cold. When that happens, God's love cannot flow through your heart, and you will become a phony Christian.

Genuine love demands toughness in moments of crisis.

- *Open rebuke is better than love carefully concealed. Faithful are the wounds of a friend, but the kisses of an enemy are deceitful. Proverbs 27:5-6*

Words to Remember

🌹 Fill in the blanks

Open rebuke _____ _____ than _____ _____ _____. Faithful are the _____ of a friend. Proverbs 27:5-6

Read Romans 2:5-11 "But in accordance with your hardness and your impenitent heart you are treasuring up for yourself wrath in the day of wrath and revelation of the righteous judgment of God, who will render to each one according to his deeds: eternal life to those who by patient continuance in doing good seek for glory, honor, and immortality; but to those who are self-seeking and do not obey the truth, but obey unrighteousness; indignation and wrath, tribulation and anguish, on every soul of man who does evil, of the Jew first and also of the Greek; but glory, honor, and peace to everyone who works what is good, to the Jew first and also to the Greek. For there is no partiality with God."

6. What happens to the shackles on your heart if you reject God's truth concerning the importance to **SEE** and examine your heart?

🕊 **SEE**. *I must SEE what is really in my heart. (Asking God to expose the root cause of my sinful thoughts and actions. So I'm not defiled and I don't defile others.) Looking carefully lest anyone fall short of the grace of God; lest any root of bitterness springing up cause trouble, and by this many become defiled. Hebrew 12:15*

7. Is there partiality with God if you are a stay home mom, business woman or a pastors wife according to Romans 2:5-11?

8. Write out Romans 2:5-11

Read 1 John 1:9 "If we confess our sins, He is faithful and just to forgive us our sins and to cleanse us from all unrighteousness "

9. Brokenness before Christ for our sin, drives us to confess. What then does God do for us?

Words to Remember

10. Fill in the blanks

If we confess our sins, He is _____ and _____ to forgive us our _____ .

When sin abounds grace does much more. The grace of God is the hope. Surely He has borne our griefs and carried our sorrows; yet we esteemed Him stricken, smitten by God, and afflicted. But He was wounded for our transgressions, He was bruised for our iniquities; the chastisement for our peace was upon Him, and by His stripes we are healed. Isaiah 53:4-5

11. What step must you **first take** to begin healing in your mind? Circle the one that applies to your heart.

- Swirl around in bitterness, unforgiveness, rehashing what another person has done, beating myself up from my own failures.

- Embrace God's healing truth from His Word to **SEE, GIVE, FORGIVE, FORGET and BE SET FREE.**

First Two Tools to Freedom

"SEE ": Learn how I must **SEE** the truth about what is in my heart, so I'm not defiled.

Looking carefully lest anyone fall short of the grace of God; lest any root of bitterness springing up cause trouble, and by this many become defiled. Hebrew 12:15.

"GIVE": Learn how **I must GIVE** the hurt, holding record of wrong, resentment and the sinful burden to the Lord.

The Lord is near to those who have a BROKEN HEART and saves such as have a contrite spirit. Psalms 34:18. For godly sorrow produces repentance leading to salvation, not to be regretted; but the sorrow of the world produces death. Corinthians 7:10.

Read Psalm 119:101-104 "I have restrained my feet from every evil way, that I may keep Your word. I have not departed from Your judgments, for You Yourself have taught me. How sweet are Your words to my taste, Sweeter than honey to my mouth! Through Your precepts I get understanding; therefore I hate every false way"

12. What should we restrain our feet from according to Psalm 119?

Fill in the blanks:

Surely He has borne our _____, and carried our _____; yet we esteemed Him _____ smitten by _____, and _____. But He was _____ for our transgressions, He was _____ for our _____; the chastisement for our _____ was upon _____, and by His _____ we are _____. Isaiah 53:4-5

Read Psalm 103:11 "For as the heavens are high above the earth, so great is His mercy toward those who fear Him."

13. Have you embraced the grace, hope and healing that Christ is offering you? How big is God's mercy toward you and toward others?

14. It's time to be real people of God. God is serious about you. Let's be people who are serious about God. What does getting serious about God mean to you? Read 1 John 1: 6-7

 SEE. I must SEE what is really in my heart. (Asking God to expose the root cause of my sinful thoughts and actions. So I'm not defiled and I don't defile others.) *Looking carefully lest anyone fall short of the grace of God; lest any root of bitterness springing up cause trouble, and by this many become defiled. Hebrew 12:15*

15. *I sought the LORD, and He heard me, and delivered me from all my fears. Psalm 3*
    Which of the following tend to motivate the way you react? Circle those that apply.

Negative thoughts	Hurt
Insecurity	Lack of trust
Guilt	Need to control
Defensiveness	Pride
Doubt	Comparing myself to others

Review

Review this Chapter on Knowing God's heart. Reflect on the truths you have learned.

* This Week's memory verse: He _____ the _____ and _____ up _____ wounds.
  Psalm ___:3

* What have you learned about God's heart toward you?

* What encouraged you?

* What challenged you?

* Does this chapter give you the desire to seek the Lords love, truth and healing for your life?

"In the next chapter we will take a closer look at **Anger**."

"Stories of real people, real hurts, real healing, and a real SAVIOR"

I Needed To Be
Healed and Set Free

"!PRAISE GOD! God is really using **Healed & Set Free** to bring women into a closer fellowship with Jesus. I am a volunteer counselor for a non-profit group in Sacramento, WEAVE (Women Escaping a Violent Environment). I thought this study would be good for me to give to victims of domestic violence. I felt I should complete the study before I started recommending it to others. Well, to make a long story short, I needed to be "Healed and Set Free" from a history of beatings from my first husband, as well as promiscuity, alcohol abuse, rape, abortion, and divorce (all before the age of 20 - I'm 38 now). I knew I had been through a lot in my life, but I didn't know I needed to give all those past hurts and the anger to the Lord. When I did, I was able to live, really live, for the first time in my Christian life.

"I heard the Lord call to my heart to start a study. I spoke with my pastor, and he said to go for it! I did, and now there is a study on Tuesday evenings at Calvary Chapel Laguna Creek. Last night 3 of the ladies revealed they gave their hurts and anger to the Lord and are beginning to walk in victory, they who have been Christians most of their lives."

Set Free to Really Live The Christian Life ~ Sherry, California

I've Learned I need to ,
Forgive

"Thank you so much for sharing the richness of God's word in the stufy Healed and Set Free. Our group has grown a lot. I have done many Bible studies but the topic of the hurting heart and what hinders our being the kind of people we want to be has been life changing for me. Working through the issues that wound me, being able to GIVE them to Jesus and being free from the past hurts has given me such peace. Knowing our loving God desires us to cleanse our hearts daily so the enemy doesn't creep back in has been another great lesson. This is a life learning experience, knowing people will disappoint us and that we daily need to forgive and daily seek His forgiveness for ourselves. Thank you for your study. The application of His mighty word has been such a blessing to myself and many others."

Set Free From The Past Hurts, Kim.

SEE, GIVE, FORGIVE, FORGET, BE SET FREE

You shall know the truth and the truth shall make you free.
John 8:32

Broken Vessel

Broken vessel on the floor, you must wonder
why you're there and what you're broken for?
Was it by the hand of man? You'll never see.
But if by the hand of God, you shall surely see.
Broken vessel.

Broken vessel there's a way that seems easy, it seems fair,
but it's not the way.
If it's by the path of man, you'll never see.
But if by the hand of God, you shall surely see.
Broken vessel.

Broken vessel understand your life is in the hollow of
His hand.
And without brokenness and suffering you'll never know
just what it means
To serve your Maker and the Living God, for by His stripes
of suffering,
He felt your pain and misery, He knows the brokenness
you're going through
Because this Master Potter has been there just like you.

Dave Messenger

Chapter 3

Letting Go
of Anger

———— 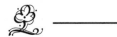 ————

*The wise woman builds
her house, but the foolish
pulls it down with her
hands.*

Proverbs 14:1

———— 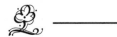 ————

There are four main tools we will weave into the very fiber of our hearts day by day: **SEE, GIVE, FORGIVE, FORGET,** and **BE SET FREE.** Thinking about the past will never change the past. But you can change your future and Be Set FREE from your past. As you deal with your past and present hurts, you can either embrace the truth and let go of the burdens you carry, or carry your burdens and reject the truth and the freedom it brings. The choice is yours. Getting real with God is the first step you need to always take as you face deep, dark hurts that have chipped away at your peace for 1 year, 10 years, 20 years, and some 50 years. God's love is bigger then all of our hurts and fears. You will have many blessings in front of you as God's truth unfolds in your heart and Sets you Free.

Let's Day By Day Go over the Four Steps to Keep Our Hearts Clean

🎗 Tools To Become Set Free

- **Tool #1 "SEE ":** I must **SEE** the truth about what is in my heart, so I'm not defiled.

  Looking carefully lest anyone fall short of the grace of God; lest any root of bitterness springing up cause trouble, and by this many become defiled. Hebrew 12:15.

- **Tool #2 "GIVE":** I must **GIVE** the sin in repentance, knowing Christ is waiting to take it. (I must be sorry enough to change and choose to go God's way over my own way.)

  For godly sorrow produces repentance leading to salvation, not to be regretted; but the sorrow of the world produces death. 2 Corinthians 7:10

- **Tool #3 "FORGIVE":** I must **FORGIVE**, as I am forgiven by Christ. (Forgiving those that hurt, bruised, wronged, hurt, rejected, betrayed or harmed me whether unintentionally or deliberately.) Ask God to Forgive you for holding unforgiveness and know that He will.

  Bearing with one another, and forgiving one another, if anyone has a complaint against another; even as Christ forgave you, so you also must do. Colossians 3:13

- **Tool #4 "FORGET":** I must **FORGET** by remembering to no longer dwell on the hurt.

  Brethren, I do not count myself to have apprehended; but one thing I do, forgetting those things which are behind and reaching forward to those things which are ahead. Philippians 3:13.

🎗 **BECOME SET FREE:** Christ will open the shackles from my past hurts showing me the truth so I can become a cleansed vessel that is Healed and Set Free.

  You shall know the truth, and the truth shall make you free. Therefore, if the Son makes you free, you shall be free indeed. John 8:32-36.

SATAN IS DEFEATED AND THE SHACKLES ARE GONE AND YOU ARE FREE!

Week 3 Day 1

> *Bow your heart before the Lord in prayer before completing today's Bible study. Ask God to help give you understanding about the truth of anger.*

The Destruction of Anger

Anger is a very powerful emotion, one of the strongest of human passions. When anger arises, it demands a response. Anger does not go away on it's own. If denied, it finds ways to express itself and tends to form roots of bitterness. Anger expressed without self-control is destructive, hurting many who stand in its way. You may be angry with yourself, with God or with those you love and trust. We'll look at the guidelines God has set for us to follow in our anger. We'll also see how God can help when our anger has turned into bitterness from past hurts and continues to affect our lives today.

When we give our lives to Christ our Savior we bring all the past hurts with us. We can have a root of bitterness deeply seated in our hearts that causes us trouble. The effects of bitterness, which are seen in many different areas of our lives, cripple us so much we are unable to look beyond our hurts!

God is slow to Anger

But He, being full of compassion, forgave their iniquity, and did not destroy them. Yes, many a time He turned His anger away, and did not stir up all His wrath. Psalm 78:38

1. Why are you grateful for God's compassion towards you?

"For My name's sake I will defer My anger, and for My praise I will restrain it from you, so that I do not cut you off. Isaiah 48:9

2. Why is God slow to anger?

So the Lord became angry with Solomon, because his heart had turned from the Lord God of Israel, who had appeared to him twice, and had commanded him concerning this thing, that he should not go after other gods; but he did not keep what the Lord had commanded.1Kings 11:9-10

3. Why was God angry with Solomon?

Learning God's Word

This week's memory verse:

🥀 SEE: Learn how I must SEE the truth about what is in my heart, so I'm not defiled.

Looking carefully lest anyone fall short of the grace of God; lest any root of bitterness springing up cause trouble, and by this many become defiled; Hebrew 12:15

4. How can a heart turn from the Lord? Give practical examples.

5. You may have allowed other gods into your life. Little gods – such as self-absorption, gossip, being critical of others, wanting to be better than others, having spiritual pride, compulsive overeating, compulsively overspending, abusing drugs or alcohol or other things – may be a source of comfort. What false gods do you **SEE** that may have crept into your life.

6. Are you willing to give up these false gods? Explain how you can do this according to God's will.

7. Record the seven things that are detestable to God from Proverbs 6: 16-19.

These six things the LORD hates, Yes, seven are an abomination to Him:

__ _____ ____, a lying tongue, _____ _____ ___ _____

_____, a heart that devises wicked plans, _____ _____ __ ___ __ _____

__ ___, a false witness who speaks lies, ___ ___ ___ ___ _____ ____ _____.

Who knows the power of Your anger? For as the fear of You, so is Your wrath. So teach us to number our days, that we may gain a heart of wisdom. Psalm 90:11-12

8. Should you be afraid of God's anger?

9. What should we be doing with each day God gives us according to the above verses?

If You, LORD, should mark iniquities, O Lord, who could stand? But there is forgiveness with You, that You may be feared. Psalm 130:3-4

10. How was the psalmist able to have hope in the face of God's anger?

Learning God's Word

This week's memory verse:

🌹 SEE: Learn how I must SEE the truth about what is in my heart, so I'm not defiled. *Looking _____ lest anyone _____ short of the grace of God; lest any _____ of bitterness springing up cause trouble, and by this many become _____; Hebrew 12:15*

Therefore, let it be known to you, brethren, that through this Man is preached to you the forgiveness of sins; Acts 13:38

11. How can we be saved from God's anger and experience His forgiveness?

But God demonstrates His own love toward us, in that while we were still sinners, Christ died for us. Much more then, having now been justified by His blood, we shall be saved from wrath through Him. For if, when we were enemies, we were reconciled to God through the death of His Son, much more, having been reconciled, we shall be saved by His life. And not only that, but we also rejoice in God through our Lord Jesus Christ, through whom we have now received the reconciliation. Romans 5:8-11

12. How can we follow God's example given to us concerning those who have sinned against us?

Learning God's Word

This week's memory verse:

🌹 _____: I must _____ the hurt, holding record of wrong, resentment and the sinful burden to the Lord.

_____

_____

_____ *Hebrew ____:_____*

Week 3 Day 2

> *Bow your heart before the Lord in prayer before completing today's Bible study. Ask God to let you SEE what is really in your heart that may still be making you angry.*

Jesus' Anger

Jesus had the same emotions we do. The Bible says He wept. He became angry when He saw things that were wrong in this world. He used His anger to see that justice was done. We must follow Jesus' example regarding the expression of anger.

> *Seeing then that we have a great High Priest who has passed through the heavens, Jesus the Son of God, let us hold fast our confession. For we do not have a High Priest who cannot sympathize with our weaknesses, but was in all points tempted as we are, yet without sin. Hebrews 4:14-15*

1. Did Jesus ever sin when He was angry?

2. What should we hate and be angry at, the sin or the sinner?

3. Is there anything about your painful memories that you are still angry about? Describe what still lingers.

_____

_____

_____

_____

_____

_____

_____

_____

_____

_____

_____

_____

_____

Doing Unto Others

If someone rolls their eyes at you, squint back. If someone is nice to you, you're nice. If someone is your friend, be their friend. If someone is hateful, you're rude back. Does getting back make things better? Do you feel good after a verbal fight? Not really, except Satan would want to make us believe that lie along with our flesh.

Look again at what Jesus said - *"Love your enemies, do good to those who hate you"* Luke 6:27. *"Bless those who curse you, do good to those who hate you, and pray for those who spitefully use you and persecute you." Matthew 5:3.* That doesn't seem right or fair, If someone hurts me. I want to get even or mad.

Jesus wants us to know the joy and freedom of love and its power to overcome evil. Through the strength that our Lord Himself gives us. We learn to follow Jesus as He was bearing the sins of the world on the cross, the suffering was so great, He cried out in agony. He was dying. But when He looked at that mob He didn't hate them, He loved them. He forgave them. And He prayed God to forgive them," Father, forgive these people, for they don't know what they are doing," His enemies hated. But Jesus forgave, Jesus concept of love overpowering hate.

4. How did Jesus respond to those who hated Him, beat Him, verbally abused Him, physically abused Him and yes even sexually abused Him as they removed his clothes and-hung Him naked on the cross for everyone to see?

5. Give practical ways Christ wants your attitude to reflect Matthew 5:3 towards those who have hurt you?

Learning God's Word

This week's memory verse:

SEE: Learn how I must SEE the truth about what is in my heart, so I'm not defiled.
Looking _____ lest anyone _____short of the grace of God; lest any _____ of bitterness springing up cause trouble, and by this many become _____;
Hebrew 12:15

Pulling Out the Bitter Roots

We are made in the likeness of God, created by God to do his will. God wants to bless you and make you fruitful in all your ways. When we forgive others only from our MOUTH the roots of bitterness, roots of hatred and roots of unfogiveneess are only cut off at the top of this ugly plant that is growing into many areas of our lives. We need to aggressively pull out this root that's deep down into the soul of our heart where it took seed. This only happens when we humble ourselves in brokeness before Christ in repentance so the bad seed will die at the root. Then we can replace that bitter root with God's good seeds and become set free, to really live the abundant Christian life. Then we will know the meaning of forgiving the unacceptable, not just with our MOUTH but from our HEART. The abundant life is offered to all of us, but few live the abundant life.

1. Define *bitterness* using a dictionary.

- What can you SEE is really in your heart that may still be making you angry about the hurt?

2. *Psalms 34:18-19 says, The LORD is near to those who have a broken heart, And saves such as have **a contrite spirit.** Many are the afflictions of the righteous, But the LORD **delivers him** out of them all.*

- Define *contrite* using a dictionary.

- Define *remorseless* using a dictionary.

- Define *relent* using a dictionary

3. What is the condition of your heart today? What do you SEE growing in your heart? *(contrite, remorseless or relent)*

4. What do you want to be delivered or set free from? Explain.

Learning God's Truth

This week's memory verse:

_____: Learn how **I must SEE** the _____ about what is in ____ heart, so I'm not defiled.

Looking _____ lest anyone _____short of the grace of God; lest anyone fall short of the grace of God; lest any root of bitterness _____ up cause trouble, and ____ _____ many become _____; _____ ____ :____

AUTHOR'S REFLECTION
Over the Edge

We are so programmed to bury our true feelings that we never really let go of them. We bury them deeper and deeper, not ever realizing those hurts will eventually begin to motivate all of our actions. We are sent "over the edge" without any control over our emotions as we lash out at those who love us the most.

That is exactly what happened to me. Rather than being the loving wife I wanted to be, I would lose control of myself and go "over the edge" by picking a fight with my husband. *"I hate the things I do and I do the things I hate." Romans 7:15 This was exactly how I felt.*

The bitter memories from being molested and raped continued to creep into my mind. It was choking out my peace. I would fall apart and go "over the edge". I would become depressed or I would get mad at the world, with my world consisting of my loving husband and two sweet kids. I just couldn't seem to control how I reacted. Those buried feelings were always right there, ready to explode. I needed to learn to get a grip. I wondered if there would ever be a change in me.

Sometimes I would be yelling, screaming mad, full of anger, with the whole house looking at me through eyes of fear. I was so blinded at the time that I would think to myself, "What's wrong with them?" I never thought for a moment that I might be the problem.

Anger, frustration and hurt would consume me. I didn't know it at the time, but my anger was just a deep root of bitterness from all my past hurts. My "over the edge" emotions were caused by long ago hurts I wasn't willing to **SEE**. I needed to **SEE** what was in my heart so I could begin to deal with the anger.

My life was filled with silent secrets. I thought, " I'm okay about my past," mean while I would mull over the past hurts in my mind. I was afraid to open up my heart to anyone. I continued to send myself into very unhappy moods. I would pick apart everything that was a drag about my life, my marriage and my kids. I was very critical of everyone. Everything was an issue with me at that time. Looking back, it was a wonder my husband Rick would even come home at night. *The wise woman builds her house, but the foolish pulls it down with her hands. Proverbs 14:1. Foolishly*, I was destroying my own home with my own hands.

It was Time

The truth is revealed to us when we get real with God, and now, finally, I was willing. It was time. God had been ready to set me free all the while, but NO! I had continued to be my own worst enemy. At last I was willing to get real with God and to SEE what was truly in my own sinful heart. When I was ready, God began showing me how I was hanging on to all of the hurts and wrongs that others had committed against me. I had become infected with the deadly poison of bitterness.

It felt so good to get that sliver out of my heart and to be healed and set free. God's grace and forgiveness came into my heart toward those that hurt me. My forgiving those who molested and raped me did not make those crimes any less wrong. But, my forgiving them allowed me to have what I needed – a correct relationship with Jesus. I traded my hurt for wholeness.

- *The Lord is near to those who have a broken heart, and saves such as have a contrite spirit. Many are the afflictions of the righteous, but the Lord delivers him out of them all. Psalms 34:18-19*

We live in a world gone wrong, a world that was created perfect, but now suffers the ravages of sin. Man's inhumanity to man, moral failures, diseases and violated relationships characterize our broken world.

It's one thing to shake our heads at the mess the world is in it. It is quite another to confront the reality of sin in our own lives. When we stand in the middle of a storm in our life, it seems as if the storm becomes our way of life. We cannot see a way out. We feel defeated, broken, hopeless and depressed.

God's Way Opens the Shackles and Sets You Free!

Will your brokenness produce a destructive, angry woman or will you yield up that brokenness to the resources of Christ Jesus the one who calms the winds, heals the brokenhearted and forgives the most grievous of sins? The choice is yours. I have learned I can **be angry at the sin but forgive the sinner**. We will take a closer look at forgiving the unacceptable in the next chapter.

The Effect of the Past

The effects of my past hurts and " over the edge" emotions were such a part of my life for so long that I continued to overreact for the sake of overreacting. I didn't know any other behavior when I was stressed or disappointed. I would just blow up. Even though I knew God spoke specifically to women about not pulling their house down with their hands or mouth (Proverb 14:1), I did it anyway! Convicted of my disobedience and aware that my overreacting didn't please God, my heart became unsettled in my constant behavior of "over the edge" emotions. I felt like a hypocrite- a pretender. I realized I needed to change. I started praying each day that I would have self-control. And still I would lose it! Real change began when I started not only to pray about my lack of self-control, but to confess it as a sin each time I did it. And asking God to cut this destruction out of my life. Purging my life of a major sin (1John 3:3) took place, in part, because I faced my sin regularly in prayer. Do you see the progression? Sin led to confession, which led to change.

I was a Christian woman, going to church, and praying with other people after the services. My husband Rick was teaching a home Bible study at this time. I knew it was sinful of me to act this way. I'd be so kind and patient toward my kids in front of others but behind closed doors I would be rude and impatient. I was so afraid that my kids would grow up and look at me as a hypocrite. That's when I cried out to God to help me with my destructive behavior. I could not continue to tell others, "Do as I say, not as I do". Even though God could see my darkest parts He still loved me. I was relying upon His love to free me from my chains. I wanted to love God with a joyful obedience. I must live it. My strongest testimony is my daily walk.

Two things were necessary for me to change this destructive behavior of Anger

SEE - why I was letting myself get so upset. Either I was not trusting God or I was keeping a record of wrongs towards another person.

GIVE - I had to give my struggle with "over the edge" anger to God in prayer everyday. I prayed for self-control. Every time I lost control I would apologize to Rick and the kids then ask Christ to forgive me. I began to have self-control over my actions and destructive emotions. I found I had to practice self-control one day at a time. I still have stress and disappointments, and I will until the day I meet Jesus face to face. However I can now choose how to act or react to stress and disappointments. *For godly sorrow produces repentance to salvation, not to be regretted; but the sorrow of the world produces death. 2 Corinthians 7:10*

Week 3 Day 3

> *Bow your heart before the Lord in prayer before completing today's Bible study. Ask Him to reveal any sins in your life that might be separating you from Him, then ask Him to forgive you and know that He will.*

Every Wise Woman Builds

Proverbs 14:1 reads, Every wise woman builds her house. Needing building instructions for making my house a home, lets start with the positive aspect of building. "To build" means, literally, to make and to set up a house and this verse refers not only to the structure and upkeep of the home, but also to the family itself. You see, a home is not only a place: its also people.

One insightful scholar explains the verse this way:

Although the Hebrew word for "house" and "home" is the same, "home" is the preferred word here. A house is not always a home and this verse does not speak of house construction, masonry, or carpentry but of home building: the knitting together of family and the day- by-day routine of creating a happy and comfortable place for a family to live.

And who is responsible for the quality of life in that place where the family lives? The woman! She sets the mood and maintains the atmosphere inside the home. In fact, this Proverb teaches, if the woman is wise, she diligently and purposefully creates that atmosphere. She doesn't just hope it will happen.

Avoid the negatives

Every wise woman builds her house, but the second half is just as important: The foolish woman pulls it down with her hands. To pull down a home means to break or destroy it, to beat or break it down, to ruin it.

> #1, A woman can cause great damage actively: What, for instance, does anger out of control do? It throws, it slams, it tears, and anger, out of control, also speaks words that break, hurt, destroy, and bring pain to a heart.

> # 2, The second way to ruin a home is passive: by simply failing to work. We can slowly erode the foundation of our home by our laziness, by never getting around to it. By neglect, by forgetting to pay a bill or two, by successfully putting things off, by not spending enough time at home. One of the greatest dangers and a problem is watching soap operas. Too much time in idleness.

1. Search your heart and your home. Are you more like the "wise woman" or the "foolish woman"?

2. What specific steps can you take to make your home a haven, a refuge, a retreat, a hospital for your loved ones? To build your home into what God wants it to be? What step will you take this week?

3. Reread Proverbs 14:1 and think about the contrast shown there. What three negatives will you start eliminating so you can build your home into all God wants it to be?

Has God been speaking to you about anger in your life? It's not God's will for you to keep a record of wrongs toward others or to be filled with resentment, anger, filthy language, gossiping, hypocrisy or being critical of others. Confess these areas now and ask for God's forgiveness. What does God promise us if we use the Christian bar of soap. (Thank You God!) *If we confess our sins, He is faithful and just to forgive us our sins and to cleanse us from all unrighteousness." 1 John 1:9.*

Being filled with all unrighteousness, sexual immorality, wickedness, covetousness, maliciousness; full of envy, murder, strife, deceit, evil-mindedness; they are whispers, backbiters, haters of God, violent, proud, boasters, inventors of evil things, disobedient to parents, undiscerning, untrustworthy, unloving, unforgiving, unmerciful; who, knowing the righteous judgment of God, that those who practice such things are deserving of death, not only do the same but also approve of those who practice them. Romans 1:29-32

4. Write down each unrighteous act that could come into our lives as you reflect back at Romans 1:29-32

Now the works of the flesh are evident, which are: adultery, fornication, uncleanness, lewdness, idolatry, sorcery, hatred, contentions, jealousies, outbursts of wrath, selfish ambitions, dissensions, heresies, envy, murders, drunkenness, revelries, and the like; of which I tell you beforehand, just as I also told you in time past, that those who practice such things will not inherit the kingdom of God. Galatians 5:19-21

5. Give examples from your own life when the expression of your anger came from your sinful nature.

Also, to have a happy home, and build your home, be sure to make mealtime fun, A young reader who wasn't having fun at dinner wrote to "Dear Abby"

Dear Abby:

*Is the dinner table a place for gripes and problems? I am 12 years old, and I am sick and tired of having my dinner spoiled by a lot of unpleasant conversation every night. I know my parents have to get it out of their system but at the dinner table?... We're just **asking** them to please let us have a nice dinner with pleasant conversation.*

{Signed} FED UP

Abby shared this bit of wisdom

Dear Fed Up:

*I hope this letter will remind parents to make mealtime a happy time. Concentrate on what you're eating and not on what's **eating you**!*

Write down what God has shown you it's time to **GIVE** *to him in prayer.*

_____

_____

_____

_____

_____

_____

_____

_____

_____

_____

_____

_____

_____

_____

_____

_____

_____

_____

_____

_____

_____

_____

_____

_____

_____

_____

_____

_____

_____

_____
_____
_____
_____
_____
_____
_____
_____
_____
_____
_____
_____
_____
_____
_____
_____
_____
_____
_____
_____
_____
_____
_____
_____
_____
_____
_____
_____

Word's to Remember

Fill in the blanks.

✥ _____ *carefully lest anyone _____ short of the grace of God; lest any _____ of bitterness springing up cause trouble, and by this_____ become defiled; Hebrews 12:15*

SEE, GIVE, FORGIVE, FORGET, BE SET FREE

Week 3 Day 4

> *Bow your heart before the Lord in prayer before completing today's Bible study. Ask Him for the strength to be honest with yourself in how you express your anger.*

Our parents' example

Anger is an emotion. As children growing up, we watch and imitate the way our parents expressed their anger. Although we cannot blame our parents for the way we express our anger, it may help us to understand how our behaviors may have been learned. Answer the following questions to discover what you may have learned from your parents.

1. In what ways did your father or step-father express his anger?

2. In what ways did your mother or step-mother express her anger?

3. What was it like for you to be around each of your parents when they were angry?

4. How do you express your own anger?

5. Which of your parents are you most like when you express your anger?

Learning God's Truth

This week's memory verse:

___: Learn how ___must ___ the truth about ___ is in my ___, so ___ ___ _____.
Looking _____ lest anyone _____ short ___the ____ of God; lest any root of _____ springing up _____ trouble, and by this many become defiled;
_____ 12:15

6. Ask those who live with you or know you best, what it is like for others to be around you when you express your anger. What were their responses?

7. In what ways would you like to express your anger differently?

God's Example

In the Book of Proverbs God gives us some guidelines to follow when expressing anger. Look these up in your Bible and match each Proverb with its Scripture reference.

Proverbs 15:1   *A fool gives vent to his anger, but a wise person keeps himself under control.*

Proverbs 16:32   *An angry man starts many quarrels.*

                       A hot temper leads to many sins.

Proverbs 29:11   *A gentle answer turns away angry feelings.*

                       Harsh words stir up anger.

Proverbs 29:22   *A patient man who controls his temper is stronger than a warrior.*

8. How can you apply the wisdom of Proverbs to help you express your anger differently?

Learning God's Truth

This week's memory verse:

🌹 ____: Learn how ____must ___ the truth about ___ is in my ____, so ____ ___ _____.
Looking _____ lest anyone _____ short ___the ____ of God; lest any root of _____ springing up _____ trouble, and by this many become defiled;
_____ 12:15

Week 4 Day 1

> *Bow your heart before the Lord in prayer before completing today's Bible study. Ask Him for the help of the Holy Spirit to enable you to* **SEE** *what's really in your heart concerning justified thoughts.*

Self Control or Out of Control

Look inside your heart. You may need to deal with one attitude that, if it were improved, if it were transformed by God, it would enhance the atmosphere of the home. Elizabeth George shares,"For me, gossip was a serious struggle. Even though I knew God spoke specifically to women about not gossiping (1Timothey 3:11 and Titus 2:3), I did it anyway. Convicted of my disobedience and aware that my gossip didn't please God, I tried some practical remedies like taping little notes on the telephone ("is it true, is it kind, is it helpful?") and setting guidelines for my speech. I even prayed each day that I wouldn't gossip. And still I gossiped! Real change began when I started not only to pray about gossip, but to confess it as a sin each time I did it, and ask God to cut gossip out of my life.

But the fruit of the spirit is love, joy, peace, patience, kindness, goodness, faithfulness, gentleness, self-control. Against such there is no law. And those who are Christ's have crucified the flesh with its passions and desires. If we live in the spirit, let us also walk in the Spirit. Galatians 5:22-25

1. Write down the nine fruits of the spirit.

2. Proverbs emphasizes self-control in expressing anger. What is self-control a result of?

But also for this very reason, giving all diligence, add to your faith virtue, to virtue knowledge, to knowledge self-control, to self-control perseverance, to perseverance godliness, to godliness brotherly kindness, and to brotherly kindness love. For if these things are yours and abound, you will be neither barren nor unfruitful in the knowledge of our Lord Jesus Christ. 2 Peter 1:5-8

3. What does self-control lead to?

4. What are the ways you can choose to control what comes out of your mouth when you are angry?

5. Self-control is something that takes practice. Think of a time when you became angry this past week. Did you respond with self-control or out-of-control? If you had used self-control in this situation, what would have been prevented or if you use self control what happened?

_____

_____

_____

_____

_____

_____

_____

_____

_____

_____

_____

_____

_____

_____

_____

_____

_____

_____

_____

_____

_____

_____

_____

_____

_____

_____

_____

AUTHOR'S REFLECTION
Falling ∽∿∽∿∽∿∽∿∽∿∽∿∽∿∽∿∽∿∽∿∽∿∽∿∽∿∽∿∽
Down

When I was a little girl growing up, I loved to go roller-skating all the time with my best friend Karleen. When I first started skating I would spend most of my time falling down and getting up, falling down and getting up, and falling down again. OUCH! Those falls really hurt! However, each time I went skating I became a little better. I would keep track of the times I fell down and eventually, with practice, my falls became fewer and fewer. At last, one Saturday I skated the entire time without falling once. I was so excited. But just a few weeks later I was leaving the skating rink with a broken arm. I had tripped over someone else's skates and down I went. Let him who thinks he stands take heed lest he fall. 1 Corinthians 10:12. After my arm healed, I was right back out there skating. I would have great days where I wouldn't fall at all, and other days when I would fall.

I compare my skating days with my Christian walk. The day I gave my life to Christ was the day I started to practice my Christian walk. Most of the early times were spent falling down and getting up, falling down and getting up. With each decision in my life I was able to choose to follow God's will or my own will. When I would follow my own negative emotions and wrong thinking I would fall hard. But praise Jesus! God is patient in teaching us and no matter how many times we fail a test, He always presents us with an opportunity to take that test again. God's desire is for us to learn His way and to choose His way for our lives. The more we practice applying His Word to our lives, the better prepared we will be when we are under stress, when hurtful comments come, or when we are in a trial. The more we choose to follow the Spirit and not the flesh, the less we will fall. But when we do fall, it is very important not to isolate ourselves. When we have fallen, it is easy to get discouraged and believe Satan's lies. We need other Christian friends to encourage us in order to turn our eyes back toward Jesus. When we fall and are broken, God will use our brokenness to lead us to His righteousness, His will and His plan for our lives. God promises to give us the strength when we need to get up again. *(I can do all things through Christ who strengthens me. Philippians 4:13)*

Just like with skating, the more times we get up and try again, the better we become and the less we will fall, soon enjoying the excitement of not falling down so often. It's the same with living our lives God's way. The more we get up and try again, the easier it will become and the less we will fall and the more joy we will have. *(For we are His workmanship, created in Christ Jesus for good works, which God prepared beforehand that we should walk in them. Ephesians 2:10.) (Commit your works to the LORD, and your thoughts will be established. Proverbs 16:3)*

SEE, GIVE, FORGIVE, FORGET, BE SET FREE

Week 4 Day 2

> *Bow your heart before the Lord in prayer before completing today's Bible study. Ask Him to show you His wisdom and heart toward those who betrayed you.*

The Desire to Get Even

When people are hurt, their first reaction is usually anger. The expression of this anger may be an attempt to hurt others as they hurt you. If people believe that the actions of others against them were sinful in God's eyes, they may feel justified in getting even.

1. *Do not rejoice when your enemy falls, and do not let your heart be glad when he stumbles; Lest the LORD see it, and it displease Him, and He turn away His wrath from him. Proverbs 24:17-18*

   What does the Bible say about getting even?

   • *Beloved, do not avenge yourselves, but rather give place to wrath; for it is written, "Vengeance is Mine, I will repay," says the Lord. Romans 12:19*

   • *since it is a righteous thing with God to repay with tribulation those who trouble you, 2 Thessalonians 1:6*

2. Is there anyone in your experience that you would like to see hurt as you hurt? If so, how have you responded to this anger?

"You have heard that it was said, 'You shall love your neighbor and hate your enemy.' But I say to you, love your enemies, bless those who curse you, do good to those who hate you, and pray for those who spitefully use you and persecute you, that you may be sons of your Father in heaven; for He makes His sun rise on the evil and on the good, and sends rain on the just and on the unjust. For if you love those who love you, what reward have you? Do not even the tax collectors do the same?" Matthew 5:43-46

3. What are some of the ways God wants you to respond to those who have wronged you or your Dad, mom, step-dad, step-mom, brother, step-brother, sister, step-sister, cousin, family member, neighbor, ex-friend, ex-boyfriend or other Christians?

4. Memorize the three scriptures below. When the desire to get even enters you mind use these scriptures remind yourself of God's will for you.

Pray Blessings On Your Enemies

Pray showers of blessings on those who cursed you, spitefully used you, and persecuted you. Pray that God will bless their hands, bless their family, and bless their job. Every time you think of them do not mull over the pain, but pray showers of blessings on them. Apply Matthew 5:44 to your prayer life. This scripture seems just the opposite of what our human flesh wants to do to our enemies. I began doing this toward someone who deeply hurt me and before long my heart was sincerely filled with God's love toward this person.

In fact I wanted to bless them by making them a pumpkin pie for Thanksgiving!

- *Therefore, if your enemy is hungry, feed him; if he is thirsty, give him a drink; for in so doing you will heap coals of fire on his head. Do not be overcome by evil, but overcome evil with good. Romans 12:20-21*

- *And be kind to one another, tenderhearted, forgiving one another, just as God in Christ forgave you. Ephesians 4:32*

- *Bearing with one another, and forgiving one another, if anyone has a complaint against another; even as Christ forgave you, so you also must do. But above all these things put on love, which is the bond of perfection. Colossians 3:13-14*

Bitter Roots

Hurtful memories leave many people feeling angry. If your hurtful experience was recent, your anger may be fresh. If your hurtful experience was years ago, this anger may have formed roots of bitterness in your life. People often remain angry with those who betray them.

5. Is there anyone in your life with whom you are still angry? Pray and ask the Lord to reveal this truth to you. What is still lingering? Write your prayer on the empty sheet provided. This is important to expose the root cause of your pain.

_____

_____

_____

_____

_____

_____

_____

_____

_____

_____

_____

_____

_____

_____

Learning God's Word

This week's memory verse:

____: Learn how ____must ____ the truth about ___ is in my ____, so ____ ___ _____.

Looking _____ lest anyone _____ short ___the ____ of God; lest any root of _____ springing up _____ trouble, and by this many become defiled; _____ 12:15

Words to Remember

• Fill in the blanks from the verse in the second Tool **GIVE**

2 Corinthians 7:10. ~ For godly sorrow _____ repentance _____ to salvation, not to be _____: but the _____ of the world _____ death.

6. *Let all bitterness, wrath, anger, clamor and evil speaking be put away from you, with all malice. Ephesians 4:31*

- • Is BITTERNESS in your life?

- • Is ANGER in your life?

- • Is CLAMOR in your life?

- • Is EVIL SPEAKING in your life?

But now you yourselves are to put off all these: anger, wrath, malice, blasphemy, filthy language out of your mouth. Colossians 3:8

7. What are you to do with your old anger?

Pain from the past

Many times when we are filled with anger toward those who have hurt us physically, emotionally, or verbally, we end up striking out. It is a painful thing to see how the anger we hold in our hearts can affects all our other relationships. We use that anger toward those who live with us. We strike out at the people who love us the most, usually our family members and friends.

8. Is this true in your life?

9. Pray and confess it to the Lord, asking for a new start in this area of your life.

10. What happens if you do not get rid of this anger according to the following verses?

- • *Looking carefully lest anyone fall short of the grace of God; lest any root of bitterness springing up cause trouble, and by this many become defiled; Hebrews 12:15*

Learning God's Word

This week's memory verse:

🖋 ___: Learn how ___must ___ the truth about ___ is in my ___, so ___ ___ ____.

Looking _____ lest anyone _____ short ___the ____ of God; lest any root of _____ springing up _____ trouble, and by this many become defiled; _____ 12:15

- *He who says he is in the light, and hates his brother, is in darkness until now. He who loves his brother abides in the light, and there is no cause for stumbling in him. But he who hates his brother is in darkness and walks in darkness, and does not know where he is going, because the darkness has blinded his eyes. 1 John 2:9-11*

11. Has God been speaking to you about any areas of anger concerning your hurtful experience that you have not let go or given over in repentance? If so, what do you need to do?

And have no fellowship with the unfruitful works of darkness, but rather expose them. Ephesians 5:11

If we say that we have fellowship with Him, and walk in darkness, we lie and do not practice the truth. But if we walk in the light as He is in the light, we have fellowship with one another, and the blood of Jesus Christ His Son cleanses us from all sin. 1 John 1:6-7

12. How do we leave the darkness of anger?

- Bitterness in your heart cannot be hidden or denied. It must be addressed. God commands you to get rid of it. Bring it out of the darkness and into the light.

13. Quiet your heart and ask God to show you any areas of bitterness left from your painful experience. Ask Him to show you any person with whom you may still be angry. In the space below, or on a separate piece of paper, complete the letter to God, telling Him why you have been angry with this person and specific ways this person has hurt you. What has been in the darkness for so long must be brought out into the light so God can heal you and set you free.

Dear God,

I am angry with_____ for hurting me when

_____

_____

_____

_____

_____

_____

_____

_____

Week 4 Day 3

Bow your heart before the Lord in prayer before completing today's Bible study. Ask Him for the help of the Holy Spirit to enable you to SEE what's really in your heart concerning wrong attitudes.

Put off the Old Self

God gives us every opportunity to make the right choices. As Christians we should desire to apply Colossians 3:8 to our lives and begin day by day to practice the Truth in our Christian walk. I desire to be obedient in my relationship to Christ because I'm the one who receives comfort from the obedience. When I go my own way, I'm the one who suffers.

1. *But now you yourselves are to put off all these: anger, wrath, malice, blasphemy, filthy language out of your mouth. Colossians 3:8*

   - Have you put off ANGER?

   - Have you put off WRATH?

   - Have you put off MALICE?

   - Have you put off BLASPHEMY?

   - Have you put off FILTHY LANGUAGE out of your MOUTH?

2. Do you have any ideas of how you want to practically apply Ephesians 4:23-29 to your life?

Fill in the Blanks:

⸴ Therefore, putting away _____,"Let each one of you speak truth with his neighbor," for we are members of _____ _____.
Let no _____ _____ _____ out of your mouth, but what is _____for necessary _____, that it may impart grace to the _____.Ephesians 4:23-29

Be renewed in the spirit of your mind, and that you put on the new man which was created according to God, in true righteousness and holiness. Therefore, putting away lying, let each one of you speak truth with his neighbor, for we are members of one another. Be angry, and do not sin: do not let the sun go down on your wrath, nor give place to the devil. Let him who stole steal no longer, but rather let him labor, working with his hands what is good, that he may have something to give him who has need. Let no corrupt word proceed out of your mouth, but what is good for necessary edification, that it may impart grace to the hearers. Ephesians 4:23-29

3. Write out the ways your mind is renewed as you apply Ephesians 4:23-29 to your relationship with others, with your actions, with your hands, and with your mouth as you put on the new man according to Ephesians 4:23-29.

_____

_____

_____

_____

_____

_____

_____

_____

_____

_____

_____

_____

_____

_____

_____

_____

_____

_____

_____

_____

_____

_____

_____

_____

_____

_____

The wise woman builds her house, but the foolish pulls it down with her hands.
Proverbs 14:1

Counting your Blessings

We all have so much to be thankful for that we need to learn to stop and count our blessings in the middle of a bad day. It's such a good way to get back our perspective.

The blessing of the Lord makes one rich, and He adds no sorrow with it.
Proverbs 10:22

Thank-you Letter from a Child

Dear mom and dad,

Thank you for loving me, thank you for snuggling me, thank you for hugging me, thank you for sharing the most important thing of all a relationship with Jesus Christ. If you would not of I would be lost in sin. Thank you for being with me when I went through difficulties.

I love you!

Signed a 8 year old girl, Jessica Brown

Author's Thankful List:

1. I am Thankful to Jesus, our great Savior, for eternal life.
2. I am Thankful for the window of time I get to spend with my children as they grow up.
3. I am Thankful my husband and I know marriage is not perfect, but we can love each other unconditionally because we allow God's love to reign in our marriage.
4. I am Thankful God's word is perfect, flawless and has healed me from my past.

The blessing of the Lord makes one rich, and He adds no sorrow with it.
Proverbs 10:22

My Thankful Heart

Write down four things you are content with and thankful for in your life.

1.

2.

3.

4.

Share it with your husband or a friend today. Share your blessed heart with another. It will brighten their day.

Week 4 Day 3

> *Bow your heart before the Lord in prayer before completing today's Bible study.*
> *Pray for His will in your relationship with your husband.*

AUTHOR'S REFLECTION
No Marriage is 〜〜〜〜〜〜〜〜〜〜〜〜〜〜〜〜〜〜〜〜〜〜〜〜〜〜〜〜〜
Perfect

Rick and I aren't perfect by any means. Many challenges still confront us. God's love will flow through us if we are willing to lay down our selfish wills and let God's will take over. I must not dump my frustrations out on my husband, my kids or others. Today, we have an incredible marriage and I am madly in love with my husband. Rick is my number one human relationship. It takes work to make a marriage incredible. God's healing power is available to each and every one of us. I am living proof of a life that has been Healed and Set Free by God's Word. God is Truth and only the truth can set you free. Remember that it's your choice to embrace or reject the Word of God and the freedom it brings.

God healed the burdens from my past hurts by showing me how I was hanging on to all the justified wrongs from my past. Yes, the wrongs were wrong, but as a Christian woman the most important thing for us to do is keep our relationship with Christ right. I forgave those wrongs! Why? Those questions will be answered as we take a closer look at forgiving the unacceptable in the next chapter.

Admonish the young women to love their husbands Titus 2:4

Practical Love ~~~ How can a wife nurture a heart of love, a heart prepared to support her husband in practical ways "until death us do part"?

One Author describes it in the following ways:

> *Decide to make your husband your number one human relationship* - Our relationship with our husband is meant to be more important than the relationship we enjoy with our parents, friends, a good neighbor, a brother or sister, a best friend, and even our children --- and the way we use our time should reflect the rank order!

> I learned a lot about this kind of decision while reading a story about a mother and her married daughter, Jill Briscoe and Judy Goltz. Right before her daughter was married, Jill sat her down and told her that, once she was married, she couldn't come running home and she was no longer to be dependent on her parents - for anything!

> Then the daughter wrote: "When Greg and I were first married, I almost automatically reached for the telephone whenever I had a certain problem or very good news to share. Usually before I finished dialing your number, Mom, I realized what I was doing, and I made sure Greg knew about it first before calling you."

> Judy also asked her mother, "Do you remember the time Greg and I had a newly - married tiff and I called you in tears? The first thing you said to me was, " Judy, does Greg know you are calling me?"

Bravo! This mother who voluntarily stepped out of a number one relationship with her daughter and showed her the way to make her husband her new number one human relationship! After all, God said that we are to "leave and cleave" - to leave our parents and cleave to our mate. (Genesis 2:24)

Begin to choose your husband over all other human relationships – Again, this includes your children.

"It's Too Late Now"

Today's letter will have a somber tone. I'm about to tell you a sad story... of a woman who put her children ahead of her husband......

These last two years he's been especially lonesome. Reason? His wife has literally latched onto their youngest daughter. She's one of those hang on to your children for dear life mothers and last year when the last one enrolled at the university, she came unglued....Now the lady is turning to her husband, hoping....

When was the last time they were close? He simply can't remember.. All those years in second place he'd make a life of his own. Had to...Not right. Of course it isn't. But...all these years his wife has been talking to him, at him, seldom with him.....Think of the fun they could be having now if they had developed a friendship.

I know too many men who, when their children came, turned down lonesome road. And when you've gone too long single file, its hard coming back to double. So much has happened alone it just seems easier to say; " It's too late now".........

You're wise to keep checking priorities.... You can be bother mother and wife. But the wise woman remembers she will begin and end as a wife.

Ask of your lifestyle, *Am I spoiling my husband rotten?*

- Pray for him daily
- Plan for him daily
- Plan special deed of kindness
- Plan special dinners
- Plan special times alone
- Prepare the home
- Prepare your greeting

Mrs. Billy Graham is a wife who knows the value of protective time with her husband. Everything is geared toward Billy when he is in their home in Montreal. Ruth refuses to have a firm schedule when Billy is there.... The daily routine is carefully designed around her husband.... A neighbor of the Grahams wrote, " Because Ruth is out of circulation when Billy comes home, her friends call him 'The Plague.'" How's that for a goal?

1. Why not pause and pray for your husband ---your number one friend-- right now? Thank God for the love He has placed in your heart for your husband, and ask for His help in sharing it with your husband. After you say "amen," plan to do something special for your husband today that sends a message of friendship from your heart to his.

Guarding Your Home from Becoming a War Zone

Wives making their husband look forward to coming home.
Husbands making their wives look forward to them being at home.

Our homes need to be a place we enjoy coming home to, a place of refuge for the hearts of all who live there. Fighting, unkind words and critical looks shouldn't be brought into our Christian homes where it will damage or destroy relationships. There is plenty of war going on in the world outside of our homes. Guard your homes from becoming a war zone.

🌽   *Let your gentleness be known to all men. The Lord is at hand. Philippians 4:5*

My List for making my Husband, Rick, look Forward to coming home:

The wise woman builds her house, but the foolish pulls it down with her hands. Proverbs 14:1

1. Have a sweet heart of unfailing love.

2. Use kind and encouraging words and don't try to be his Holy Spirit.

3. Edify my husband by looking for and pointing out the good things in his life.

4. Respect my husband as the head of our home.

5. Show him how much I love him in word and in action, to render to him what is his.

Rick's List for making me look forward to him being at home:

Husbands, love your wives, just as Christ also loved the church and gave Himself for it. Ephesians 5:25

1. Be the spiritual leader in word and prayer.

2. Show how valuable and priceless she is to me in word and action.

3. Show loving care and concern by listening to and sharing with my wife.

4. Show her my affection with kindness and with hugs and kisses.

5. Show loving care and concern for our children.

6. Be willing to help around the house.

Resolving Conflicts (God's Way)

- You must be willing to resolve the conflict, to tell the truth in love, and to do whatever the Bible requires resolving the conflict. Ask God to give you a willing heart to resolve conflicts, to reconcile, to be a peacemaker.

- Where you are weak, He promises He will make you strong. *My grace is sufficient for you, for My strength is made perfect in weakness. 2 Corinthians 12:9*

- You must choose to restrain your own anger in every conflict. *I can do all things through Christ who strengthens me Philippians 4:13*

- You must listen to the other person instead of arguing to prove your own point. *Let every man be swift to hear, slow to speak, slow to wrath. James 1:19*

- You must confess your own faults instead of blaming others. *And why do you look at the speck in your brothers eye, but do not consider the plank in your own eye. First remove the plank from your own eye, and then you will see clearly to remove the speck out of your brother's eye. Matthew 7:3,5*

Taking It Out on My Husband for 20 Years

I was molested in the third grade. Because of this sin against me, I sinned in my teenage years by being sexually active. I was trying to fill the void in my heart, but I ended up getting pregnant. I had an abortion, piling sin on top of sin.

I didn't realize these sins affected every area of my life including my relationship with God, my relationship with my husband, and especially any relationship with other men. I felt dirty, like I had a smelly yuck all over me and my whole life. God knew I could not go on like that. He led me to this Bible study even though I thought I didn't need it. He opened my eyes and revealed to me things I never realized I was doing.

All the pain I had felt over being molested and over the abortion, I had been taking out on my husband for 20 years. Every time I looked at him it reminded me of my past hurts.

Through this study I am free. That is the word that keeps coming to my mind - Free! By being obedient to God, being in the Word, and studying this workbook , God has set me Free. Follow those steps and you can be Healed too. Thank you, Tammy, for letting the Lord use you in such a special way.

Healed and Set Free - Pam, Idaho

SEE, GIVE, FORGIVE, FORGET, BE SET FREE

Week 4 Day 5

Review

Review this Chapter on Letting Go Of Anger. Reflect on the truths you have learned.

🦢 SEE: I must ___ the truth about ___ is in my ____, so ____ ___ _____.

Looking _____ lest anyone _____ short ___the ____ of God; lest any root of_____

springing up _____ trouble, and _ this many become defiled; _____ 12:15

- God's anger is...

- The thing about my experience that makes me angry is...

- I want to respond to this anger by...

- I will practice self-control when I am angry by...

- For a long time I have had anger toward...

- I desire to know more about Forgiving the Unacceptable towards
  _____ in the next chapter.

The next step in getting rid of this root of bitterness is to forgive people who have hurt you. Forgiveness is not easy, especially when the hurting may have been with you for years. The next chapter will reveal God's plan for learning how to forgive others.

"Stories of real people, real hurts, real healing, and a real SAVIOR"

Shackles of Anger and Bulimia

I can't express the hatred and anger that I held in a dark hole in my heart toward my brothers. I have four older brothers, three out of the four abused me sexually. It started when I was quite young, five or six years old. My oldest brother is 10 years older than I am. He would take me into the back bathroom when my parents were gone and pay me pennies to do things to him and allow him to do things to me. I knew it was wrong, but I truly trusted him, he said it was okay. Small incidents (if any sexual abuse is small,) went on with my second brother. The youngest of my brothers forced intercourse on me. I remember fearing I was pregnant by him when I was only in the fifth or sixth grade. I would do hurtful things to my body to make sure the baby wouldn't survive, just in case I was pregnant. For some reason I still trusted them. I knew it was wrong and yet I thought it was normal or okay.

I had to face my brothers each and every day at home. Even after they moved out we would still have many family get-togethers. In order to survive I tucked all of my hatred, anger and fear deep down in my heart. I never dealt with these feelings but I knew they were there because of the way I treated my husband. I would lash out in anger at him for no reason. I thought sex was dirty and only for the pleasure of the man. My husband didn't understand why I hated sex and hated being intimate with him. I didn't know about God's perfect plan for intimacy in marriage.

Another way this abuse affected my adult life was through an eating disorder. I am bulimic, which I thought was just a sickness like alcoholism. I felt this was the only area in my life I could control. I would eat nothing or eat a lot and then throw it up, feeling I was in control. Through this study I found out I wasn't in control of my eating, instead my eating was controlling me. I also found out being bulimic is giving into the flesh, and I was sinning every time I threw up.

A few years after I was married, my husband received Christ. Through my husband, some months later, I too received Christ. Our relationship did a complete turn around, still I knew the deep dark holes in my heart were still there. Years passed and I thought the anger toward my husband and children was just how it was going to be. This is me, I thought.

I started the Healed and Set Free Bible study for my eating disorder. I thought I might get something out of it with regard to my brothers' abuse. A lot of emotional issues started coming out as I began the study. The deep dark holes in my heart were exposing themselves. I had told myself I would never forgive my brothers for what they had done to me. They had probably long forgotten that any of this had ever happened. I was still angry, still remembering, still carrying around all of this baggage.

One day during the study, I shared my memory of the pennies and how much it had affected me. When another woman in the study said she had the same experience, all my emotions came flooding back. I was crying uncontrollably. Tammy Brown stopped the study, and we prayed and prayed as I gave the hurt and fear over to Christ, asking for help and strength to be Set free from the past hurts. I was finding out that I couldn't do it without God's help.

The Turning Point

I think the turning point for me was when one of the women in the Healed and Set Free Bible Study shared what God had shown her, sin is sin is sin. God was telling me it doesn't matter if you are sinning by not forgiving, or living in the flesh by letting food and self-centeredness control your life. I knew what my brothers did was not okay, but was sin. I learned I was sinning just as much as my brothers did by not forgiving them. And God wanted me to forgive them. I was also sinning by being bulimic. I now know I can control this through prayer and asking God daily to kill my flesh.

As I completed the Bible study, I truly prayed in my heart for forgiveness toward my brothers. I knew God was healing my heart. My hatred has turned into compassion. God has laid their lives and their families' lives on my heart. I have been praying for their salvation and that I would be able to share God's Word with them. I want to show them how God has changed my life and my heart.

Just three weeks after I finished the Healed and Set Free study my brother received Christ as his savior. God has completely restored our relationship. If I had been asked five years ago if I would ever see myself having compassion toward my brothers, I would have said, 'NEVER!' Through God's Word and being in prayer with Him, He has allowed me to leave all of this at the foot of the cross, and maybe use this to minister to others. My marriage and relationship with my family isn't perfect, but I live day by day and continue to seek God for the strength to love my husband and children the way God has designed for me. God has changed my life and my heart, and I have been Healed and Set Free.

Brand new woman

SEE, GIVE, FORGIVE, FORGET, BE SET FREE

A. Ignorant disobedience: you do not know what you are doing is sinful.

B. Willful disobedience: you know what you are doing is sinful and you continue to sin.

The Path

The pain has crushed me, stifled me,
taken my last breath.
I stand in confusion and wonder,
will I ever trust, ever love again?
NEVER, I say.

I leave doors open,
never to walk through them,
Or slam doors to block out intrusion.
I am a fortress alone.
I need no one.

Yet a small, still voice whispers,
only a sigh above the wind.,
rustling in the limbs of the weeping willow tree.
Pain becomes only one of TWO things,
It is up to YOU.

It grows to HATE:
It's path covered with concrete blocks,
Or it grows to LOVE,
Whose path is covered with soft, delicate roses,
Along the path to love, a few petals must fall.

Jonnie Landis

Chapter 4

Forgiving the Unacceptable

Bearing with one another and forgiving one another, if anyone has a complaint against another; even as Christ forgave you, so you also must do.

Colossians 3:13

There are four main tools we will weave into the very fiber of our hearts day by day: **SEE, GIVE, FORGIVE, FORGET,** and **BE SET FREE.** Thinking about the past will never change the past. But you can change your future and Be Set FREE from your past. As you deal with your past and present hurts, you can either embrace the truth and let go of the burdens you carry, or carry your burdens and reject the truth and the freedom it brings. The choice is yours. Getting real with God is the first step you need to always take as you face deep, dark hurts that have chipped away at your peace for 1 year, 10 years, 20 years, and some 50 years. God's love is bigger then all of our hurts and fears. You will have many blessings in front of you as God's truth unfolds in your heart and Sets you Free.

Let's Day By Day Go over the Four Steps to Keep Our Hearts Clean

🦢 Tools To Become Set Free

- **Tool #1 "SEE ":** I must **SEE** the truth about what is in my heart, so I'm not defiled.

    Looking carefully lest anyone fall short of the grace of God; lest any root of bitterness springing up cause trouble, and by this many become defiled. Hebrew 12:15.

- **Tool #2 "GIVE":** I must **GIVE** the sin in repentance, knowing Christ is waiting to take it. (I must be sorry enough to change and choose to go God's way over my own way.)

    For godly sorrow produces repentance leading to salvation, not to be regretted; but the sorrow of the world produces death. 2 Corinthians 7:10

- **Tool #3 "FORGIVE":** I must **FORGIVE**, as I am forgiven by Christ. (Forgiving those that hurt, bruised, wronged, hurt, rejected, betrayed or harmed me whether unintentionally or deliberately.) Ask God to Forgive you for holding unforgiveness and know that He will.

    Bearing with one another, and forgiving one another, if anyone has a complaint against another; even as Christ forgave you, so you also must do. Colossians 3:13

- **Tool #4 "FORGET":** I must **FORGET** by remembering to no longer dwell on the hurt.

    Brethren, I do not count myself to have apprehended; but one thing I do, forgetting those things which are behind and reaching forward to those things which are ahead. Philippians 3:13.

🦢 **BECOME SET FREE:** Christ will open the shackles from my past hurts showing me the truth so I can become a cleansed vessel that is Healed and Set Free.

    You shall know the truth, and the truth shall make you free. Therefore, if the Son makes you free, you shall be free indeed. John 8:32-36.

SATAN IS DEFEATED AND THE SHACKLES ARE GONE AND YOU ARE FREE!

Week 5 Day 1

Bow your heart before the Lord in prayer before completing today's Bible study. Ask Him to help you SEE and understand the truth about the fallen angel, Satan.

God's Truth

The cross shows the love of God. From the cross God is saying to each one of us, I love you. I love you. I love you. God provided forgiveness for people who were bound to fail but who would want to return to Him to seek His mercy and forgiveness. God sent His Son, Jesus, to be the sacrifice for all our sins. Christ bore your sins on the cross. Every sin you have ever committed, every evil thought you have ever had is on that cross.

God can not lie and God's highest priority is for you to be in a trusting, loving relationship with Him. Thus God, determining to show more abundantly to the heirs of promise the immutability of His counsel, confirmed it by an oath, that by two immutable things, in which it is impossible for God to lie, we might have strong consolation, who have fled for refuge to lay hold of the hope set before us. Hebrews 6:17-18

Satan's Lie

Because you have been forgiven you can choose to share this forgiveness of Jesus with others. If you chose not to receive God's forgiveness or forgive others, you are saying you believe that Christ's sacrifice and His death on the cross weren't enough. You have believed a lie from Satan who is the father of all lies. He was a murderer from the beginning, and does not stand in the truth, because there is no truth in him. When he speaks a lie, he speaks from his own resources, for he is a liar and the father of it. John 8:44. Satan's highest priority is the destruction of your Christian life.

As people in Christ we need to resist the devil and his lies and stand strong in the days to come when we are lead by the spirit into the wilderness to be tempted.

Learning God's Word

This week's memory verse:
 Bearing with one another, and forgiving one another, if anyone has a complaint against another; even as Christ forgave you, so you also must do. Colossians 3:13

You Need to Know What God's Word says About Satan

1. **Satan is your adversary.**

Fill in the blanks: *Be sober; be vigilant, because your _____ the devil walks about like a _____ lion, seeking whom he may devour. 1 Peter 5:8*

2. **Satan is the thief.**

Write out: *John 10:10*

3. **Satan fills your heart to lie.**

Fill in the blanks: *But Peter said, "Ananias, why has Satan filled your _____ to ____ to the Holy Spirit and keep back part of the price of the land for yourself? Acts 5:3*

4. **Satan is a cunning snake.**

Write out: *Genesis 3:1:*

5. **Do not fear.**

Read Revelation 2:10: *Do not fear any of those things which you are about to suffer. Indeed, the devil is about to throw some of you into prison, that you may be tested, and you will have tribulation ten days. Be faithful until death, and I will give you the crown of life. Revelation 2:10*

6. **God is greater.**

Fill in the blanks: *Greater is ____ that is in you (Jesus) than ____ that is in the world (Satan). 1 John 4:4*

7. Write out James 4:7

Read Job 1:12 *So Satan went out from the presence of the Lord. And the Lord said to Satan, "Behold, all that he has is in your power; only do not lay a hand on his person." Job 1:12*

(Satan had to receive permission from God to attack Job.)

You are in a Spiritual War.

The battles we face and the power of Satan are ongoing. The footsteps of Satan creep in to our homes to bring destruction. He will do whatever he can to stop you from being Healed and Set Free from hurts in the past that affect you today. Satan is like a hit man and he wants to take you out. This is no game. You are in a spiritual war for your freedom.

What the Snake Knows about You.

Do you know your own flesh, weaknesses, fears, insecurities, and struggles?

Write down and recognize the follow about yourself in order to guard yourself from Satan's attacks.

8. He knows your flesh. When does your flesh get stirred up?

9. He knows your weaknesses. Recognize your weaknesses by writing them down?

10. He knows your fears and insecurities. What lies has Satan been whispering in your ear to activate your fears and insecurities?

11. He knows your every struggle. What struggles continue to tempt or lead you to failure?

12. He knows when, where, and how to most effectively attack you. Can you see where Satan is launching his attacks against you? If so, where.

Greater is He that is in you (Jesus) than he that is in the world (Satan). 1 John 4:4
Therefore, submit to God. Resist the devil and he will flee from you. James 4:7

Learning God's Word

This Week's tool:

🔖 Tool #2 GIVE: I must **GIVE** the sin in repentance. Knowing Christ is waiting to take it (I must be sorry enough to change and choose to go God's way over my own way.)

For godly sorrow produces repentance leading to salvation, not to be regretted; but the sorrow of the world produces death. 2 Corinthians 7:10

Week 5 Day 2

> *Therefore strengthen the hands which hangs down, and the feeble knees, and make straight paths for your feet, so that what is lame may not be dislocated, but rather be healed. Hebrews 12:12*

Footsteps of Satan in Your Home

1. Is the enemy launching attacks your way? Do you recognize it as the snake? Lets continue to look a little deeper to recognize your weaknesses, fears, insecurities and struggles. If the snake knows them you need to know them to resist Satan from continuing to be effective in his attack.

2. Are the footsteps of Satan in your home? Summarize the temptations he throws at you.

3. Do you know that the footsteps of Satan are crafty, tempting, and deceitful? Explain three ways he wants to keep you from obeying, trusting, and following God.

4. Do you hear the footsteps of Satan? He wants to sift you like wheat in your marriage or single life. List the ways he does this.

Learning God's Word

This Week's tool:

Tool #3 FORGIVE: I must **FORGIVE**, as I am forgiven by Christ. (Forgiving those that hurt, bruised, wronged, hurt, rejected, betrayed, or harmed me whether unintentionally or deliberately.) Ask God to Forgive you for holding unforgiveness and know that He will.

Bearing with one another, and forgiving one another, if anyone has a complaint against another; even as Christ forgave you, so you also must do. Colossians 3:13

> *Bow your heart before the Lord and ask Him to reveal any sins in your life that might be separating you from Him, then ask Him to forgive you and know that He will.*

Satan wants us to follow the Wrong Answers

One of the hissing snake's most deceitful attacks, as he slips in with his crafty ways, is to smoothly tempt you to forget you have an enemy at all. When you fall for this lie, it will lead you to embrace all the wrong answers. When hurts come into our lives we are sure we can figure it out. We think we know what life is all about. The world's ungodly wisdom of healing is offered through the snake, hissing at us, tempting us to try and fix ourselves.

Remember he knows where to launch his attack in your life.

5. **Wrong Answers** (Circle the ones that have crept into your life)

   * Denying myself, punishing myself

   * Turning to false gods or wrong attitudes

   * Using medications, feeling depressed or worthless

   * Blaming everyone else, being discontent with my life or my marriage

   * Getting even

   * Giving the cold shoulder

   * Pretending it doesn't bother me, thinking no one else struggles with the past

   * Stuffing it deep into my heart and not accepting that it ever happened

   * Running to shopping fixes

   * Running to food fixes or starving myself

   * Running to parties or sex

   * Longing for death

   * Thinking others don't like me and being self absorbed

I haven't seen one person healed by the world's wisdom. Dealing with your hurts in your own way just leads to a heart of sorrow. It's the wrong answer.

> We like sheep have gone astray; we have turned, every one, to his own way; and the Lord has laid on Him the iniquity of us all. Isaiah 53:6

The Right Answer

When hurts come into our lives from the actions of someone's unacceptable sin, usually a root of bitterness usually begins to grow from that broken heart, that word hurled to wound, that unseen evil pushed on a child, or the pain of being rejected.

How can we stop that root from growing and consuming our lives? The right answer is to follow the truth and the truth will set you free. In Hebrews 4:12 it say's, " For the word of God is living and powerful, and sharper than any two-edged sword." The right answer is to get a sharp sword and cut that root out of our life. That sword is God's word.

1. Being filled with the knowledge of His will in all wisdom an spiritual understanding; that you may have a walk worthy of the Lord, fully pleasing Him, being fruitful in every good work and increasing in the knowledge of God. Colossians 1:9-10

Write down how you have actively applied the following Healed and Set Free tools to your heart in order to be filled with the knowledge of His will?

🌿 I can now **SEE** _____

🌿 I have **GIVEN** _____

🌿 I have **FORGIVEN** _____

🌿 I desire to **FORGET** _____

🌿 I have been **SET FREE** from _____

The thief does not come except to steal, and to kill, and to destroy. I have come that they may have life, and that they may have it more abundantly. John 10:10

2. When the footsteps of Satan come into your home, ask yourself if these three words are in action and you will know he is there:

STEAL   **KILL**   **DESTROY**

Learning God's Word

This Week's tool:

🌿 Tool #2 GIVE: I must _____ the sin in repentance. Knowing Christ is waiting to take it   (I must be sorry enough to change and choose to go God's way over my own way.)

For _____ produces _____ leading to salvation, not to be regretted; but the sorrow of the world produces death. ___ Corinthians ___:10

JUNK DRAWER

A dear friend taking the Healed and Set Free Bible study shared this story with me.

Most every home has a junk drawer, somewhere to throw odds and ends, screwdrivers, pencils, pens and all the items you don't know where else to put. She hadn't realized that she had been keeping a junk drawer tucked away in her heart ever since her stepfather had sexually abused her at a very young age. From that point on and throughout her life, she learned to put broken trusts, painful memories and all the hurts that still lingered into the junk drawer of her heart when she didn't know what else to do with them. Her heart became filled with unforgiveness, bitterness and keeping track of the wrongs that others had committed against her.

She was continually reminded in each chapter of the Healed and Set Free study that she needed to see what was really going on in her heart and get real with the hurts where they still lingered. As she completed the Bible study homework, God began to show her that she needed to clean out the junk drawer of her heart. After being a Christian for over 20 years, she was being faced with the contents of the junk drawer she had tucked away in her heart. She tossed out the unforgiveness and resentment by receiving God's forgiveness. She then forgave her stepfather and others who had wronged her.

Now my dear friend knows how to keep the junk drawer in her heart empty. She was able to SEE, GIVE, FORGIVE, FORGET AND BE SET FREE! She is not only enjoying the freedom of not having a junk drawer in her heart, but also in having a heart that has been Healed and Set Free.

"By His Stripes we are Healed"

SEE, GIVE, FORGIVE, FORGET, BE SET FREE

Learning God's Word

This Week's tool:

Tool #3 FORGIVE: I must _____, as I am forgiven by Christ (Forgiving those that hurt, bruised, wronged, hurt, rejected, betrayed or harmed me whether unintentionally or deliberately. Ask God to Forgive you for holding unforgiveness and know that He will.

Bearing with one another, and _____ one _____, if anyone has a _____ against another; even as Christ forgave you, so you also must do. Colossians 3:13

Week 5 Day 3

> *Bow your heart before the Lord in prayer before completing today's Bible Study.*

Satan offers pleasures

No matter what kind of pleasures Satan offers you, his ultimate intention is to ruin you. Your destruction is his highest priority.

The thief does not come except to steal, and to kill, and to destroy. John 10:10

1. Has the thief sneaked into your home with temptations cleverly disguised as harmless pleasures? Explain.

Therefore, submit to God. Resist the devil and he will flee from you. James 4:7

2. How do you resist the devil?

Therefore take up the whole armor of God, that you may be able to withstand in the evil day, and having done all, to stand. Stand therefore, having girded your waist with truth, having put on the breastplate of righteousness, and having shod your feet with the preparation of the gospel of peace; above all, taking the shield of faith with which you will be able to quench all the fiery darts of the wicked one. And take the helmet of salvation, and the sword of the Spirit, which is the word of God. Ephesians 6:13

3. How do you stand against the devil in God's Armor?

Learning God's Word
This Week's Memory Verse:
🎵 _____ _____ _____ another, and _____ one another, ___ anyone has a
_____ against _____; even as _____ _____ you, so you also _____ do.
_____ 3: ___

Don't Waste Your Pain; Use It To Bring Glory to God.

Don't stop your tears. Let them cleanse you. Don't stop the pain. Let the pain in your heart drive you deeper into God's love and God's truth. Draw near to God and He will draw near to you. Lots of brokenhearted people just give up and walk away. Don't let that be you.

You need to SEE that God's hand is there to SET YOU FREE.

4. Fill in the blanks: *You are _____ workmanship, created in Christ Jesus for good works, _____ God prepared beforehand that we _____ walk in them. Ephesians 2:10*

5. What are you to walk in according to Ephesians 2:10?

6. Study the story of Joseph who was betrayed by his family in Genesis 37-50

   • His brothers hatred him because they were jealous. Genesis 37:4

   • He was sold into Egypt by his brothers. Genesis 37:25-30

   • He won esteem in Egypt. Genesis 39:1-23

   • He interpreted pharaoh's dream. Genesis 41:1-37

   • He became pharaoh's Prime Minister. Genesis 41:38-46

   • He recognized his brothers. Genesis 42:1-8

   • He revealed his identity. Genesis 45:1-16

   • He dealt kindly with his brothers. Genesis 50:15-21

Satan meant all of this for evil. His intention was to destroy Joseph, but God meant it for good. Joseph was willing to trust God and to let God work in his life through his brokenness. He let his pain drive him deeper into God.

7. Write out Matthew 19:26

And we know that all things work together for good to those who love God, to those who are called according to His purpose. Romans 8:28

8. Do you see how the hurts or failures can work together for good in the calling and the purpose God has planned for your life? If so, how?

Week 5 Day 4

> *Bow your heart before the Lord in prayer before completing today's Bible study. Ask Him to help you apply the tools to the eyes of your heart to SEE and understand the truth.*

AUTHOR'S REFLECTION
Forgiving the Unacceptable

Perhaps my brokenness brought me to the end of myself. To become strong in the broken place in our lives demands that we do two things that seem to be opposites: *hang in there and let go.*

As a result of sexual abuse. I isolated myself by withdrawing into a shy little girl. My second grade teacher even informed my mom that I was retarded. In a sense, she was probably right. As a seven-year-old I was dealing with a very abnormal issue. I wasn't showing up at school with the normal cares of a second grader. My mind was not on what snack I was going to eat after school or innocent childhood secrets like which girl likes which boy. I was dealing with unacceptable secrets, shame, guilt, death threats, and sexual threats to silence me. I was paralyzed with fear. I didn't trust anyone enough to share what was happening to me. I grew a root of bitterness and hate towards my uncle, and for twenty years I suffered in silence and fear.

My silence was broken when I became a Christian and shared my painful experience with my husband Rick. He listened to me talk, as I was able to tell him about my memories, heartache, anger and resentment. I had pushed it down so deep in my heart that once I began to talk and pray about it, I was overwhelmed with grief. But once it was out, it felt good. I didn't stop the tears; I let them cleanse me. I hung in there as I learned to let go and to forgive.

- *Confess your trespasses to one another, and pray for one another, that you may be healed. The effective, fervent prayer of a righteous man avails much.* James 5:16

- *Blessed are those who mourn for they shall be comforted. Matthew 5:4*

Learning God's Word

This Week's Memory Verse:

🌹 _____ ____ ____ *another, and* _____ *one another,* ___ *anyone has a* _____ *against* _____*; even as*_____ _____ *you, so you also* _____ *do.* _____ *3:* ___

Pot of ∿∿∿∿∿∿∿∿∿∿∿∿∿∿∿∿∿∿∿∿∿∿∿∿∿∿∿∿∿∿∿∿∿
Boiling Water

My past did in fact affect me. I hated those that hurt me so much I prayed God would send them to hell to burn! The bitterness also affected all other areas of my life. I was like a pot of boiling water and you would never know when a splash of "hot water" would slosh out and burn someone. Bitterness, rage, hatred, resentment, defensiveness and insecurities filled my heart. I was tired of being filled with trash.

I knew it was time to face the pain and face my unforgiving heart that was taking over my life. I could no longer accept the way I was living. I was ready to get real with Jesus Christ and ask God for help. I needed to become broken before Him and I needed to trust Him with my hurts. I wanted a new beginning.

Jesus Christ started moving me on a journey toward healing. I'm so thankful I went on that journey even though it was one of the most difficult journeys I've ever made. I needed to be completely healed and set free because Satan had me in bondage, and he wasn't going to let me go easily. I had to fight for my freedom.

I see now that one day at a time, God began to take me on this journey and use the four steps of SEE, GIVE, FORGIVE, FORGET, and BE SET FREE to heal me. He created in me a pure heart, and granted me a new start. You may be tempted to think you don't want to go on this journey. That is a lie from the pit of hell. Remember Satan doesn't want to see you Healed and Set Free.

Step One — SEE

🦋 SEE the truth of what sins are in your own heart. Asking God to expose the root causes of your sinful thoughts that could be springing up and defiling your heart.

I had to **SEE** the truth of what sins were in my own heart. At first I tried to justify my feelings. But after many tears, lots of prayer and learning God's Truth in His Word, I finally realized my sins of "hate and unforgiveness" were no different than the sins my uncle had committed. SIN IS SIN.

---

1. Have any of the following filled your heart? (*Circle all that apply*)

Fear - hurt - defensiveness - anxiety - insecurities - self-pity- resentment - doubt - pride jealousy -desire to get even - bitterness - comparing myself to others - need to control.

---

2. Read Hebrews 12:15: *Looking diligently lest anyone fall short of the grace of God; lest any root of bitterness springing up cause trouble, and by this may become defiled;*

Step Two — GIVE

I had to **GIVE** my bitterness, hate and everything to Christ. This was the hardest part for me because I had built a thick wall of resentment in my heart. But I knew the way I was living as a Christian was no longer acceptable. With God's help I began to GIVE my sinful burden to the Lord.

My heart began to heal when I asked for forgiveness for my unforgiving heart. This wasn't to be a one-time thing, but the beginning of a painful journey. I needed to SEE the truth about what was in my heart that was causing trouble and defiling me. I knew I had to GIVE it to Christ as it began to arise in my heart.

I continue to apply Psalm 32:5 and James 5:16 in my life to this very day. I have no desire to let my ugly sinful nature take over my life.

3. Are you ready to GIVE your bitterness, your hate and your hurts to Jesus today? We needed to become broken before God and open up our hearts and let the Healer set us free.

4. Read 2 Corinthians 7:10: *For godly sorrow produces repentance leading to salvation, not to be regretted; but the sorrow of the world produces death.* *2 Corinthians 7:10*

5. Write out Psalm 32:5

6. Fill in the blanks: _____ *your trespasses to one another, and* _____ *for one another, that you may be healed. The effective, fervent* _____ *of a righteous man avails much.* *James 5:16*

Step Three — FORGIVE

🌿 I need to **FORGIVE** others, As I am forgiven by Christ. (Forgiving those that hurt, bruised, wronged, hurt, rejected, betrayed or harmed me whether unintentionally or deliberately.) Ask God to Forgive you for holding unforgiveness and know that He will.

7. Read Colossians 3:13 *Bearing with one another, and forgiving one another, if anyone has a complaint against another; even as Christ forgave you, so you also must do.*

I need to be sorry enough to change my way of thinking and choose God's way over my own way. Of course the memories are still there, but the feeling of hate and the hollow feelings that unacceptable hurts bring is gone. Because I have forgiven others from my heart, I don't even think about those memories now. It's not worth it! It's time to FORGET the past and remember to look forward, keeping my eyes on Jesus.

8. Are you ready to Forgive those that have heart you? Pray and tell Christ about it.

Step Four — FORGET

🌿 FORGET by remembering to no longer dwell on your past hurts but look to the future.

I had to learn to **FORGET** and not dwell on my past hurts. This happened only after my heart was truly healed from the unforgiveness and the unacceptable shame and anger I held in my heart from the past hurts. This is the easiest step for you to take to have a fresh start in God's truth and love. But you will need to be alert and on your guard. Recognize it as an attack from Satan when you are tempted to remember and dwell on your past hurts. Instead, remember to forget. There is such freedom for your heart and soul in forgetting the past and looking forward to your future.

9. Fill in the blanks: *Brethren, I do not count myself to have apprehended; but one thing I do, forgetting _____ things which _____ behind and reaching forward to __ things which ____ ahead, Philippians 3:13*

Forget until the Lord wants to use the memories for His glory, to show and comfort others that have a brokenheart. We have a great Healer that can Heal them also.

The Victory to BE SET FREE

BE SET FREE from the shackles that have kept you in bondage to all the hatred, shame and bitterness by believing and trusting in God's Truth found in God's Word.

10. Read John 14:6: *Jesus answered, "I am the way and the truth and the life." John 14:6*

11. Write out John 8:32::

You will experience freedom when you get rid of the junk drawer in your heart where records of wrongs are kept. You will then become an open vessel that is Healed and Set Free!

Remember now, O Lord, I pray, how I have walked before You in truth and with a loyal heart, and have done what is good in your Sight. Isaiah 38:3

AUTHOR'S REFLECTION
Satan is Defeated, the Shackles are Gone and I'm Free

The crime of molestation sent my uncle to prison for fifteen years. The effects of being molested put me in a prison of bitterness and despair for twenty years. Even to the end, my uncle was not remorseful for his actions and is still in bondage to his sin. But Praise Jesus Christ! He has shown me a better way. I am remorseful for my sins of hatred and unforgiveness. He has freed me from my bondage.

Jesus Christ healed my bitterness toward my uncle and turned the unacceptable into compassion. Jesus Christ healed my hatred toward my uncle and turned the unacceptable into forgiveness. Jesus Christ healed my heart from the prayer that my uncle would burn in hell forever to praying he would inherit everlasting life. Would I ever trust my uncle alone with a child? Never! It would be extremely unwise to leave him alone with a child. God tells us to use wisdom concerning others whose weaknesses can harm others.

Although the memories will always be there, the emotional grief has been healed. I have been Healed and Set Free by Jesus Christ. I am not to meditate on those memories. I am to meditate on the purity of God's Word and fill my mind and heart with God's Truth. I still pray one day my uncle will surrender his life to Christ. I am fearful for his soul. The prison walls he lives in now will seem like paradise compared to prison walls of eternal hell

I know I'm forever Transformed, Tammy Brown

"Our basic problems are not social or due to lack of education, our problems are in our hearts."

- Billy Graham

Week 6 Day 1

Bow your heart before the Lord in prayer before completing today's Bible study. Ask Him to help you by the power of the Holy Spirit to SEE what is in your heart concerning forgiving and being forgiven so you may GIVE it to Christ.

A Forgiving God

Who forgives all your iniquities, Who heals all your diseases, Psalm 103:3

Who is a God like You, pardoning iniquity and passing over the transgression of the remnant of His heritage? He does not retain His anger forever, because He delights in mercy. He will again have compassion on us, and will subdue our iniquities. You will cast all our sins into the depths of the sea. Micah 7:18-19

1. What truths are revealed about God and the forgiveness He extends to us in the above verses?

I acknowledged my sin to you, and my iniquity I have not hidden. I said, "I will confess my transgressions to the Lord," and you forgave the iniquity of my sin. Psalm 32:5

Iniquities prevail against me; as for our transgressions, You will provide atonement for them. Psalm 65:3

For You, Lord, are good, and ready to forgive, and abundant in mercy to all those who call upon You. Psalm 86:5

2. What does God do when we confess our sins?

If we confess our sins, He is faithful and just to forgive us our sins and to cleanse us from all unrighteousness. 1 John 1:9

"Repent therefore and be converted, that your sins may be blotted out, so that times of refreshing may come from the presence of the Lord, Acts 3:19

"To Him all the prophets witness that, through His name, whoever believes in Him will receive remission of sins." Acts 10:43

3. Who can receive God's forgiveness?

Learning God's Word

This Week's tool:

🌹 Tool #2 GIVE: I must _____ the sin in repentance knowing Christ is waiting to take it.   (I must be sorry enough to change and choose to go God's way over my own way.)

For _____ sorrow produces _____ leading to salvation, not to be regretted; but the sorrow of the _____ produces _____. 2 Corinthians 7:10

Forgive and be Forgiven

Apply the following parable to your own experience by putting yourself in the place of the unforgiving servant. Your master is God. Your fellow servant is someone from your experience that you have been unable to forgive.

Then Peter came to Him and said, "Lord, how often shall my brother sin against me, and I forgive him? Up to seven times?" Jesus said to him, "I do not say to you, up to seven times, but up to seventy times seven.

"Therefore the kingdom of heaven is like a certain king who wanted to settle accounts with his servants and when he had begun to settle accounts, one was brought to him who owed him ten thousand talents. But as he was not able to pay, his master commanded that he be sold, with his wife and children and all that he had, and that payment be made. The servant therefore fell down before him, saying, 'Master, have patience with me, and I will pay you all.' Then the master of that servant was moved with compassion, released him, and forgave him the debt.

"But that servant went out and found one of his fellow servants who owed him a hundred denari; and he laid hands on him and took him by the throat, saying, 'Pay me what you owe!' So his fellow servant fell down at his feet and begged him, saying, 'have patience with me, and I will pay you all.' And he would not, but went and threw him into prison till he should pay the debt.

"So when his fellow servants saw what had been done, they were very grieved, and came and told their master all that had been done. Then his master, after he had called him, said to him, 'You wicked servant! I forgave you all that debt because you begged me. Should you not also have had compassion on your fellow servant, just as I had pity on you?' And his master was angry, and delivered him to the torturers until he should pay all that was due to him.

"So My heavenly Father also will do to you if each of you, from his heart, does not forgive his brother his trespasses." Matthew 18:21-35

1. From what debt has your master released you or for what sin has God forgiven you?

2. Who is the person you can't forgive and why?

Learning God's Word

This Week's tool:

Tool #3 FORGIVE: I must _____, as I am forgiven by Christ. (Forgiving those that hurt, bruised, wronged, hurt, rejected, betrayed, or harmed me whether unintentionally or deliberately.) Ask God to Forgive you for holding unforgiveness and know that He will.

Bearing with one another, and _____ one _____, if anyone has a _____ against another; even as Christ forgave you, so you also must do. Colossians 3:13

(Continue to reflect back to Matthew 18:21-35 as you answer the following Questions)

3. In the parable how did the servant treat his fellow servant?

4. What happened to the servant who would not forgive?

5. What happens when we are unwilling to forgive from our hearts?

6. How will Jesus treat you if you don't forgive your fellow servant from your heart?

God the Almighty Judge

God is the only one who can forgive people's sins against Him. He is the almighty judge. He judges the motives of the hearts of people and refuses to forgive those whose hearts have rejected Him right into eternity.

God can refuse to forgive others because He is God. We are in no position to refuse anyone forgiveness because God has forgiven us so much.

Week 6 Day 2

> *Bow your heart before the Lord before completing the following statements that apply to you. Ask God to help you SEE what conditions you may have set up before you are willing to forgive.*

For you were once darkness, but now you are light in the Lord. Live as children of the light." Ephesians 5:8

1. I will forgive the person who hurt me if...

2. I will forgive my mother or step-mother if...

3. I will forgive my father or step-father if...

4. I will forgive my sister if ...

5. I will forgive my brother if...

6. I will forgive my boy friend or ex-boy friend if...

7. I will forgive my friend or ex-friend if...

8. I will forgive the person involved in the abortion if...

9. I will forgive my boss or co-worker if...

10. I will forgive myself if...

Learning God's Word

This Week's Memory Verse:

_____ ____ ____ another, and _____ one another, ___ anyone has a _____ against another; even as_____ forgave you, so you also _____ do. _____ 3:13

Forgiving Others Even If They Are Not Sorry

It is difficult to forgive others if they are not sorry for what they have done. You may want to set up conditions before you forgive someone for their part in hurting you. You may want that person to show remorse or to confess guilt before you are willing to forgive.

Examine your heart for a moment and ask yourself the questions, "Who am I really seeking to please?" "Am I seeking to please God, or am I more concerned with being a friend of the world and with pleasing my own negative thoughts and others negative thoughts?"

Bearing with one another, and forgiving one another, if anyone has a complaint against another; even as Christ forgave you, so you also must do. Colossians 3:13

1. What is the condition for forgiveness?

And whenever you stand praying, if you have anything against anyone, forgive him, that your Father in heaven may also forgive you your trespasses. But if you do not forgive, neither will your Father in heaven forgive your trespasses. Mark 11:25-26

2. Are you still required to forgive others if they are not sorry for hurting you?

Therefore, if you bring your gift to the altar and there remember that your brother has something against you, leave your gift there before the altar and go your way. First be reconciled to your brother, and then come and offer your gift. Matthew 5:23-24

3. If you know that someone has something against you, are you to wait for that person to come to you before asking for forgiveness?

Learning God's Word

This Week's tool:

Tool #2 GIVE: I must _____ the sin in repentance. Knowing Christ is waiting to take it   (I must be sorry enough to change and choose to go God's way over my own way.)

For_____ sorrow produces_____ leading to salvation, not to be regretted; but the sorrow of the _____ produces _____. 2 Corinthians 7:10

You have heard that it was said, "You shall love your neighbor and hate your enemy." But I say to you, love your enemies, bless those who curse you, do good to those who hate you, and pray for those who spitefully use you and persecute you. Matthew 5:43-44

4. If someone wants to burn the bridge and not reconcile, how can you apply Matthew 5:43 to your life?

And they stoned Stephen as he was calling on God and saying, "Lord Jesus, receive my spirit." Then he knelt down and cried out with a loud voice, "Lord, do not charge them with this sin." And when he had said this, he fell asleep. Acts 7:59-60

5. Who was able to forgive others before he saw signs of repentance?

6. Have the people who brought heartache and pain into your life asked for forgiveness? Are you willing to forgive them even if they are not sorry or remorseful? Why or why not?

Chains I've grown To Know

The sun is just above the hill and I can see You crying.
Your breath has swept away the chill and
I know you are smiling through Your tears.
And these CHAINS that I have grown to know
Have fallen BROKEN into the snow and the
Fears that once tormented me
You've cast them far into the sea.
I can SEE the face of Jesus.
I can FEEL the hands of God
Now I know what true belief is.
To fall lost in LOVE with You
The words with which You called to me are the purest I've heard spoken. Son, it's been a long, long time Come and bring your weary, broken heart back home. I've caused such an awful mess and all you speak is tenderness. I've caused You so much pain and grief but all you show is love for me. Thank You. Thank You. Thank You for saving me.

Zach Blickens

SEE, GIVE, FORGIVE, FORGET, BE SET FREE

A Lesson in Forgiveness

The chapter on forgiveness was a struggle for me. After all, the hurts were so deep how could I possibly forgive everyone who hurt me, especially my relatives. My husband and I were deeply hurt by the actions of his brother and sister-n-law. We were told that we were not welcome to live in their neighborhood when we were seeking out a new home. Their children were discouraged from playing with our children. The list went on! We could not understand the pain being hurled our way from them, it hurt. We were so fed up that we did not speak to them for an entire year, we even moved across town just to get away from them. We avoided family functions, just so we wouldn't run into them.

While in the forgiveness chapter I prayed hard for the Lord to help me see all of the people I was harboring anger against. I did not want to include these in-laws because I felt that this anger was truly justified! I prayed and forgave everyone else, except them. I could not move on to the next chapter because the Lord was ministering to my heart to repent and forgive my in-laws. His presence in my heart was so strong one day that I became broken with the weight of this guilt for harboring anger. I sat at my computer and obeyed the Lord, I wrote a letter of apology to my in-laws for not embracing forgiveness toward them. I could not take the silence or anger any longer.

I gave the letter to my husband and asked him to read it. I told him that this would mean no more resentment, anger or bickering with his brother, it would all come to a halt with us. He didn't talk to me for an hour, it was the longest hour of my life, I think! I just prayed that the Lord would open his heart so that he could forgive too. After an hour he came upstairs and got his coat on. When I asked him where he was going, he said he was going to deliver this letter to his brother in person. When he walked out of the room I cried. I had obeyed the Lord and He opened the way! In the letter I had written that we all needed to get together for a family hug. A few hours after my husband delivered the letter his brother called and said that they would like to cash in on that hug. They came over to our home and through God's love another family was healed. Thank you, Lord, for ministering to my heart and teaching me how to truly forgive.

Another family Healed - Cheryl

SEE, GIVE, FORGIVE, FORGET, BE SET FREE

Learning God's Word

This Week's Memory Verse:

_____ ____ ____ another, and _____ one another, ___ anyone has a _____ against another; even as_____ forgave you, so you also ____ do. _____ 3:13

Week 6 Day 3

Thank the Lord that He becomes the Light in this dark and dying world, and for choosing to become light and, truth to you personally.

Father, Forgive Them, Luke 23:34

God wants us to forgive because He has forgiven us. He wants us to show mercy to others because He has shown us His mercy. You may be suffering with the internal injuries of a broken heart or bruised feelings. Even if the wound is old, the sliver lodged in long ago is still hidden under your skin, reminding you of the hurt yet unforgiven.

We've Broken the Body, Now Lets Break The Spirit

Of all the scenes around the cross, this one is so powerful, yet so heartbreaking. What kind of people would mock a dying man? The criminal on the cross-mocked Christ. "Aren't you the Christ? Save yourself and us!" The passers-by mocked the crucified Christ with insults that were meant to bruise and hurt. "We've broken the body, now let's break the spirit!"

Did you see what Jesus did? He did not fight back. He did not desire to threaten. He did not let any guile be found in His mouth and say I'll get you. No, these words were not found on Christ's bloody, beaten lips. Christ, who had a body consumed with pain, and lungs longing for air, could speak with such love, "Father, forgive them."

Did you hear what Jesus said? He left us with His example. He entrusted himself to God who judges justly. He demanded no apology. He sought no revenge. He humbly spoke on their behalf:

- *Father, forgive them; for they do not know what they are doing." Luke 23:34*

The second part of Jesus' statement "For they do not know what they are doing" allows us to see with the heart and eyes of Christ. Our beaten Savior considered this death-hungry crowd not as murderers, but as confused and lost sheep, in need of a shepherd. He did not get angry but saw that in their hearts, they did not know what they were doing. Anger never does anyone any good. When we get angry at others or get angry at God, it just causes us to become defiled. Look to Christ's example on the cross. If the Son sets you free, you are free indeed.

Learning God's Word

This Week's tool:

🌰 Tool #2 GIVE: I must _____ the sin in repentance, knowing Christ is waiting to take it. (I must be sorry enough to change and choose to go God's way over my own way.)

For _____ sorrow produces _____ leading to salvation, not to be regretted; but the sorrow of the _____ produces _____ . 2 Corinthians 7:10

But love your enemies, do good, and lend, hoping for nothing in return; and your reward will be great, and you will be sons of the Most High, For He is kind to the unthankful and evil. Therefore be merciful, just as your Father also is merciful. Luke 6;35-3

1. What are the results of showing mercy to others?

For judgment is without mercy to the one who has shown no mercy. Mercy triumphs over judgment. James 2:13

2. What are the consequences of not showing mercy to others?

3. Look up and write out the definition of judging.

But why do you judge your brother? Or why do you show contempt for your brother? For we shall all stand before the judgment seat of Christ. Romans 14:10

For we must all appear before the judgment seat of Christ, that each one may receive the things done in the body, according to what he has done, whether good or bad. 2 Corinthians 5:10

4. Why are we not to judge our brother?

Learning God's Word

This Week's tool:

Tool #3 FORGIVE: I must _____, as I am forgiven by Christ. (Forgiving those that hurt, bruised, wronged, hurt, rejected, betrayed, or harmed me whether unintentionally or deliberately.) Ask God to Forgive you for holding unforgiveness and know that He will.

Bearing with one another, and _____ one _____, if anyone has a _____ against another; even as Christ forgave you, so you also must do. Colossians 3:13

Judge not, that you be not judged. For with what judgment you judge, you will be judged; and with the measure you use, it will be measured back to you." Matthew 7:1-2

5. How will we be judged if we judge others?

"And why do you look at the speck in your brother's eye, but do not consider the plank in your own eye? Or how can you say to your brother, 'Let me remove the speck from your eye and look, a plank is in your own eye? Hypocrite! First remove the plank from your own eye, and then you will see clearly to remove the speck from your brother's eye." Matthew 7:3-5

6. Taking the plank out of your own eye includes looking at the ways you have hurt others by your own failures. Ask God to show you the ways you have hurt others and record what comes to your mind. Ask Christ to forgive you and know that He will.

Past gossiping, judging, verbal, physical or sexual abuse, outburst of anger, unforgiveness, lying, stealing, ect.)

- Towards another brother or sister in Christ

- Towards a family member

- Towards a co-worker

- Towards a child or step-child

- Toward old classmates

When you have been forgiven much, you love much

SEE, GIVE, FORGIVE, FORGET, BE SET FREE

Make straight paths for your feet so that what is lame may not be dislocated, but rather be healed. Pursue peace with all men, and holiness, without which no one will see the Lord looking diligently lest anyone fall short of the grace of God; lest any root of bitterness springing up cause trouble, and by this many become defiled. Hebrew 112:13-15

What about You?

Do you desire to see the truth about what God says about forgiveness concerning your hurts and your sins? You don't have to live your life damaged or destroyed because of your past failures or past experiences. You can be freed from bondage by God's love, God's truth and God's forgiveness. You can grow into a deeper and sweeter relationship with Jesus Christ during this time. It is time for you to forgive and let go of the unacceptable sin from others or yourself. This is necessary for your healing.

First, you must **SEE** what is in your heart. Second, you must **GIVE** the sin in repentance to the Lord. Third, you must **FORGIVE** those your angry with. Fourth, **FORGET** by remembering to no longer dwell on the past. You will **BE SET FREE** by Christ to enjoy a fresh, new beginning. You must now press on to a higher calling in Jesus Christ.

Bow your heart before the Lord in brokenness asking Him to reveal any sins in your heart that might be defiling you, then ask Him to forgive you and know that He will.

Write down your thoughts.

_____

_____

_____

_____

_____

_____

_____

_____

_____

_____

_____

_____

_____

_____

_____

_____

_____

_____

_____

_____

_____

Week 6 Day 4

Bow your heart before the Lord in prayer before completing today's Bible study. Surrender any bitterness in your heart that has kept you in shackles from old hurts.

Forgiven Much, Love Much

Peace floods your heart when you have been forgiven. And so it does when you forgive others. You replace the anger and hatred in your heart with love and peace toward those that have spitefully used you. The memories don't go away, but the feelings that you once held in your heart do go away. That is when you ENJOY freedom.

But I say to you who hear: Love your enemies, do good to those who hate you, bless those who curse you, and pray for those who spitefully use you. Luke 6:27-28

Not returning evil for evil or reviling for reviling, but on the contrary blessing, knowing that you were called to this, that you may inherit a blessing." 1 Peter 3:9

1. How are we to treat those who have hurt us? Explain how you can apply these verses to your life.

Not returning evil for evil or reviling for reviling, but on the contrary blessing, knowing that you were called to this, that you may inherit a blessing For "He who would love life And see good days, Let him refrain his tongue from evil, and his lips from speaking deceit let him turn away from evil and do good; let him seek peace and pursue it. For the eyes of the Lord are on the righteous, and His ears are open to their prayers; but the face of the Lord is against those who do evil." 1 Peter 3:9-12

2. Will God hear your prayers if you have unforgiveness in your heart?

No one has seen God at any time. If we love one another, God abides in us, and His love has been perfected in us. 1John 4:12

3. If we choose to love each other, what happens in our relationship with God?

Learning God's Word

This Week's tool:

🥀 Tool #2 GIVE: I must _____ the sin in repentance, knowing Christ is waiting to take it. (I must be sorry enough to change and choose to go God's way over my own way.)

For _____ sorrow produces _____ leading to salvation, not to be regretted; but the sorrow of the _____ produces _____. 2 Corinthians 7:10

Can you now forgive them as Christ has forgiven you? *"Father, forgive them, for they do not know what they do." Luke 23:34.*

4. Are you ready to forgive those who have hurt you? Why or why not?

When you forgive others you are a witness to them of Christ's forgiveness in this world. Christ died for all those who have hurt you in the past, those who are hurting you now, and those who will hurt you in the future. Are you willing to say, "I am in Him, so I must now forgive. He died and suffered agony, so I will not forget. The price of my forgiveness came at the highest cost."

Write your prayer here releasing them from your judgment, and releasing yourself from the shackles of anger and bitterness. Come before God broken and with a sincere heart, turn your sorrow into grace and forgiveness so you may be Healed and Set Free.

_____

_____

_____

_____

_____

_____

_____

_____

_____

_____

_____

_____

_____

_____

_____

_____

_____

_____

_____

The Hate Hurt My Mind, Body and Soul

Can you imagine a woman being a Christian for 20 years and not fully understanding the very basic Christian principle of forgiveness? Well, I can't imagine it either, except that's what I did. The hatred I held in my heart towards my step-father has hurt me—mind, body, and soul.

I really believed I was justified in my unforgiveness and that God understood. My husband had tried for years to explain forgiveness to me. For reasons I don't understand, I had been blinded for so long.

I now have been SET FREE! God has shown me that forgiving somebody is not saying that what they did is okay. It is never okay to hurt a child. When we open the little black corner of our hearts where we hold onto unforgiveness, we let God shine His light in. This becomes a very humbling and healing experience. Once we let God into our whole heart we begin to SEE that we have been forgiven completely by God for our sins.

When God forgives us, He is not saying that what we did was okay, He is saying that He sent Jesus to shed His blood and die for all our sins. All sins. Abusing a child is a sin. Holding unforgiveness in your heart is a sin. Jesus died for all sins. SEE, GIVE, FORGIVE, FORGET, BE SET FREE - 4 important tools

           I know I have been Set Free, Debbie.

SEE, GIVE, FORGIVE, FORGET, BE SET FREE

Learning God's Word

This Week's tool:

Tool #3 FORGIVE: I must _____, as I am forgiven by Christ. (Forgiving those that hurt, bruised, wronged, hurt, rejected, betrayed, or harmed me whether unintentionally or deliberately.) Ask God to Forgive you for holding unforgiveness and know that He will.

Bearing with one another, and _____ one _____, if anyone has a _____ against another; even as Christ forgave you, so you also must do. Colossians 3:13

Forgiving Others Without a Confrontation

So many times I was convinced that if I could only meet with the person who hurt me and let them know how much they hurt me, then maybe I could forgive them. It was a lie to think that I needed to have a meeting in order to forgive, in order to heal. I never met with my uncle or the guy that raped me. I met with God and took care of my unforgiving heart and bitterness with Him. It is a matter of keeping my relationship right with God.

1. Think of a person who triggers ungodly reactions in you. Pray and ask God to Help You SEE the root cause of these feelings. When God show you, go through the four Healed and Set Free tools to freedom and GIVE them to God.

2. Pray and ask God to show you other things you've been stuffing down in your hidden heart. Deal with these things and, by faith, believe that God has cleansed you. Don't allow these things to come back again by thinking and meditating on them. (Look up Philippians 4:8 and write it out.)

3. Write out two scriptures that particularly ministered to you from this chapter and use them to help you apply them to forgiving the unacceptable things that others have committed or unacceptable acts you have done..

A.

B.

Learning God's Word

This Week's Memory Verse:

🌸 _____ ____ ____ *another, and* _____ *one another,* ___ *anyone has a* _____ *against another; even as* _____ *forgave you, so you also* ____ *do.* _____ *3:13*

Week 6 Day 5

Review

This week's memory verse:

Bearing with one another, and _____ one another, if anyone has a complaint against another; even as Christ _____ you, so ___ also____ do. Colossians 3:13

Write a short paragraph summarizing what you have learned on the subject of forgiving the unacceptable.

Bow your heart before the Lord in prayer, asking Him to help you let go of all the past and to examine your heart daily as you embrace His word.

_____

_____

_____

_____

_____

_____

_____

_____

_____

_____

_____

_____

Share with those in your life how the Healer is opening the shackles on your heart.

Learning God's Word

This Week's tool:

🌹 Tool #3 FORGIVE: I must _____, as I am forgiven by Christ. (Forgiving those that hurt, bruised, wronged, hurt, rejected, betrayed, or harmed me whether unintentionally or deliberately.) Ask God to Forgive you for holding unforgiveness and know that He will.

Bearing with one another, and _____ one _____, if anyone has a _____ against another; even as Christ forgave you, so you also must do. Colossians 3:13

With Guns To Our Heads, My Life Would Be Forever Changed

I grew up in Orange County. I was the youngest of three children, and I had two very loving and honest parents. My parents were always doing something wonderful for our neighbors or community. My dad was a college professor and politician, and he was so honest, that he was sometimes snubbed by corrupted people. My mom always seemed to be even keeled and I never remember her ever complaining about anything. My dad was teacher of the year, man of the year, whose who in Orange County, distinguished citizen of Costa Mesa. People truly found strength in my parents and although they weren't walking with the Lord, they were extremely Christlike in example and deed. They did however, instill a concept which has taken me many years to think about. They told me that "God helps those who help themselves." I was sure it was biblical, and so I began my process of being independent and helping God by being as self-sufficient as possible.

College Years

My college years came, and I went off to Cal Poly, SLO, and got involved immediately with intervarsity. I again had a ministry to jump into: I lead Bible studies in the dorm's, trained students to lead, went on short term missions, and tried to prove to everyone that I was that unique christian totally sold out for God. Since I had grown up with such stability, it was easy for me to be disciplined and be a do gooder. I had a hard time understanding why all christians weren't as busy as I was. I was very independent (I never wanted a boyfriend) and the one thing I never wanted anyone to associate me with was one of those sweet, only think of boyfriends and babies type of girls, I wanted to be thought of as brilliant, independent, self-sufficient, fun, adventurous. I never wanted to lean too hard on God's grace. There was work to be done, and I certainly wasn't going to sit around and be idle. I was often really frustrated with christians who didn't seem to have it all together and I'd have to say I was very judgmental.

The Terror in Peru

God had other things to teach me about. Who He really is and His deep love for me, Loren. My junior year, since things seemed to be getting a little too easy at college, I decided to go abroad for a year of interchange. I went to Peru, at a Catholic University, and took all my classes in Spanish and had everything transferred back, so I wouldn't be missing a year. (I had to finish in four years or I was afraid of being looked at as a sloth). I really prayed about going, and to this day I know the Lord's hand was in it. But for different reasons then I had planned. God was about to break my pride and teach me of His love.

My parents came for Christmas and I traveled with them through South America, It was great.When I came back, there was still one month until school started. My other friends had gone off for the entire summer,and my peruvian friends didn't travel like we did. Here I was, having lots of time and I did use it wisely. I prayed a lot, and read God's Word. I felt so useless just doing this. I wasn't ministering, or talking to people about the Lord. So when some friends came back early and asked me to travel with them, of course I said yes. I can witness to them. We went to a famous city in Peru,and the three of us went to some ruins. Upon coming back down, my life was about to be changed forever. On the way down, three men with guns came up from behind us, and demanded all our money, jewelry, credit cards, etc. Then, with guns to our heads, they proceeded to rape us. Now it could have been much worse then what they did. They could have beaten us, or brutally hurt us.When they finished, they told us to lie down on our stomachs and not move or they would shoot. I thought about heaven, and wondered what it was going to fell like dying with a bullet in my back. They did leave, as we made our way back to the town, people taunted us,and made fun. They blamed us, and didn't help us, not to even use a phone. The police did find the attackers, but let them go for a single bribe and told us laughingly that if we wanted them in jail, we would have to go get them. Incredible! We were told by the program directors not to tell a soul about what happened. They threatened us by saying that they'd take away our credits at school if we went home or leaked what had happened. They blamed us—saying we must have been promiscuous... I didn't tell my parents, and we went to secular counselor who told me I should go have sex to get over the whole ordeal. I held alot in because God helps those who help themselves.

The reason I tell you all this is because this year in Peru was probably the most life changing incident in my life. When Moses killed the Egyptian, his life was changed forever, as well as Esther who conceded to marrying a king and David when he killed Goliath. It changed my personality, my career, who I might have married. I didn't tell my parents because I wanted to get through this myself. I didn't want to be a crybaby about it. God helps those who help themselves.

I was a Mess

When I got home, I was a mess. I became very with drawn, depressed, introspective. I tried to tell friends about my experiences in Peru, and they listened once. But I needed to talk a lot,and people are busy, and so I felt I couldn't tell anyone. I became a bit cynical. I started noticing in myself that I now didn't feel so independent. I desperately cried out to God. I needed people and you know what? He heard me. Through the whole ordeal. I had this awesome sense that God cried out with me. I was his child and He hurt with me. When we cry out to Him, he heals us. As Christians, we have that hope, and God was with me the entire way. The entire experience was so incredibly humbling, I realized that I couldn't do it on MY OWN. I began to see why some people are the way they are regarding their weaknesses. I grew more compassionate as Christ had compassion on me. I saw that Christ came for the sick, not those who are well. Even though this was a rough time in my life, it was a sweet time in the Lord. I started to see God as my Father, and not a partner in my christian work.

My Wounds Were Healed

As my wounds were healed, I began plunging into ministry again. I met this wonderful Christian guy (Craig). Alek came along very quickly. Jonathan came 2 1/2 years after Alek, and then 2 1/2 years after Alek, came Nathanael. So in 5 years we've had 3 kids, which will humble anyone. When Alek came, I was amazed at how dependent he was on me. It kind of took me by surprise. Since then, I'm starting to understand our relationship with God. It's been very humbling setting aside my own wants and desires for His glory to do the mundane services of raising a family. Pain is relative- my hurtful experiences in Peru were no more difficult then the the frustrations of every day living. I'd have to say that serving my husband, and my children has been difficult at times. But it has helped me understanding our relationship with our creator. He is our heavenly Father, and we are his children. I've learned what a joy it is to share my hard times with other believers and have them pray with me. I need others and I need God each and every second of my life. I don't have it all together, and praise God that He is able, more than able, to accomplish what concerns me today.

Healed and Set Free Bible study, gave me more tools to fight the enemy. I believe true healing cannot occur until we **SEE** the wickedness of our own heart and then **GIVE** it to the Lord. When we are weak He is strong --Amen.

I can't wait to lead other women through this study!

Set Free by God's love and truth,~Loren, California

Self Preservation

Many things have been done - or words were said
That pierced the heart - like a bullet of lead
And thought the event came - and soon was gone
The sting of it all - lingered on and on.

Dwelling on the past - though time has marched on
Will make us miserable - no mood for a song
Because peace and joy - Satan is stealing
Thus, he alone prospers - if we hold an ill-feeling.

We must forgive others - in a way that is right:
Leaving their flaws - for only God's sight.
Sometimes it's impossible - to humanly do
So we call on the Holy Spirit - to see us through.

When the Lord forgives us - our slate is wiped clean.
God doesn't hold grudges - or see us as mean.
Yes, He gives us a chance - for a whole new start.
He holds no memory - of our mistakes in his heart.

If we can't forgive - like the Lord intended
We have a miserable life - which can't be mended.
Because an unforgiving heart - is real devastation
And forgiving completely - is self-preservation.

- author unknown

Conquering Depression

*Anxiety in the heart of
man causes depression, but
a good word makes it glad.
The righteous should
choose his friends carefully,
for the way of the wicked
leads them astray.*

Proverbs 12:25-26

There are four main tools we will weave into the very fiber of our hearts day by day: **SEE, GIVE, FORGIVE, FORGET,** and **BE SET FREE**. Thinking about the past will never change the past. But you can change your future and Be Set FREE from your past. As you deal with your past and present hurts, you can either embrace the truth and let go of the burdens you carry, or carry your burdens and reject the truth and the freedom it brings. The choice is yours. Getting real with God is the first step you need to always take as you face deep, dark hurts that have chipped away at your peace for 1 year, 10 years, 20 years, and some 50 years. God's love is bigger then all of our hurts and fears. You will have many blessings in front of you as God's truth unfolds in your heart and Sets you Free.

Let's Day By Day Go over the Four Steps to Keep Our Hearts Clean

Tools To Become Set Free

- **Tool #1 "SEE ":** I must **SEE** the truth about what is in my heart, so I'm not defiled.

    Looking carefully lest anyone fall short of the grace of God; lest any root of bitterness springing up cause trouble, and by this many become defiled. Hebrew 12:15.

- **Tool #2 "GIVE":** I must **GIVE** the sin in repentance, knowing Christ is waiting to take it. (I must be sorry enough to change and choose to go God's way over my own way.)

    For godly sorrow produces repentance leading to salvation, not to be regretted; but the sorrow of the world produces death. 2 Corinthians 7:10

- **Tool #3 "FORGIVE":** I must **FORGIVE**, as I am forgiven by Christ. (Forgiving those that hurt, bruised, wronged, hurt, rejected, betrayed or harmed me whether unintentionally or deliberately.) Ask God to Forgive you for holding unforgiveness and know that He will.

    Bearing with one another, and forgiving one another, if anyone has a complaint against another; even as Christ forgave you, so you also must do. Colossians 3:13

- **Tool #4 "FORGET":** I must **FORGET** by remembering to no longer dwell on the hurt.

    Brethren, I do not count myself to have apprehended; but one thing I do, forgetting those things which are behind and reaching forward to those things which are ahead. Philippians 3:13.

BECOME SET FREE: Christ will open the shackles from my past hurts showing me the truth so I can become a cleansed vessel that is Healed and Set Free.

    You shall know the truth, and the truth shall make you free. Therefore, if the Son makes you free, you shall be free indeed. John 8:32-36.

SATAN IS DEFEATED AND THE SHACKLES ARE GONE AND YOU ARE FREE!

Week 7 Day 1

> *Bow your heart before the Lord in prayer before completing today's Bible study. Ask Him to open your heart to the truth about conquering depression.*

• What does the Bible say about Depression?

The Bible tells us depression is the common lot of man and is a normal reaction in life. You can find a lot of comfort in the Old and New Testaments pertaining to depression. You will read in both the Old and New Testaments about saints suffering from and conquering depression in their lives. While Scripture reminds us we are only human, it also encourages us to realize we don't always have to be depressed. We are to focus our minds on God, maintain our faith, trust in Him, and keep our eyes on eternity, not ourselves. Putting things in perspective are necessary steps in resolving or avoiding depression.

• How can I keep up my spiritual life when I feel so low? Shouldn't I just abandon it for awhile until I get my problem solved?

Never, but never abandon your spiritual life while trying to solve your problems. Satan would have you believe it is unspiritual, sinful and shameful to be depressed. Satan would have you believe you can solve your problems with your own strengths. Satan wants to keep you from the fellowship of other Christians and from the spiritual growth and maturity that comes from seeking God in your time of need. Don't allow the feelings of depression to keep you from dealing with the cause of the depression. To keep your spiritual life up when you are feeling down, you must recognize and fight the depression, seeing it as a symptom that something is wrong and needs attention. You need the resources of Christ to enable you to SEE the problem and to GIVE it to Him, ask for His help and healing. I can do all things through Christ who strengthens me. Philippians 4:13

For those who have a broken heart

• *The LORD is near to those who have a broken heart, and saves such as have a contrite spirit. Psalm 34:18*

God's Love for You

• *Therefore, if anyone is in Christ, he is a new creation; old things have passed away; behold, all things have become new. 2 Corinthians 5:17*

You need to know without a doubt that the Father loves you. He gave you His love through Jesus Christ, and He has called you as a Christian to be His workmanship, created in Christ Jesus to be a vessel of His love. God wants to use your life in a special way to comfort others, as you have been comforted. *A merry heart does good, like medicine, but a broken spirit dries the bones. Proverbs 17:22*

For I know the thoughts that I think toward you, says the LORD, thoughts of peace and not of evil, to give you a future and a hope. Jeremiah 29:11

1. What are the thoughts of Jesus toward you?

Are not two sparrows sold for a penny? Yet not one of them will fall to the ground apart from the will of your Father. And even the very hairs of your head are all numbered. So don't be afraid; you are worth more than many sparrows. Matthew 10:29-31

2. Do you know the number of hairs on your own head? Who does? Do you believe there is anything too small or trivial to bring before God in prayer?

Understanding the Broken Spirit

The Bible is full of stories of people with broken hearts and broken spirits. They are filled with sorrow and mourning during different seasons in their lives. Depression, grief and sorrow can grip our own hearts when things don't work out the way we planned. A friend may talk behind our back, we may lose someone to death, or someone we love might walk away from Christ. Emotions flood our hearts and we need to cry out to God in times of despair. Suffering comes to all of us, and yet no one can suffer for us. However, we can be supported in our difficult times by the prayers, compassion and understandings of loved ones and friends. God created us and gave us our emotions. The Bible tells us we are to "Rejoice with those who rejoice, and weep with those who weep." Romans 12:15 It is when we are too proud to admit our needs to others that we are in the greatest danger.

Then Jesus came with them to a place called Gethsemane, and said to the disciples, sit here while I go and pray over there. And He took with Him Peter and the two sons of Zebedee, and He began to be sorrowful and deeply distressed. Then He said to them, My soul is exceedingly sorrowful, even to death. Stay here and watch with Me. He went a little farther and fell on His face, and prayed, saying, O My Father, if it is possible, let this cup pass from Me; nevertheless, not as I will, but as You will. Matthew 26:36-39

3. What two emotions flooded Jesus' heart and mind?

4. Does it comfort you to know that even Jesus had times of sorrow and could be deeply distressed? If so, how.

For we do not have a High Priest who cannot sympathize with our weakness, but was in all points tempted as we are, yet without sin. Let us therefore come boldly to the throne of grace, that we may obtain mercy and find grace to help in time of need. Hebrews 4:15-16

5. Does it comfort you to know Christ understands your weaknesses and struggles and wants to help you in times of need? Why does Jesus understand?

6. How do we come boldly before His throne of grace?

Learning God's Truth

This week's memory verse:

_____ in the heart of man _____ depression, but a good _____ makes it glad. The righteous should choose his friends carefully, for the way of the wicked leads them astray. Proverbs 12:25-26

In the Garden of Gethsemane Jesus knew He would face Calvary the next morning, where on the cross, He would bear the sins of the world. On the cross would be the first and only time Jesus would ever experience separation from His Father. *"My God, My God, why have You forsaken Me?"* Matthew 27:46. This was the cup He prayed to have taken from Him. In His darkest hour, Jesus, not wanting to be alone, asked for the presence and prayers of Peter, James, and John. Although Jesus sought God in prayer, He also desired the prayers and support of his closest friends in His hour of crisis. Likewise, you are to seek God in prayer during your time of need as well as seek out those who can pray with you and for you. Just as you need a friend, be willing to be a friend and look for opportunities to comfort and pray for others who are suffering.

He knelt down and prayed, saying, "Father, if it is Your will, take this cup away from Me; nevertheless, not My will, but Yours, be done." Then an angel appeared to Him from heaven, strengthening Him. And being in agony, he prayed more earnestly. Then His sweat became like great drops of blood falling down to the ground. When He rose up from prayer, and had come to His disciples, He found them sleeping from sorrow. Luke 22:42-45

7. What difficult circumstances or cups have you asked God to remove from your life?

8. What does Christ Jesus' words "not My will, but Yours, be done" mean to you in your difficult circumstances?

9. Was the cup removed from Jesus? What did Jesus do more earnestly?

10. Has God's answer in your circumstances been yes, no, or wait? Explain

11. Do you believe God's plans for you are good even if you don't understand them at this moment?

Learning God's Truth

This week's memory verse:

_____ in the heart of man causes _____, but a good word makes it glad. The righteous _____ choose his friends carefully, for the way of the _____

12. What if Jesus had walked away from His cup and not submitted to God's will? What hope would we have for eternal life?

13. Which friends did Jesus choose to have with him during His greatest time of agony, and what did He ask of them?

14. Do you follow Jesus' example and call upon friends to pray with you and for you, or do you isolate yourself from your friends? Explain.

– If you do not have a friend to pray with, stop right now and take a few moments to pray, ask the Lord to show you someone who can be a prayer partner. If you let your burdens go unrelieved, they may lead to depression.

Learning God's Truth

This week's memory verse:

🌿 _____ in the _____ of man causes _____, but a good word makes it glad. The righteous should choose his _____ carefully, for the way of the wicked leads them _____. *Proverbs 12:25-26*

My eyes flow and do not cease, without interruption, till the LORD from heaven looks down and sees. My eyes bring suffering to my soul because of all the daughters of my city. My enemies without cause hunted me down like a bird. They silenced my life in the pit and threw stones at me. The waters flowed over my head; I said, "I am cut off!" Lamentations 3:49-54

15. Depression can come when we feel we have been cut off in some way. Have you ever been cut off in a relationship? Explain.

_____

_____

_____

_____

_____

_____

_____

_____

_____

_____

_____

_____

_____

_____

_____

_____

_____

_____

My face is flushed from weeping, and on my eyelids is the shadow of death; although no violence is in my hands, and my prayer is pure. O earth, do not cover my blood, and let my cry have no resting place! Surely even now my witness is in heaven, and my evidence is on high. My friends scorn me; My eyes pour out tears to God. Oh, that one might plead for a man with God, as a man pleads for his neighbor! For when a few years are finished, I shall go the way of no return, Job 16:16

16. Have you ever had a friend criticize you? Explain how you can relate to what Job went through with his friends.

When I Forgave, I Could Forget.

Testimony on release from the temptation of suicide

July, unbearable in Virginia. Hot, muggy, not a breeze in sight. I walk the cliff, my eyes traveling to the distant shore, then float with beads of sunlight back across the James River to rest on the rocks below. All is peaceful, all that is except my own heart.

The problems of MY world are suffocating me. I rebel in full armor, breastplate of hostility and sword of hate, I will not surrender this space.... I plant my feet firmly and watch myself slowly crumble as Satan fights to win this monumental battle.

I walk for hours not seeing, not hearing, not even dreaming. My heart is dying...beat by beat for the world and people have become a game. If the world assigns classes to everyone and if people use and abuse you and put you to shame, what is the sense of life?

There is only one step before I will fee the rocks at the bottom of the cliff.

Satan plays the game well: "DIE!"

But Jesus gave the Word: "LIVE!"

Why are you cast down, oh my soul? And why are you disquieted within me? *Hope in God; For I shall yet praise Him, the salvation of my countenance and my God. Psalm 43:5*

From this tiny beginning the seed was watered. It was nurtured by none other than Jesus himself.

Days turned into weeks, weeks into months as I hung onto threads. Reading the Bible, I attempted to strangle God into admitting He was with me. Scripture stayed with me as I ate, as I went to bed.

And then I started going to a Bible study and was able to share the pains and heartaches of my life. Having been raised in an alcoholic home, I had many insecurities, much self-pity, and great fears. But with others who had also suffered, I began to see that only the Lord could heal me. But I had to do my part. I had to be able to give all my pain to Him. The hardest thing for me was surrendering my bitterness for that was the crusted protective coating I had put around my heart. But as I began to let go of anger and hatred, I was able to forgive those who had harmed me. When I forgave, I could forget. And God could then bring true healing into my life.

I gave my pain to Him ~ Jonnie, Idaho

SEE, GIVE, FORGIVE, FORGET, BE SET FREE

Learning God's Truth

This week's memory verse:

_____ in the _____ of man causes _____, but a good word makes it glad. The righteous should choose his _____ carefully, for the way of the wicked leads them _____. Proverbs 12:25-26

Week 7 Day 2

> *Bow your heart before the Lord in prayer before completing today's Bible study. Ask Him to let you SEE and GIVE to Him what may be leading to depression in your life.*

Responsibility and Accountability

"I desire that the younger guide the house." 1 Timothy 5:14

As one Christian woman puts it. This verse has special meaning to me as a woman, I found a verse that worked its way into my unorganized heart. There was no way I could miss the word "guide" as I read, *"I desire that the younger women guide the house". 1 Timothy 5:14.* Furthermore, the way of this statement was clear: The young women of Timothy's church were *"'idle', wandering about from house to house, and not only idle but also 'gossips' and busybodies, saying things which they ought not" 1 Timothy 5:13.* Their loose, undisciplined behavior led those outside the church to think and speak poorly of Christianity. (Verse 14) Obviously, having a home to manage would contribute positively to these women's lives by, at the very least, eliminating the opportunity for these negative behaviors.

To "guide a house" means to be the head of or to rule a family, "to guide the home". The one who manages a house, the householder. Yet this management has built in accountability, describing as it does the work of a steward or a servant. The woman who manages her house is "not the head" of the home. Her husband is if she is married; God is if she is not. Instead, she is the house manager.

God holds us accountable. What a blessing it is to us when we serve Him well in this capacity! And what a blessing we are to our family when we properly manage the house: In fact, Martin Luther wrote, "The greatest blessing... is to have a wife to whom you may entrust your affairs." That's what being a home-manager is all about!

Titus 2: 4-5 has given us women an assingment to *Love their husband, to love their children, to be discreet, chaste, homemakers, good, obedient to their own husband, that the Word of God may not be blasphemed.*

1. Reread 1 Timothy 5: 3-16. Make a list of what God values in His women. Pray and ask God what you can do to be the best house manager for God and your family? Then plan your day to accomplish it.

"She watches over the ways of her household." Proverbs 31:27

As one woman says, "One of my most appalling memories is neglecting my household, as, hour after hour, I stayed curled up on our couch reading and reading and reading anything and everything. Reading was a passion for me, something of far greater importance to me than a mere hobby or interest. And as I read, my two little girls wearing only diapers, roamed around the house, unsupervised, untrained. There I sat my house ignored, my husband and children neglected sifting through my new Bible to look up the Scripture references about work and why God thought it was so important. Soon I grabbed my marker to highlight another guideline God has given me as one of His homemakers. The verse simply said, She watches over the ways of her household, and does not eat the 'bread of idleness'."

So what are some of the specific things you and I are to watch over in our home? Maybe your list is like mine says one woman, " In my home, I am the one who watches over safety, health, sanitation, cleanliness, and security, (Whenever I'm gone, I leave instructions on the refrigerator door reminding my husband and two children to lock the doors at night because that's my job when I'm home.)" Another House manager says, "I oversee the money recording, saving, supervising, giving, spending, and stretching it. As house manager I have the following list to take care of: clothing needs and mending, the appliance warranties and service contracts, and the food planning, shopping, and preparation. This list also includes watching over the nutrition and selecting the types of foods and beverages for my family. And all the while I intently watch over the attitudes and unexpressed needs of each family members. I never tolerate -- harsh, cruel words in our home. No name calling or picking apart each others weakness."

One other house manager keeps an open eye to upcoming events and trying to anticipate future needs.

2. Married or not watches over the ways of her household and refuses to eat the bread of idleness (Proverb 31:27). Do you see God's assignment to watch over your home and the people in it? Do you see the value of every meal prepared, every rug vacuumed, every piece of furniture dusted, every floor mopped, every load of laundry washed, folded, and ironed. Is it your hearts desire to pay the price of watching and working? If your married ask your husband what he wants you to watch over? (*I will make him a helper. Genesis 2:18.*)

Lets look at how to manage our home by watching over your home, rather than eating the bread of idleness.

First, understand that home management is God's best for us ~~~ Every company has a manager to oversee and manage the customer service, quality control, and the employees. If not, the company would "fall apart". In the same way choosing to manage our home is choosing God's way. He is simply calling us women to do it. Home management is His plan, His way: its His good and acceptable and perfect will for us (Romans 12:2). If we don't manage our homes they too will "fall apart".

Second, decide to take home management seriously ~~~ Why? One Christian woman say, I realized that as much as I wanted to I couldn't run out the front door of my home, leaving it in a shambles, and go over to the church to do the work of ministry. I came to understand that God has charged me with the stewardship of managing my home, and He uses this primary area of ministry to train me for managing other areas of ministry. At home, as I try to live according to God's instructions for me – instructions I find in His written Word – I develop faithfulness and learn to follow through. At home I become a faithful steward (1 Corinthians 4:2).

Once I have shown myself to be a faithful manager at home, I am free to run out the door and do the work of ministry outside my home. All is well at home. Everything is under control. The people are cared for and the place is cared for. My management responsibilities on the domestic front are fulfilled.

And let me be clear: I'm not talking about years and decades spent at home waiting for the children to grow up and leave so we have less at home to manage. That option wouldn't teach our children much about the importance of being a contributing member of the body of Christ, the Church.

On a daily basis, management of a home happens for me when I have a schedule. Plan a time for devotions, for example most American's brush their teeth and teach their children to brush their teeth every morning. It's scheduled into the day, because they don't want bad breath or their teeth to decay. Isn't your spiritual life and relationship with God more important then your teeth? If you don't schedule a devotional time and teach your children to have a devotional time each day, your life and their life will decay and the fragrance of your lives will be worse then bad breath.

Also plan a time for household jobs to do together with your children, time reserved for cultivating a relationship with your husband and children, and time to be involved in ministry at church.

3. Think about your own homemaking skills. What lesson(s) (if any) would you like to learn from an older woman? If you work outside the home, who could give you some pointers on new skills for better "management at home"? Ask God to lead you to the right woman and to enable you to follow through on what you learn.

4. We can't share what we don't posses. We can't help children learn, read, study, discuss, memorize, or recite the Bible if we're not doing this ourselves. What are you doing or what will you do to fill you're own heart with the law of the Lord. Develop a step - by - step plan, start small, but start! What will you read? What will you teach your children?

Teach your children how to build their own room, which is their "little house". When I clean the house, Caleb and Jessica clean their room and help with household jobs. They each have their own dirty - clothes basket and from the time they were 9 years old they could dump in soap, and turn the dials on the washing machine. They have washed their own clothes, folded them, and put them in the drawers. This is all preparation for real life.

Decide to begin building. It's never too late to begin or- begin and - begin again- to build your house, to create a wonderful home. Only our enemy, Satan, would want us to think other wise. We can begin at any time even today!

The Power of the Tongue

Death and life are in the power of the tongue. Proverbs 18:21

5. What does criticizing or gossiping do to a relationship?

The heart of the righteous studies how to answer, but the mouth of the wicked pours forth evil. Proverbs 15:28

6. What practical steps can you take to be mindful and avoid criticizing or gossiping about someone else?

Therefore comfort each other and edify one another, just as you also are doing 1 Thessalonians 5:11

But encourage one another daily, as long as it is called today, so that none of you may be hardened by sin's deceitfulness. Hebrews 4:13

7. What does the Bible instruct us to do for one another?

I recall to my mind, therefore, I have hope. Through the Lord's mercies we are not consumed, because His compassions fail not. They are new every morning; great is Your faithfulness. "The LORD is my portion," says my soul, "therefore, I hope in Him!" The LORD is good to those who wait for Him, to the soul who seeks Him. It is good that one should hope and wait quietly for the salvation of the LORD. Lamentations 3:21-26

8. What does it mean to your heart that Christ's compassions fail not?

9. What is new every morning?

10. What does it mean for you to give others new mercies when they fail you?

11. Have anger, lack of patience, lack of faith, a sharp tongue, or the wrong attitude been a part of your life this week? If so, how?

Keep your tongue from evil, and your lips from speaking deceit. Depart from evil and do good; seek peace and pursue it. Psalm 34:13-14

12. You are responsible for your own choices and actions in seeking to keep your relationship right with God. Write down one time you made that right choice to obey God's word in a difficult situation. What was the outcome?

13. Write down a time you made the wrong choice and followed after your own desires and ways. What was the outcome?

I Needed God's Help and Forgiveness to Stop This Horrible Habit

When I took the "Healed and Set Free" Bible Study, one of the things I really wanted to do was stop gossiping because I knew it was not what God wanted in my life. It made me feel bad about myself even though I thought I gossiped to make myself feel better. Throughout this study, I knew that I needed God's help and forgiveness to stop this horrible habit. During one of our study sessions, Tammy Brown told us that in the past, she had also wanted to stop gossiping and shared with us how God had shown her a practical way that would help her stop gossiping. When she thought about gossiping she imagined that there was a baby monitor that was turned on and the person she was gossiping about had the other part of the monitor and could hear everything she said! So I decided to make myself a reminder so that I could try, with God's help, to stop gossiping. I wrote "Baby Monitor" in big letters on a card with a check mark for each hour of the day so that I could track my progress. As the day goes by, and I see that I'm progressing toward my goal of a "gossip-free day," it gives me incentive to stick with it. I'm not perfect, and I'm working on breaking the habit, but with God's help, I know I can do it!

Desiring to put off the old self- Jenny, Idaho

Guilt Leads to Depression

Guilt comes as a result of breaking one of God's laws. When guilt remains in your heart, it will lead to depression. If you have broken one of God's laws then God desires for you to come to Him in confession and repentance. When you confess your sin to Christ and repent, Christ is faithful to cover your sin with His blood and extend His forgiveness to you. This is Christ's example for you to follow. In Christ you can be forgiven and set free from your guilt. In Christ's strength you can refuse to keep a record of wrongs done to you and forgive others as you have been forgiven.

If you choose to ignore your own sin, you have not removed your guilt. By keeping a record of wrongs done to you, you have added to your sin, and have thereby added to your guilt. By refusing to forgive, you are refusing to be forgiven. If you haven't gotten rid of the sin, you haven't gotten rid of the guilt or shame. The choice is yours to make. You can choose to have Christ set you free from your sin and guilt, or you can choose to ignore your sin and guilt and be in bondage to bitterness, depression and unforgiveness.

Guilt can be used for your good by God to encourage you to SEE what is in your heart and GIVE it in confession to Him. Ignoring your guilt will affect your relationship with God. It will cause you to become entangled in a web of self-condemnation, self-pity or self-justification as you are inwardly overcome by guilt, anxiety and increasing depression. For whoever desires to save his life will lose it, but whoever loses his life for My sake will find it. Matthew 16:25. God has given you a way to conquer depression and become Healed and Set Free.

Peter answered and said to Him, "even if all are made to stumble because of You, I will never be made to stumble." Jesus said to him, "assuredly, I say to you that this night, before the rooster crows, you will deny Me three times." Peter said to Him, "even if I have to die with You, I will not deny You!" And so said all the disciples. Matthew 26:33-35

1. What was Peter confident he would never do? In the end, what did Peter do?

For the good that I will to do, I not do; but the evil I will not to do, that I practice. Romans 7:19

2. Have you ever said "I would never do that," and then found yourself doing exactly what you said you would never do? If so, how?

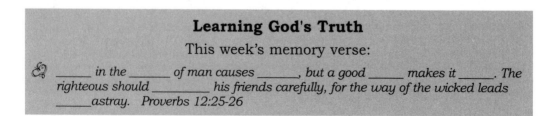

Learning God's Truth

This week's memory verse:

_____ in the _____ of man causes _____, but a good _____ makes it _____. The righteous should _____ his friends carefully, for the way of the wicked leads _____ astray. *Proverbs 12:25-26*

3. Would identifying with Peter give you a heart of compassion toward the shortcomings and failures of others? If so, how?

4. Have you ever stumbled and gossiped, kept a record of wrongs, failed to show mercy, used drugs, alcohol, filthy language, sharp words, or had angry outbursts? What happens to your heart and emotions when you stumble and do something that you know is wrong?

Now I rejoice, not that you were made sorry, but that your sorrow led to repentance. For you were made sorry in a godly manner, that you might suffer loss from us in nothing. For godly sorrow produces repentance leading to salvation, not to be regretted; but the sorrow of the world produces death. 2 Corinthians 7:9-10.

5. What does godly sorrow produce? What does sorrow of the world produce?

6. Using a dictionary what does it mean to repent?

For though you wash yourself with lye, and use much soap, yet your iniquity is marked before Me," says the Lord God. Jeremiah 2:22

7. In this example, what attempt is made to conceal guilt?

Learning God's Truth

This week's memory verse:

_____ in the _____ of man causes _____, but a good _____ makes it _____. The righteous should _____ his _____ carefully, for the way of the wicked leads _____astray. Proverbs ___:__-__

Therefore, brethren, having boldness to enter the Holiest by the blood of Jesus, by a new and living way which He consecrated for us, through the veil, that is, His flesh, and having a High Priest over the house of God, let us draw near with a true heart in full assurance of faith, having our hearts sprinkled from an evil conscience and our bodies washed with pure water. Hebrews 10:19-22

8. How are you to draw near to God? How do you have your heart sprinkled from an evil conscience?

Not by works of righteousness which we have done, but according to His mercy He saved us, through the washing of regeneration and renewing of the Holy Spirit. Titus 3:5

9. Are you saved from hell by your works of righteousness or according to God's mercy?

From Jesus Christ, the faithful witness, the firstborn from the dead, and the ruler over the kings of the earth. To Him who loved us and washed us from our sins in His own blood. Revelation 1:5

10. Who loves you and washes away your sins in His own blood?

I acknowledged my sin to You, and my iniquity I have not hidden. I said, "I will confess my transgressions to the LORD," And You forgave the iniquity of my sin. Psalm 32:5-7

11. What do you need to do to be forgiven?

Learning God's Truth

This week's memory verse:

🕮 _____ in the _____ of man causes _____, but a good _____ makes it _____. The righteous should _____ his friends carefully, for the way of the wicked leads _____astray. Proverbs 12:25-26

Understanding Your Emotions During Your Cycle or the Zone

The difference in estrogen levels in a woman's body during various times of the month correlates to a predictable pattern of behaviors and emotions.

1. The **first** **week** of her cycle or zone she is outgoing, ambitious, and self-confident. ~ *Life is peaceful.*

2. The **second** **week** she is hopeful, easygoing, with an inner strength and a sense of well being. ~ *Life is fun.*

3. The **third** **week** she lacks coordination, longs for peace, is impatient, gloomy and depressed. ~ *Life is sad.*

4. The **fourth** **week** she is very irritable, touchy sexually, withdrawn and lacks self-confidence. ~ *Life is war.*

Some of us struggle more than others during certain times of our cycle. Maybe you need to mark your calendar to help you and your family become more aware of what will be going on inside your body from day to day and week to week. This will help you and your family to not take the mood swings too seriously. It will allow you to see what may be causing you to be depressed, gloomy, irritable, withdrawn, or have a lack of patience at certain times of the month.

What have you noticed about your own personal cycle and how it effects your moods?

Week 7 Day 3

> *Bow your heart before the Lord in prayer before completing today's Bible study. Ask Him to free you from the shame of the past.*

Shame from the past

Many times when we have a painful past, we may reject ourselves for having this wound, and experience shame, discouragement, and even despair.

"Do not fear, for you will not be ashamed; neither be disgraced, for you will not be put to shame; for you will forget the shame of your youth, and will not remember the reproach of your widowhood anymore. For your Maker is your husband, The LORD of hosts is His name; and your Redeemer is the Holy One of Israel; He is called the God of the whole earth. For the LORD has called you like a woman forsaken and grieved in spirit, like a youthful wife when you were refused," says your God. "For a mere moment I have forsaken you, but with great mercies I will gather you. With a little wrath I hid My face from you for a moment; but with everlasting kindness I will have mercy on you," says the LORD, your Redeemer. Isaiah 54:4-8

1. What sins or shame from your youth linger in your heart?

2. What attitude should you have about the shame of your youth according to Isaiah 54:4-8?

Learning God's Truth

This week's memory verse:

_____ in the _____ of man causes _____, but a good word makes it glad. The righteous should choose his _____ carefully, for the way of the wicked leads them _____. *Proverbs 12:25-26*

3. How does God gather you?

But we have renounced the hidden things of shame, not walking in craftiness nor handling the word of God deceitfully, but by manifestation of the truth commending ourselves to every man's conscience in the sight of God. 2 Corinthians 4:2

4. Is there hidden shame in your life today? Are you ready to walk away from it and commit yourself to the truth? Write down the hidden shame you need to give over to Christ. Take that step to let the old go and the new come! You no longer need to wear the clothes of shame. Christ died for all the shame from your past. Can you believe His death on the cross was enough for you to begin to wear the clothes of purity?

_____

_____

_____

_____

_____

_____

_____

_____

_____

_____

_____

_____

_____

_____

_____

_____

_____

_____

_____

_____

_____

_____

Warnings of a Heart weighed down

"But take heed to yourselves, lest your hearts be weighed down with carousing, drunkenness, and cares of this life, and that Day come on you unexpectedly.   Luke 21:34

5. Are there any particular thoughts or questions concerning your experience that repeatedly plague your mind or causes your heart to be weighted down?

6. What will happen if you let these anxieties continually dwell in your heart?

7. Are you "carousing" around in an ungodly relationship?

8. Does "drunkenness" numb or heal the pain? Does drinking solve problems or create more problems?

9. Have any "cares of this life" come upon you? Turning back to Chapter 4, are you seeking wrong answers to solve the cares of your life?

Casting all your care upon Him, for He cares for you. 1 Peter 5:7

10. What does God want you to do with your anxieties?

To walk in God's will for you means to spend time daily in God's Word, discovering His will, and then obeying what He has told us.

You number my wanderings; put my tears into Your bottle; are they not in Your book?
Psalm 56:8

11. What does God do with all your tears? What does it mean to you to know God cares this deeply about what is going on in your life and that your tears are precious to Him?

In my distress I called upon the LORD, and cried out to my God; He heard my voice from His temple, and my cry came before Him, even to His ears. He sent from above, He took me; He drew me out of many waters. Psalm 18:6,16

12. What prayer would you offer up to God in praise concerning any truths you have learned?

_____

_____

_____

_____

_____

_____

_____

_____

_____

_____

_____

_____

_____

_____

_____

_____

_____

_____

_____

_____

_____

_____

Fear of Contracting AIDS Gripped My Heart

I had been physically and sexually abused for ten years before I met and married my husband. So, from day one, I brought a lot of bitterness and unforgiveness into my marriage. I was very closed off because I didn't want to be vulnerable. Not knowing where to turn for help, my husband eventually became fed up with me. One night, while working out of town, he committed adultery. That night changed our lives forever. He contracted AIDS.

Fear gripped my heart; fear of losing my husband, fear of being alone, fear of raising my children alone and fear of contracting AIDS. At that point in our lives we realized something had to change. We both repented and gave our lives to Christ Jesus as our personal Savior. However, there were still a lot of burdens weighing down my heart.

Anxiety in the heart of man causes depression. Proverbs 12:25.

I decided to take the Healed and Set Free Bible Study. Within the very first few weeks, I could feel the Lord lifting the burden from my heart as He began to show me my own sins of unforgiveness by holding on to all my hurts.

Bearing with one another, and forgiving one another, if anyone has a complaint against another; even as Christ forgave you, so you also must do. But above all these things put on love, which is the bond of perfection. And let the peace of God rule in your hearts, to which also you were called in one body; and be thankful. Colossians 3:13

When I read this verse, I understood. I was sinning by holding my hurts in my heart. God's truth was the only thing that was going to set me free from my own past sins and hurts. I wanted to get real with God. I could SEE I was just as guilty and now I could GIVE these sins to God. I allowed myself to FORGET the past, and BE SET FREE by Jesus from the shackles of fear, bitterness and unforgiveness.

This Bible study taught me to claim God's promises and hide them in my heart. Praise God! I have been Healed and Set Free. God's mercy and love touched our marriage and our lives in a very real way. Today we are living each day for Christ Jesus.

🥀 Changed Woman - Idaho

🥀 SEE, GIVE, FORGIVE, FORGET, BE SET FREE

Week 7 Day 4

Bow your heart before the Lord in prayer before completing today's Bible study. Ask Him to free you from the prison of depression.

The Prison of Depression

Then they cried out to the LORD in their trouble, and He saved them out of their distresses. He brought them out of darkness and the shadow of death, and broke their chains in pieces. Psalm 107:13-14

1. What helped the prisoners in their deepest gloom? How did God respond to their change of heart?

But God be thanked that though you were slaves of sin, yet you obeyed from the heart that form of doctrine to which you were delivered. And having been set free from sin, you became slaves of righteousness. Romans 6:17-18

2. What does it mean to obey God's word from the heart in peaceful and in struggling times?

3. What does it mean to be a slave to sin?

Stand fast therefore in the liberty by which Christ has made us free, and do not be entangled again with a yoke of bondage. Galatians 5:1

4. Can you SEE if you are entangled with a yoke of bondage? Be Specific

Pray for those that are entangled:

Jeanne Hendricks, wife of Dallas Theological Seminary professor Howard Hendrick, spent a season in intense prayer for one of her children. During his later adolescence, her son went through what Jeanne called a " blackout" period. He was unenthusiastic, moody, and depressed, communicating only with single - syllable responses. " This was one of the most traumatic times of my life," Jeanne admits. "He was so far from the Lord and from us. I felt like the devil himself was out to get my child. I prayed as I never had before." Mrs. Hendricks shared that, during the half year when this situation continued, she covenanted with God to give up her noon meal. As she fasted each day, she prayed for her son for one hour until God broke through to him.

5. Do you know someone that needs you to pray for them? Take time to pray for them today!

All My Mama's Unhappiness is ∾∾∾∾∾∾∾∾∾∾∾∾∾∾∾∾∾∾ Because of Daddy

It was Monday, June 13, 1994. It had been a painful couple of months; as we sold our new home in Boise, made major job changes and condensed a large three bedroom home into a small two bedroom apartment in Twin Falls. My husband of six years chose that time to inform me he thought it would be best if he didn't live with his wife and baby. He suggested we "date again" and he didn't mean each other. In a matter of seconds, my life and my son's life changed forever. I could write a book on anger, bitterness, fear, hatred, devastation and loneliness. The reality of divorce is sin. And sin, whether we ourselves transgress or someone else does the transgressing against us, produces absolutely nothing good unless we can forgive and forget in order to be healed and set free.

I came to the first session of a confidential Bible study not knowing exactly what was in store for me. I was nervous and knew nothing about the other women and was sure "I didn't fit in here." They were all so "put together". They were smiling, they knew each other, and they certainly loved the Lord. Why had I come? Tammy handed out booklets as we introduced ourselves and discussed the importance of confidentiality. She put my mind at ease by making it clear we did not have to share anything we didn't want to and we did not have to read or pray out loud if we felt uncomfortable in any way.

Well, I didn't need healing. The divorce was four years ago. I had coped well and did what I had to do. Of course, I blamed my ex-husband for everything. If he hadn't committed adultery with that "woman" I wouldn't be in this situation, and my son would have a father at home, and we could be a normal family. Someday I planned to tell my son what a terrible dad he had and all of mama's unhappiness was because of "daddy". I didn't need healing. My ex-husband just needed to stay as far away as possible from me and my son.

Honesty with myself was my goal

I read chapter one. Honesty with myself was my goal. My first studies were somewhat difficult and uncomfortable. I had answered "Yes" to all the questions! Where did these questions come from? As I read and answered honestly, my heart was softened. I was broken and my emotions flooded over me. I believe to this day that God revealed to me, alone in my bedroom that night, that I had a lot of issues to deal with regarding my past. Also, that He was with me and would remain with me no matter what was to happen.

I became closer to the Lord, reading and praying and learning about how much He really does love me. However, being a selfish sinner, I wanted the Lord all to myself. I did not want Him to love my ex-husband or "that woman". After all, they were the ones who had sinned. I continued to pray that they would get what was coming to them - HELL.

As our group met, we shared more about each other and our life experiences, and I began to love these women. I was never so humbled in all my life as I was during the "session of confession" as I call it! I listened to these women talk about hurts and express emotions so powerful I could not hold back the tears. The compassion and empathy I felt with these suffering women was too close to my own painful memories. How dare we discuss these "never-talked-about" subjects! We women in Christ were doing just as He instructed us to do. We were being obedient in our walks. However ugly the past was, together we brought our darkness into the light. We confessed the sin! Let the healing begin!

The Lord made it very clear I needed to forgive many people for many things so I could be forgiven and go on with what was really important - Him! Just when I thought it was getting easier, it got much harder to obey. Forgive my ex? Forgive the woman who slept with my husband? Forgive the man who molested me as a young girl? Forgive the men who used or abused me in other relationships? Yet, time and time again Scriptures came back to me about forgiving so as to be forgiven. *"For if you forgive men their trespasses, your heavenly Father will also forgive you. But if you do not forgive men their trespasses, neither will your Father forgive your trespasses."* Matthew 6:14-15. Many nights, I prayed for those people. At first, half-heartedly "Oh, yeah, and I pray for.... Amen." Gradually, my heart filled with God and His love. I see it everywhere! My prayers now are for these people's salvation!

Only by the power of His Holy Spirit would I ever be able to forgive and pray for someone who could have caused so much pain. PRAISE THE LORD!

I am living proof that God does heal and does answer our prayers. I also know my future is so much more critical than my past, so I will not dwell on those things that no longer exist. My ex-husband and I no longer raise our voices at each other in anger. We both make sacrifices for our son. I even find myself smiling when I answer the door to greet him and often thank him for his efforts toward our son. I will never tell Steven what a terrible daddy he has or that our lives are so bad because of his father's sins; those are lies! I will and have told him only the truth. I love him so very much and there is nothing I would ever change about my life, good or bad, because I have such a precious gift!

I hear other women talking poorly about their ex-husbands; sometimes using such colorful language and harsh wishes, often demeaning them in front of their own children, and I know their pain. Only recently have I been able to see more fruits of my healing when I was privileged to share the Peace of the Lord with another young woman recently divorced asking me, "How do you cope with it?"

        A New Spirit When Healed and Set Free - Gina, Idaho

From the moment I gave my life in faith to Christ I have been blessed with so much love and so many friends. This will be my first Christmas in which the best gift I have ever received is not under the tree, but was nailed to the tree.

SEE, GIVE, FORGIVE, FORGET, BE SET FREE

Conquering the Cycle of Depression

When we are depressed, we suffer from "ingrown eyeballs." Our eyes are turned inward and we focus on our own problems and on ourselves. The more we are focused inward, the worse we feel and the harder it is to take the necessary steps to SEE the truth and allow the Lord's love and grace to flow in our lives. What advice do the following Scriptures give on how to break this cycle?

Therefore, we also, since we are surrounded by so great a cloud of witnesses, let us lay aside every weight, and the sin which so easily ensnares us, and let us run with endurance the race that is set before us, looking unto Jesus, the author and finisher of our faith, who for the joy that was set before Him endured the cross, despising the shame, and has sat down at the right hand of the throne of God. Hebrews 12:1-2

1. Where should your eyes be focused?

2. Remember Satan has come to "kill, steal and destroy". When he shoots his fiery darts your way, you must not look back, but look inside to SEE what's in your heart that could defile you. What reminders from your past such as places, songs, or smells does Satan throw in your face trying to catch you off guard to ensnare you and weigh you down? What four steps must you take to BE SET FREE?

Put off, concerning your former conduct, the old man which grows corrupt according to the deceitful lusts, and be renewed in the spirit of your mind, and that you put on the new man which was created according to God, in true righteousness and holiness. Ephesians 4:22-24

3. Concerning your former conduct, what have you put off by being renewed in your mind?

4. Concerning your present conduct, what has the Holy Spirit been showing you that needs to be put off?

For you were once darkness, but now you are light in the Lord, live as children of the light. Ephesians 5:8

5. To "live as children of the light" means God's light is within us and we are cannot hide from God, and we should not hide God from others. Are you witnessing and sharing Christ with others?

6. Do your acquaintances even know you are a Christian?

...all things are naked and opened unto the eyes of Him with who we have to give an account. Hebrews 4:13

Learning God's Truth

This week's memory verse:

🌝 _____ in the _____ of man causes _____, but a good word makes it glad. The righteous should choose his _____ carefully, for the way of the wicked leads them _____. *Proverbs 12:25-26*

7. In what areas of your life do pride or fear keep you focused on pleasing others instead of pleasing God?

8. Was Jesus concerned about pleasing man or God?

9. Write down and share your thoughts about ways that you could be a shining light to others.

_____

_____

_____

_____

_____

_____

_____

_____

_____

_____

_____

_____

_____

_____

_____

_____

_____

_____

_____

"And we, who with unveiled faces all reflect the Lord's glory, are being transformed into His likeness with ever-increasing glory, which comes from the Lord, who is the Spirit." 2 Corinthians 3:18

Week 7 Day 5

> *Bow your heart before the Lord in prayer before completing today's Bible study. Thank Him for the abundant life He offers to you.*

Celebrating Life

The thief does not come except to steal, and to kill, and to destroy. I have come that they may have life, and that they may have it more abundantly. John 10:10

Christ came to make available to all the gifts of eternal life and abundant life. All who have accepted Jesus have eternal life, but few Christians enjoy the abundant life. Satan can not steal the gift of eternal life, but he can rob you of the joy of living life abundantly. Be aware of Satan's schemes and be quick to SEE, GIVE, FORGIVE, FORGET and BE SET FREE to enjoy the gift of abundant life.

One day we will be in heaven where there will be no more tears, no more pain, and no more failures. We need to celebrate the life we have been given now, as we live in anticipation of heaven. The air you breathe is a gift from God. Celebrate your life. The husband and children you have been allowed to have are gifts from God. Celebrate your husband and children. The love you give and receive is a gift from God because God is love. Celebrate your love. Your very salvation is a gift from God and insures your future. Celebrate your future in heaven.

First Make commitments to Focus on God in Celebration: "Lord, what can I do today to live out and celebrate the fact that you are the Ultimate Priority of my life?" What can I do today to grow spiritually?

Second Make commitments to help your husband in celebration: Focus on your Husband: One way I try to help Rick by focusing on him and his responsibilities as a senior Pastor is by asking him two questions I learned from a Christian woman. " What can I do for you today?" and " What can I do to help you make better use of your time today?" You may worry (as I did initially) about what major, time consuming demands your husband might make. But I have to tell you when I asked Rick these questions all he wanted was ironed clothes to put on for the day. That's All! Rick's my number one human priority and it's my joy to help him with ironed clothes daily. And yes! There are days I don't feel like ironing. But I would say to myself, "Tam, you're ironing these clothes for Jesus, not for Rick". I sort of mentally set my precious Rick to one side, and that left me serving the Lord. Yes! Rick is the one that benefits from the ironed clothes. My heart to submit and become Rick's helper had nothing to do with Rick and everything to do with the Lord. As a familiar Scripture says, "Whatever you do (including submitting and helping my husband!), do it heartily, as to the Lord and not to men." (Colossians 3:23, emphasis added.) What a blessing to apply this scripture to honoring, submitting to and following Rick!

Sometimes, though, the requests are larger, And just a few weeks ago I had a week of "larger" demands as Rick had asked me to do many things before we were going to leave for a ministry trip. Caleb, Jessica, and I teamed up and accomplished everything on the list, along with our daily schedule of things to do. I even had time for a quick trip to the ice cream store to bless Caleb and Jessica.

And even if there is no husband in your life today, you can nurture a heart of Christlike service as you focus on helping and serving other people. Whether or not you are married, serving the people in your life pleases God and shows Christ to the world.

Ask, "Will this help or hinder my husband?" ~~~ When Elizabeth George's husband became a full time seminary student, a full time staff member at church, and also traveled extensively with a mission's Pastor, she read every book she could find about Ruth Graham, wife of evangelist Billy Graham. Because Ruth's famous husband was absent from home almost ten months a year, Elizabeth learned much from her about being alone. Listen to Mrs. Graham's wise statement: "We have to learn to make the lest of all that goes and the most of all that comes." This encouragement from a fellow helper has made me a better helper to my husband as he serves as a Senior Pastor preparing for speaking, preaching, early morning and late night counseling appointments, elders, leadership, and school staff meetings, and late night hospital visits, week after week. It has also decreased my urge to pout and give the cold shoulder to my husband.

Third make a commitment to Focus on your Children in celebration: Lord, what can I do today for Caleb and Jessica to let them know that, after Rick, they are more important than all the other people in my life?

Many times the answer to this question was "show patience," "kindness," "no nagging and losing my temper," as I scheduled specific times during each day to set aside all other activities and have a special time of playing, reading a book with them at teatime, riding bikes to the snow cone stand, or going for a horseback ride. After school I would surprise them by going out for a Reed's dairy ice cream or prepare a favorite snack for them after school.

Fourth make commitments to Focus on your Home in celebration: Lord, what can I do today regarding my home? The answer to this question is to watch over my home {as the house manager} and not eat the bread of idleness. To make my home a refuge for my family and guests.

Fifth make commitments to Focus on your Ministry in celebration: Lord, what can I do today to minister to your people? Call friends, lessons to plan, organizing women's retreat, writing, purchasing paper, and preparing food for ministry events.

Practice Your Priorities

As one Christian Author says, Each day presents many opportunities and challenges to practice our priorities. One way to simplify your moment by moment decision making might be to assign your priorities these numbers:

#1 God (spiritual growth)

#2 Your husband

#3 Your children

#4 Your home

#5 Your ministry activities

#6 Other activities

Celebrate Plan and keep the Priorities

Celebrate the life you have been given by giving your life away to others. Complete the following sentences with ways in which you can give your life away everyday.

1. I will celebrate my life by sharing the gift of helping my husband by...

2. I will celebrate my children by have a special time by...

3. I will celebrate my health.... Who can you serve and help this week ...

4. I will celebrate my love by obeying God when He lays a friend on my heart by... Who can you encourage today?

5. I will celebrate the gift of salvation... Who needs to hear about this gift?

Celebrate each and every day. Here's a list to make home a place to cherish.

☞ *I will seek daily to keep my heart clean from a junk draw.*

☞ *I will apply the tools to SEE, GIVE, FORGIVE, FORGET so I can be Healed and Set Free to celebrate my life.*

☞ I will work diligently to send every member of my family off in a good mood.

☞ I will consult my husband every day to see if there is anything special he wants me to do for him.

☞ I will keep a neat and orderly home.

☞ I will respond positively.

☞ I will meet my husband's needs.

☞ I will personally meet and greet each family member as he or she returns home.

☞ I will be predictably happy.

☞ I will make dinner for my family.

☞ I will grow daily in the areas of my assignment from God as a wife, mom, and Christian woman.

"Stories of real people, real hurts, real healing, and a real SAVIOR"

I am a Completely Different Person

I do not even know 1/8 of the things the Lord has shown and done in me through the Healed and Set Free Bible study. I am a completely different person than I was 3 months ago.

I was a victim of rape. I had been through all the topic of the Bible study except Divorce. I did go for counseling over my rape before my daughter was born. And at that time I thought it helped, but it did not HEAL any part of me. I have applied the tools SEE, GIVE, FORGIVE AND FORGET to my life. Christ has taken the wrongful and sinful feelings away. I can say, "He has HEALED me." I am no longer a slave to Satan; I am a slave, ONLY to Jesus Christ. Praise the LORD!

🌿 Set Free ~ Sheila , Philadelphia

I was Crying Out For a Reason to Live

I have always believed in my head that God is the Wonderful Counselor, but as I prayed over the past few years for healing for my painful emotional baggage, He seemed not to hear or respond. I was at the point of seeking professional counseling, disappearing for a few weeks or both, when this study was offered at my church in Minnesota. I immediately knew when I heard the title "Healed and Set Free" that this was God's answer for me so I signed up.

How do you communicate the total unhappiness, the effort living was for me? Oh, I'd wake up anticipating each day, looking forward to things I liked to do. But guess what? I didn't "like" to do anything anymore, really. I just DID out of habit. It was all an effort, I was so sad. I really didn't want to live like this - to waste my life. I was at the bottom in a dark, distrustful hole for several years, which had just gotten larger and deeper. I hung on to every little real and imagined hurt and stuffed it deep inside, feeling justified but stuck in a horrible nightmare.

I was doubtful because of the patterns and habits that had already been established but I wanted a new perspective.

This Bible study has truly been a great healing experience for me, As I wrote down my heart and shared some of my frustrations and as I and others prayed for this work to be done the garbage just faded away. I really can't remember some of the things that I thought were so big before. I am just so grateful to God for healing and leading me and for the enthusiasm He has restored to me for life and serving others. I see so many needing this study that I'm praying about becoming a leader so no one misses out. I'd like everyone to experience the abundant Christian life.

🌿 The truth set me free to live the abundant life ~ Karen, Minnesota

SEE, GIVE, FORGIVE, FORGET, BE SET FREE

How you spent your dash?

I read of a reverend who stood to speak at the funeral of his friend. He referred to the dates on his tombstone from the beginning...to the end. He noted that first came the date of his birth and spoke of the following date with tears, but he said what mattered most of all was the dash between those years. For that dash represents all the time that he spent alive on earth, and now only those who loved him know what that little line is worth. For it matters not, how much we own: the cars, the house, the cash. What matters is how we Live and Love and How we spend our dash.

So think about this long and hard, are there things you'd like to change? For you never know how much time is left. (You could be at "dash mid-range.")

We need to slow down enough to consider what's true and real, about eternal life and always try to understand the way other people feel. And be less quick to anger, and show appreciation more and love the people in our lives like we've never loved before. We need to treat each other with respect and more often wear a smile, remembering that this special dash might only last a little while. So when your eulogy is being read with your life's actions to rehash... would you be pleased with the things they say about how you spent your dash?

- Author unknown

- Are there things you'd like to change? If so, what? For you never know how much time is left. (You could be at "dash mid-range".)

Chapter 6

Living to Eat
or
Eating to Live

*Stand fast therefore in the
liberty by which Christ has
made us free, and do not be
entangled again with a
yoke of bondage.*

Galatians 5:1

There are four main tools we will weave into the very fiber of our hearts day by day: **SEE, GIVE, FORGIVE, FORGET,** and **BE SET FREE**. Thinking about the past will never change the past. But you can change your future and Be Set FREE from your past. As you deal with your past and present hurts, you can either embrace the truth and let go of the burdens you carry, or carry your burdens and reject the truth and the freedom it brings. The choice is yours. Getting real with God is the first step you need to always take as you face deep, dark hurts that have chipped away at your peace for 1 year, 10 years, 20 years, and some 50 years. God's love is bigger then all of our hurts and fears. You will have many blessings in front of you as God's truth unfolds in your heart and Sets you Free.

Let's Day By Day Go over the Four Steps to Keep Our Hearts Clean

🌼 Tools To Become Set Free

- **Tool #1 "SEE ":** I must **SEE** the truth about what is in my heart, so I'm not defiled.

    Looking carefully lest anyone fall short of the grace of God; lest any root of bitterness springing up cause trouble, and by this many become defiled. Hebrew 12:15.

- **Tool #2 "GIVE":** I must **GIVE** the sin in repentance, knowing Christ is waiting to take it. (I must be sorry enough to change and choose to go God's way over my own way.)

    For godly sorrow produces repentance leading to salvation, not to be regretted; but the sorrow of the world produces death. 2 Corinthians 7:10

- **Tool #3 "FORGIVE":** I must **FORGIVE**, as I am forgiven by Christ. (Forgiving those that hurt, bruised, wronged, hurt, rejected, betrayed or harmed me whether unintentionally or deliberately.) Ask God to Forgive you for holding unforgiveness and know that He will.

    Bearing with one another, and forgiving one another, if anyone has a complaint against another; even as Christ forgave you, so you also must do. Colossians 3:13

- **Tool #4 "FORGET":** I must **FORGET** by remembering to no longer dwell on the hurt.

    Brethren, I do not count myself to have apprehended; but one thing I do, forgetting those things which are behind and reaching forward to those things which are ahead. Philippians 3:13.

🌼 **BECOME SET FREE:** Christ will open the shackles from my past hurts showing me the truth so I can become a cleansed vessel that is Healed and Set Free.

    You shall know the truth, and the truth shall make you free. Therefore, if the Son makes you free, you shall be free indeed. John 8:32-36.

SATAN IS DEFEATED AND THE SHACKLES ARE GONE AND YOU ARE FREE!

Week 8 Day 1

> *Bow your heart before the Lord before completing today's Bible study. Ask for help, being completely honest with God and yourself concerning food.*

The battle (lifestyle of bondage)

God is intimately involved with every aspect of our lives, minds, bodies and souls. To be obsessed with our bodies or food is to live our lives in bondage. When a stronghold is in our lives we are working against ourselves and against God's design for us. We are His workmanship created in Christ Jesus.

Break that stronghold

The battle to break strongholds requires that we get up each day and pray God will kill the flesh of our own will, our own thinking and our own pride. We must pray His will and His Word would be lived out in our lives, day by day. Satan is your adversary, a very real and crafty enemy who has targeted you and is using food or pride as his weapon of destruction. Remember this is not a game. This is spiritual warfare and you are going to have to war in the spirit as Satan launches his attacks on your very life.

SEE the Stronghold

You can make the choice to change and enter into a self-controlled life with the help of God. It is necessary to:

- **SEE** the stronghold in your life.

- **GIVE** it over to God in confession, asking for His help and His strength to change.

- **FORGIVE** as Christ has forgiven you.

- **FORGET** the lies you have believed.

 BE SET FREE by God's truth for your life as you stand firm in your new choices.

Learning God's Truth

This week's memory verse:

 Stand fast therefore in the liberty by which Christ has made us free, and do not be entangled again with a yoke of bondage. Galatians 5:1

A Secret My Husband Didn't Know About

I had been praying for God to give me someone to go to for help. I had this secret even my husband didn't know about. A few times I had almost shared with a sister in Christ, but I never did. Then one day Tammy called me out of the blue and the desire to share my secret with her was so strong, I knew it was time. I told her I was bulimic and that I was really struggling.

I started the Healed and Set Free Bible study with a heart to end the slavery to this sin. The study brought out many issues from my past that I had never fully dealt with. One of those issues was being molested as a child. In the eight weeks of doing the study God has shown me so much in my life. Sin is sin is sin, no matter what. I couldn't do it alone. I needed God to help me. We need to SEE, GIVE, FORGIVE, FORGET, and BE SET FREE.

Walking in the truth - A sister in Christ

SEE, GIVE, FORGIVE, FORGET, BE SET FREE

"For whoever does the will of My Father in heaven is my brother and sister and mother." Matthew 12:50

By sitting down and going over the reasons why you eat and what you feel during and after eating, you can pinpoint areas where problems exist for you. If you are eating for any reason other than the normal feelings of hunger, food has taken an inappropriate place in your life. You need to find out why so you can **SEE, GIVE, FORGIVE, FORGET,** and **BE SET FREE**. The next set of yes or no questions is designed to help you take a closer look at what place you give food in your life.

Yes or No

___ ___ Do you starve yourself?

___ ___ Do you have uncontrollable urges to eat until you become physically ill?

___ ___ Do you have episodes where you eat an enormous amount of food in a short period of time?

___ ___ Do you make yourself vomit to get rid of the food you've eaten?

___ ___ Is it hard to eat normal meals without bingeing and purging?

Yes or No

___ ___ Do you use laxatives to control your weight or to get rid of food?

___ ___ Do you spit out food after chewing it to keep the food from getting into your stomach?

___ ___ Do you eat because you are bored, angry, or upset?

___ ___ Do you exercise out of control?

___ ___ Do you use enemas?

___ ___ Do you become preoccupied with what you eat?

___ ___ Are you unwilling to gain weight in order to stop any faulty eating pattern you might have?

___ ___ Do you eat to relieve stress or to comfort yourself if you are depressed?

___ ___ Is it hard for you to stop eating when you are full?

___ ___ Do you feel eating is a sin?

___ ___ Have others made fun of you because of your weight?

___ ___ Do you compare your weight or size with that of other women?

___ ___ Do you feel guilty about eating?

___ ___ By not eating, do you believe you are more in control than the person who overeats?

SEE, GIVE, FORGIVE, FORGET, BE SET FREE

SEE the Stronghold

> *Self-control is the ability from the Holy Spirit to say no to what is wrong and to say yes to what is right. Take each day one at a time. Face the truth about any weakness in your life. Ask for God's strength to apply self-control in this area.*

Remember the **"Falling Down"** skating story? As you begin to practice self-control by taking steps to change your eating habits, you may fall down and get up and fall down and get up again. Praise Jesus for the times you are up. Praise Jesus that His mercies are new every morning as you pick yourself up from a fall and begin again to fuel your body in a wise and healthy manner. The more you practice self-control, the easier it will become to choose to follow the Spirit and not the flesh.

1. Do you desire to embrace or reject self-control in this area of your life?

As His divine power has given to us all things that pertain to life and godliness, through the knowledge of Him who called us by glory and virtue, by which have been given to us exceedingly great and precious promises, that through these you may be partakers of the divine nature, having escaped the corruption that is in the world through lust. But also for this very reason, giving all diligence, add to your faith virtue, to virtue knowledge, to knowledge self-control, to self-control perseverance, to perseverance godliness, to godliness brotherly kindness, and to brotherly kindness love. For if these things are yours and abound, you will be neither barren nor unfruitful in the knowledge of our Lord Jesus Christ. For he who lacks these things is shortsighted, even to blindness, and has forgotten that he was cleansed from his old sins. 2 Peter 1:3-9

2. How can you have self-control to your life?

3. Do you look at your eating disorder each day with a heart to change and become an obedient child? Pray and ask the Holy Spirit to show you practical steps that you can take to begin this change, and write them down, then share these steps with the person that is helping you get out of this bondage.

Learning God's Truth

This week's memory verse:
Stand fast therefore in the liberty by which Christ has made us free, and do not be entangled again with a yoke of bondage. Galatians 5:1

AUTHOR'S REFLECTION
Bulimia Could Have Taken ∿∿∿∿∿∿∿∿∿∿∿∿∿∿∿ My Life

By the time I reached my senior year of high school, my life was out of control. I had given my life to Christ but was still doing anything that felt good to me at the time, such as partying, lying, gossiping or whatever. Jesus Christ was my Savior, but He was not the Lord, King or Master of my life. I wasn't serving Him with joyful obedience. I wasn't in the Bible desiring to feed my spirit. I was consumed by the world's ways, going down a dead end street.

It all started with my friend bragging about how she would eat as much as a horse and then vomit up her food and take laxatives to stay thin. The thought was placed in my mind and I decided to give it a try. I didn't realize the deadly consequences in a person's body and mind. I would take in large amounts of food and vomit it all up at least five times a day, just to stay thin. Why? Because I was filled with pride and I wanted to stay thin. I was consumed with self, what people thought of me and how they looked at me. I wanted to control my weight and control my life, but in reality, bulimia was controlling me. My mind became sick. I thought I was fat, but I was very thin.

Closing off my heart to God

I was determined to build thick walls around myself, retreating into the safety of trusting in myself. I decided I would close off my heart to God and I set about going my own way in the world. I continued in my sin of bulimia and filled myself with pride and self-pity. As I partied hard, my heart became hard. When I looked at myself in the mirror there was no life in my face at all. I looked like I had cut my lifeline and I was dying. I had cut God out of my life. Even though I had moved away from God, God still remained loving and faithful to me. All I had to do was reach up and take His hand and unconditionally trust Him.

Reaching out to food for comfort

The Holy Spirit was tugging on my heart. I'm not sure when or how it happened, but it did happen. I realized I was sinning in my thoughts about the importance of self. God wasn't God in my life. My belly was my god. My thinness was my god. My pride was my god. I wasn't reaching out to God for comfort when I was discouraged, stressed or lonely. I was reaching out for food to comfort me.

He is a jealous God

God will have nothing before Him in our hearts: not our families, husbands, children, careers, bellies, homes, bodies, not even our ministries. Often things can become more important to us than God. Psalms 73:25 tells us, there should be nothing upon earth that we desire more than God. If we have put ANYTHING before God in our hearts, we will never quite be able to give Him our total lives because SOMETHING will always be standing in the way. I knew I needed to make a change in my life, my thoughts and my eating habits. It was time to stop my bulimic lifestyle and start having self-control in my life. If I would not have stopped my bulimic life style, I might not be here for my husband or children. I could be **dead.** I know several women whose lives have been taken by anorexia and bulimia. These are real women who are now dead. God has healed my mind and healed my sin of bulimia. I've asked for forgiveness and confessed with my mouth my sin, and have been Set Free by God. It's just a matter of having the right perspective on food. Today when I sit down to eat, I don't feel guilty or worry I'm going to get heavy. I feed my body the food it needs to stay alive, and when I'm full, I stop eating. I know it sounds too simple, but it is that simple. It is just a matter of choice at mealtime. It is my desire to maintain a healthy body weight so when I eat, I apply the fruit of the Spirit of self-control.

Food is only to fuel the body

But the Fruit of the Spirit is love, joy, peace, longsuffering, kindness, goodness, faithfulness, gentleness, SELF CONTROL. Against such there is no law. And those who are Christ's have crucified the flesh with its passions and desires. If we live in the Spirit, let us also walk in the Spirit. Galatians 5:22

SEE, GIVE, FORGIVE, FORGET, BE SET FREE

A. Ignorant disobedience: you do not know what you are doing is sinful.

B. Willful disobedience: you know what you are doing is sinful and you continue to sin.

Week 8 Day 2

Bow your heart before the Lord in prayer before completing today's Bible study. Ask God to help you embrace what He wants to teach you.

The Dead-end Reality of Eating Disorders

Those in bondage to eating disorders can experience freedom that is life changing. Believe that God's healing is always available to those desiring recovery. There is a difference between surviving and living. This part of the study offers you hope for change.

You are starting a journey, that means you are leaving one place and moving toward another. This requires change and change can be very unsettling. Your eating disorder on the other hand is a predictable and comfortable behavior that has been with you for a long time.

While you are focusing on the uncomfortable nature of change, you will need to **look again at the dead-end reality of your eating disorder.** Yes, change and movement are scary and challenging, but you wouldn't have picked up this study and gotten this far if you didn't know, really know, **the way you are living is no longer acceptable to you.**

It's time to get real with God. He's not looking for performance, just a totally honest and open heart. It's my prayer, that as children of God meditating on the following scriptures, you will let God in as you look at the Truth of what is going on in your heart. God is the God of Truth and only the Truth will set you Free.

Words to Remember, Fill in the blanks

*Therefore let him who _____ _____ stands take heed lest he fall. No temptation has overtaken you _____ such as is common to man; but God is faithful, _____ will _____ allow you to be tempted beyond what _____ are able, but with the **temptation will _____ make the way ___ escape,** that you may be ___ to bear it..Corinthians 10:12-13*

Learning God's Truth

This week's memory verse:
Stand fast therefore in the liberty by which Christ has ____ us free, and do not __ _____ again with a ___ of bondage. Galatians _:_

Definition of Anorexia

Anorexia nervosa is a disorder in which preoccupation with dieting and thinness leads to excessive weight loss. It can be defined as self-starvation leading to a loss of body weight, accompanied by hypothermia, amenorrhea, and hyperactivity. Hypothermia results when the body's natural insulation of fat stores becomes nonexistent leaving the body cold all the time. Amnerorrhea is the absence of at least three menstrual cycles, which can be brought about by the loss of fat stores in the body. Hyperactivity may result from obsessive exercising in a frantic attempt to burn calories to lose weight.

Anorexia may not be noticed in the early stages because it often starts as an innocent diet. The individual may not acknowledge that weight loss or restricted eating is a problem. There may be a loss of appetite due to emotional states such as anxiety, irritation, anger and fear. However, in true anorexia nervosa there is no loss of appetite, just a refusal to eat. This refusal to eat can lead to severe malnutrition by denying the body essential nutrients creating long lasting effects. Complaints of rapid and irregular heartbeats are caused by not taking in enough potassium, the fuel that regulates the heartbeat.

Even though the anorexic is emaciated, they still feel fat and want to hide their "ugly, fat body." An anorexic may have ritualistic eating patterns such as cutting the food into tiny pieces and weighing every piece of food before eating. These behaviors can be found in people who are on a normal healthy diet, but in anorexics these behaviors are extremely exaggerated. These individuals want to maintain control over the only part of their life they think they have control over by starving themselves to death. The most famous case is Karen Carpenter, who died from heart failure resulting from anorexia nervosa.

Simply stated anorexia is starving yourself to death because of an obsessive fear of being fat and a desperate desire to maintain control over some area of your life. The desire to maintain a healthy body weight is fine. But the goal of an anorexic is not a healthy body weight, but having control over some area of their life. However, the reality is this obsession is controlling them, and unchecked, will bring about their death. At least 60% of all anorexics are also bulimic. Both eating disorders usually begin near the onset of puberty.

If you are anorexic, it will be easy for you to deceive yourself. The only protection against this deception is total honesty on your part, and if necessary, the wise counsel of those who truly love you.

1. Are you being honest with your self?

Learning God's Truth

This week's memory verse:
🌹 *Stand fast therefore in the liberty by which Christ has _____ us free, and do not __ _____ again with a ___ of bondage. Galatians _:_*

Warning signs of Anorexia:

1. Circle the following warning signs that describe you. Being totally honest with yourself will protect you against being deceived.

   - Intense fear of gaining weight or of getting fat.

   - Unnatural or obsessive preoccupation with food, dieting and weight.

   - Eating only small amounts of fruits or vegetables, sometimes only black coffee.

   - Eating sprees usually at night, afterwards forcing yourself to vomit.

   - Distorted perspective of how your body actually looks.

   - Feeling fat even after loosing weight.

   - Continuing to diet when already too thin.

   - Deny hunger.

   - Avoidance of social situations where food is present.

   - Prefer to eat alone.

   - Difficulty making friends or meeting strangers.

   - No longer have monthly menstrual periods.

   - Weakness, fatigue, depression and lack of energy.

   - Exercise compulsively.

   - Decreased coordination.

   - Inability to concentrate.

   - Indecisiveness.

   - Mood swings, irritability, depression.

2. Could you share the answers that you have circled with the person you are accountable to during your healing of anorexia? YES or NO

Questions about Anorexia

Question: Do I have to get heavy to get well?

Answer: You must reject the false values of society and accept your own worth, based on who you are as a person in Christ and not on what your body looks like. You'll find you must work the fruit of the spirit of self-control in your life. And no, you don't have to get heavy to get well. Your identity is in Christ not in your weight. It's a matter of the choices you make at mealtimes. Food is just fuel for your body. Food is not your enemy and food is not your companion.

Charm is deceitful and beauty is passing, But a woman who fears the LORD, she shall be praised. Proverbs 31:30

Definition of Bulimia

Bulimia is an eating disorder consisting of bingeing and purging. Bingeing is eating large amounts of food in a short amount of time. Be aware this type of eating is abnormal, the bulimic will purge her body by getting rid of all the food she has just eaten. The purging methods used can be vomiting, abusing laxatives or diuretics, taking enemas or exercising obsessively. Some will use a combination of all these purging methods.

A bulimic can severely damage her body by frequent bingeing and purging. Memory impairment, blackouts, a sense of psychological abnormality and numbness often accompany this type of behavior. Binge eating can cause the stomach to rupture. Repetitive vomiting may also cause the esophagus and larynx or voice box, to become inflamed resulting in tearing and bleeding. The glands near the cheeks can become swollen. Stomach acid constantly going over tooth enamel will eventually cause tooth decay. Daily use of laxatives will cause the body to be leached of essential nutrients. Potassium, the fuel that regulates the heartbeat, is flushed out of the body of a bulimic, creating complaints of a rapid or irregular heartbeat. A bulimic may also have irregular or no menstrual periods.

Bulimics fear they will not be able to stop eating voluntarily and fear losing all control. They carry out their bingeing and purging in secret. When around family and friends, they either don't eat or they drastically reduce their food intake. They insist they are dieting to lose just a few pounds. Since they usually maintain a normal or above normal body weight, they can hide their problem for years. Some individuals with bulimia also struggle with addictions to drugs and alcohol, and compulsive stealing. They also may suffer from clinical depression, anxiety and obsessive-compulsive disorder.

In both bulimia and anorexia, food replaces other people as a source of comfort and companionship. When you withdraw from others, Satan has you right where he wants you…isolated.

Purging is the most common warning sign with bulimia. If you are bulimic you already know it. This eating disorder can accelerate quickly and early recognition is a must in order to prevent serious physical consequences.

1. Write down verses that speak to you on pieces of paper to place in your bathroom or kitchen and take the time this week to really meditate on them.

Warning signs of Bulimia:

2. Circle the following warning signs that describe you. Being totally honest with yourself will protect you against being deceived.

- Bingeing and purging.

- Hide stashes of food such as chips, candy, etc.

- Secretive eating.

- Disappearance after meals with long visits to the bathroom after eating.

- Avoidance of social situations where food is present.

- Increased withdrawal from normal activities.

- Distorted body image.

- Fear of becoming fat.

- Deny hunger.

- Compulsive exercising.

- Use of laxatives, diet pills.

- Physical changes including dehydration.

- Blood shot eyes from vomiting.

- Abrasions on the back of the hands from induced vomiting.

- Swollen salivary glands.

- Irregular or rapid heartbeat.

- Tooth decay.

- Menstrual irregularities.

- Mood swings, depression, and irritability.

3. Could you share the answers you have circled with the one person you are accountable to during your healing of bulimia? YES or NO

Warning signs of Compulsive overeating

1. Circle the following warning signs that describe you. A compulsive overeater has over time become more intimate with food than with people. Being totally honest with yourself will protect you from being deceived.

- Lost all hope of ever being anything but large and fat.

- Concluded there's nothing else in life except the pleasure food brings.

- Single most important goal is getting the next "food fix".

- Can't stop eating because food is only source of comfort and companionship.

- Eating is out of control.

- Hide food, stashing it around the house.

- Eat in secret.

- Make jokes about your eating habits.

2. Could you share the answers you have circled with the one person that you are accountable to during your healing with compulsive overeating? YES or NO

For he who sows to his flesh will of the flesh reap corruption, but he who sows to the Spirit will of the Spirit reap everlasting life. Galatians 6:8.

Learning God's Truth

This week's memory verse:
☘ *Stand fast therefore in the liberty by which Christ has ____ us free, and do not ____ _____ again with a ___ of bondage. Galatians _:_*

Self-control is Fruitful

But the fruit of the Spirit is love, joy, peace, longsuffering, kindness, goodness, faithfulness, gentleness, self-control. Against such there is no law. And those who are Christ's have crucified the flesh with its passions and desires. If we live in the Spirit, let us also walk in the Spirit.. Galatians 5:22

1. Write down the nine words that describe the fruit of the Spirit from Galatians 5:22.

2. How can you apply the ninth word from the list in Galatians 5:22 to your meals?

3. Finish the statements that apply to you by inserting self-control.

   • If I want to over eat at meals or during the day I can remember the fruit of

   the Spirit of_____ to stop eating once I'm full.

   • If I want to vomit after meals I can remember the fruit of the Spirit

   of_____ not to vomit after meals.

   • If I want to starve myself I can remember the fruit of the Spirit of

   _____ to eat when I'm hungry and not let the food control me.

4. *"Therefore I say to you, do not worry about your life, what you will eat or what you will drink; nor about your body, what you will put on. Is not life more than food and the body more than clothing? Matthew 6:25*

5. Is life more than food?

Learning God's Truth

This week's memory verse:
🌸 *Stand fast therefore in the liberty by which Christ has ____ us free, and do not __ _____ again with a ___ of bondage. Galatians _:_*

6. Is it sinful to eat when you're hungry and your body needs fuel?

7. Food is my enemy because...

8. Food is my friend because...

9. Why do we need to eat?

10. A balanced perspective is to eat to fuel your body and to stay alive. Is this your perspective?

Learning God's Truth

This week's memory verse:

🌱 *Stand fast therefore in the liberty by which Christ has ____ us free, and do not ___ _____ again with a ___ of bondage. Galatians _:_*

11. Have you been blinded to a yoke of bondage in your life? Explain

Practical Steps to Flee the Bondage

Stand fast therefore in the liberty by which Christ has made us free, and do not be entangled again with a yoke of bondage. Galatians 5:1

A. Pray daily for the Holy Spirit to help you make the right choice concerning food.

B. Learn to listen to your body. When you're hungry eat until your full. Stop eating even if there is still food on your plate.

C. Tell one Christian person close to you, a husband, friend, or family member about the struggles you face with food. Make Jesus the focus of every conversation to break away from the bondage.

D. Place scripture in the bathroom, kitchen, and bedroom to strengthen you in your choices and decisions when you are weak.

Self-control Questions to Ask Yourself

- Why am I eating?

- Am I hungry?

- Am I Angry?

- Am I Frustrated?

- Am I nourishing my body?

- Am I eating just to fuel my body?

FROM THE WINDS AND RAIN OF ADVERSITY
COME ABUNDANT GROWTH AND A BEAUTIFUL LIFE.

- Am I still eating when my hunger is satisfied? Why?

- Am I going to stop eating when my hunger is satisfied? Why?

- Why do I need to eat each day to keep living?

- Food is not a companion and food is not an enemy. Self-control is a part of God's will for each of us. Are you going to follow your own desires or God's desires for you? Your will or God's will? Explain

_____

_____

_____

_____

_____

_____

_____

_____

_____

_____

_____

_____

_____

_____

_____

_____

_____

_____

_____

_____

Week 8 Day 3

Bow your heart before the Lord in prayer before completing today's Bible study. Ask Him to strengthen you to apply His word to your life.

Strive to Satisfy

Some people continually act on impulse, grabbing at whatever seems attractive at the time. If you strive to satisfy your impulses you will defeat yourself and the bondage will continue.

1. Write down this week's memory verse.

2. *"Therefore, whoever hears these sayings of Mine, and does them, I will liken him to a wise man who built his house on the rock: and the rain descended, the floods came, and the winds blew and beat on that house; and it did not fall, for it was founded on the rock."* Matthew 7:24-25

3. What does it mean to build your house on the rock?

4. What trial or struggles have flooded into your life?

5. Describe a time you made a choice by faith to apply God's Word to your difficult circumstance.

6. What was the outcome?

7. Do you sense that your outlook on eating has steadiness? Explain.

8. What is it about your eating that is up and down?

9. When you sense yourself becoming unstable, quickly reach out to a godly source to establish accountability. Name a godly person that fits this role _____. Decide on a Time and Place to have a special Meeting to share your struggle or stronghold and ask that person to be a safe guard when you are weak.

Learning God's Truth

This week's memory verse:
Stand fast therefore in the liberty by which Christ has ____ us free, and do not __ _____ again with a ___ of bondage. Galatians _:_

Learning from the mistakes of others.

Find someone who has shared these same struggles in their life and has gained wisdom from the past. Talk with them about their mistakes and the bad choices that led to a life of bondage. What wise choices did they eventually make and how did they apply their new choices in order to stop living in bondage?

When wisdom enters your heart, and knowledge is pleasant to your soul, discretion will preserve you; understanding will keep you, to deliver you from the way of evil,
Proverbs 2:10-12a

Write down the questions you would ask them.

_____

_____

_____

_____

_____

_____

_____

_____

_____

_____

_____

_____

_____

_____

_____

_____

_____

_____

_____

**For all the negative things we have to say to ourselves,
God has a positive answer for it.**

You say: It's impossible.
God says: All things are possible. (Luke 18:27)

You say: I'm too tired.
God says: I will give you rest. (Matthew 11:28-30)

You say: Nobody really loves me.
God says: I love you. (John 3:16 & John 13:34)

You say: I can't go on.
God says: My grace is sufficient. (II Corinthians 12:9& Psalm 91:15)

You say: I can't figure things out.
God says: I will direct your steps. (Proverbs 3:5-6)

You say: I can't do it.
God says: You can do all things. (Philippians 4:13)

You say: I'm not able.
God says: I am able. (II Corinthians 9:8)

You say: It's not worth it.
God says: It will be worth it. (Roman 8:28)

You say: I can't forgive myself.
God says: I FORGIVE YOU. (I John 1:9 & Romans 8:1)

You say: I can't manage.
God says: I will supply all your needs. (Philippians 4:19)

You say: I'm afraid.
God says: I have not given you a spirit of fear. (II Timothy1:7)

You say: I'm always worried and frustrated.
God says: Cast all your cares on ME. (I Peter 5:7)

You say: I don't have enough faith.
God says: I've given everyone a measure of faith. (Romans 12:3)

You say: I'm not smart enough.
God says: I give you wisdom. (I Corinthians 1:30)

'You say: I feel all alone.
God says: I will never leave you or forsake you. (Hebrews 13:5)

Week 8 Day 4

Bow your heart before the Lord in prayer before completing today's Bible study. Ask God to show you if there is a stronghold in your life.

Be Yourself

The world is always trying to press us into its mold. The world points its finger saying, "You have to be young, you have to be thin, you have to be rich, you have to be perfect to be worth anything." Remember God's love for you is absolutely steadfast, unlike human love. He does not give or take away His love based on appearance or performance. The Word, the Truth, says you don't have to be any of those things. Trust God and be yourself. God wants you to be yourself and to make yourself available to Him so He can work in and through you for your good and for His glory.

- **SEE** the stronghold as sin.

- **GIVE** the sin to God in confession.

- **FORGIVE** as Christ has forgiven me.

- **FORGET** the lies of Satan and the world telling you to overeat, starve, or vomit.

🌹 **BE SET FREE** by God's truth and His love for you, enabling you to be yourself.

We need to make a conscious decision in order to change. Our aim is to develop godly habits that will result in godly living.

Behold what manner of love the Father has bestowed on us, that we should be called children of God! Therefore the world does not know us, because it did not know Him. John 3:1

1. How can you apply your desire to be an obedient child in this area of eating habits?

Learning God's Truth

This week's memory verse:

🌹 _____ therefore __ the _____ by which _____ has made us___, and __ ___ be entangled_____ with a yoke of_____. *Galatians 5:1*

2. Which of the following influence or determine your choices and actions? Circle those that apply.

Fear	Insecurities	Pride	Negative thoughts
Anxiety	Hurt	Resentment	Doubt
Need to control	Guilt	Bitterness	Defensiveness

3. What happens when these thought influence your choices? What scriptures could you use to replace these thoughts?

Words to Remember

Fill in the blanks

But the fruit of the Spirit is _____, joy, peace, _____, kindness, goodness, _____, gentleness, self-control. Against such there is no _____. And those who are Christ's have crucified the flesh with its passions and desires. If we live in the Spirit let us also _____ in the Spirit. Let us not become conceited, provoking one another, _____ one another. Galatians 5:22-26

4. Does food control you or do you control your food?

5. Is overeating or starving yourself, or eating large quantities and vomiting it up, a part of God's plan for you in the area of self-control?

6. If you are ready to change, write out how you plan to apply self-control and change your eating patterns and habits in order to change your life.

Learning God's Truth

This week's memory verse:

🌸 _____ therefore __ the _____ by which _____ has made us____, and __ __ be entangled_____ with a yoke of_____. *Galatians 5:1*

7. What people or activities make you feel you need to consume large amounts of food or no food at all, in order to make you feel happy?

8. 1 Peter 4:2 tells us we "No longer should live the rest of our lives to the lust of men, but to the _____."

9. In the past I learned that I needed to be thin to be happy through the following people and things:

10. I have decided to make my happiness or acceptance from the truth of God's Word. I plan to do that in the following ways...

_____
_____
_____
_____
_____
_____
_____
_____
_____
_____
_____
_____
_____
_____
_____
_____

_____

_____

_____

_____

_____

_____

_____

_____

_____

_____

_____

_____

_____

_____

_____

_____

_____

_____

_____

_____

11. Strongholds are hard to break. It is sometimes a second-by-second choice. Is there one person in your life that you can talk to and work together with in order to break this stronghold? Name that person _____ Make plans to tell them this week.

Learning God's Truth

This week's memory verse:

_____ therefore in the liberty by _____ Christ has made __ free, and __ not be entangled again ____ a yoke of _____. Galatians 5:_

Happiness should not be based on the Opinions of Others

Some of the values you hold right now may be the same as those your culture holds. Be aware how much these cultural expectations may be influencing and defining your own expectations for personal happiness. Your personal happiness should not be based on outside judgments or the opinions of others. When your heart is surrendered to God, you will experience true joy.

I will praise You, for I am fearfully and wonderfully made; marvelous are Your works, and that my soul knows very well. Psalm 139:14

1. Take time this week to meditate on Psalm 139:14. Write this scripture down.

A sound heart is life to the body, but envy is rottenness to the bones. Proverbs 14:30

Let us not become conceited, provoking one another, envying one another. Galatians 5:26

2. Do you envy other women? Explain.

3. Summarize in one sentence why you have believed thin was more acceptable.

Learning God's Truth

This week's memory verse:

_____ therefore in the liberty by _____ Christ has made __ free, and __ not be entangled again ____ a yoke of _____. Galatians 5:_

What is True Beauty?

You can take an enormous leap forward in your spiritual life when you determine that being "useful" is more important that being "noticed". Physical appearance in terms of size or shape can tempt you to be living for the wrong reasons. You can't compare yourself to others. We are all uniquely made: some are naturally thin, some are born with a medium frame and some with a large frame, some are short while others are very tall. Your size does not determine your worth or your beauty.

When you allow a stronghold to keep you down, it also may keep you from reaching out. Let every part of your life be in Christ; your eating habits, your mind, your dress, your speech, your joys and your heartbreaks. Anchor yourself to the great "I AM" and you will be free to become who God intended you to be, a Christian who is whole, true, and at peace.

And the people said to Joshua, "The LORD our God we will serve, and His voice we will obey!" Joshua 24:24

Therefore we do not lose heart. Even though our outward man is perishing, yet the inward man is being renewed day by day. For our light affliction, which is but for a moment is working for us a far more exceeding and eternal weight of glory, while we do not look at the things which are seen, but at the things which are not seen. For the things which are seen are temporary, but the things, which are not seen, are eternal. 2 Corinthians 4:16-18

1. Can you accept that the body is perishing? Write down the evidence of how you see this happening.

2. In what way is your spirit being renewed day by day? Write down the evidence of how you see this happening.

3. What is more important to you the outward or the inward? Explain your answer.

4. What if your present moment is one of disappointment or heartache? Where will you choose to turn?

5. Will you choose the things, which are seen, or the things, which are not seen? Temporary or Eternal? Flesh or Spirit? God's will or your will. The choice is yours. What will you choose?

6. Memorize scripture that brings comfort to your heart when you feel out of control with over eating or out of control with starving yourself. Write out that scripture and hide it in your heart or place it in an area of your home as tools for strength.

Words to Remember

Fill in the blanks.

But the fruit of the Spirit is love, joy, peace, _____, kindness, _____, faithfulness, gentleness, self-control. Against _____ there is no law. And those who are Christ's have_____ the flesh with its _____ and desires. If we live in the Spirit, let us also walk in the Spirit. Let us not become conceited, provoking one another, _____ one another. Galatians 5:22-26

SEE, GIVE, FORGIVE, FORGET, BE SET FREE

Learning God's Truth

This week's memory verse:

_____ therefore in the liberty by _____ Christ has made __ free, and __ not be entangled again ____ a yoke of _____. Galatians 5:_

Week 8 Day 5

> *Bow your heart before the Lord in prayer before completing today's Bible study.*
> *Ask Him to shine His light on the darkness so you can*
> **SEE, GIVE, FORGIVE, FORGET, AND BE SET FREE.**

Caught up in God's Love

We are Christians, caught up in the love of God that surrounds us everyday. As we serve Him in the area of our calling and enjoy all the gifts of life, there is neither room nor time for living with destructive strongholds. Every part of your life, your person, your style, your direction, your eating, your thinking, let it all be in Christ.

He has shown you, O man, what is good; and what does the LORD require of you but to do justly, to love mercy, and to walk humbly with your God? Micah 6:8

1. Write three things you struggle with concerning your eating habits.

   1

   2.

   3.

Therefore, humble yourselves under the mighty hand of God, that He may exalt you in due time, casting all your care upon Him, for He cares for you. 1 Peter 5:6-7

2. Have you cast the cares of your heart upon God?

3. Name what you want to change about your eating habits. Ask God to help you each day to break any strongholds in your life.

Words to Remember

Fill in the blanks

Therefore strengthen the _____ which hang down, and the feeble _____, and _____ straight paths for your _____, so that what is lame _____ not _ dislocated, _____ rather _____ healed. Hebrews 12:12-13

4. Do you think it is God's business how you eat? Explain

For he who lacks these things is shortsighted, even to blindness, and has forgotten that he was cleansed from his old sins. 2 Peter 1:9

5. What have you been cleansed from? What is the old life style from past eating disorders?

"Now no chastening seems to be joyful for the present, but painful; nevertheless, afterward it yields the peaceable fruit of righteousness to those who have been trained by it. Therefore strengthen the hands which hang down, and the feeble knees. Hebrews 12:11-12

Desiring to Move from Bondage to Freedom?

Bring your life under the submission of Christ. Ask God to show you any lies about yourself that you have programmed in over the years, and upon which you are basing your identity. Choose to give these over to God and replace them with His truth. God does answer prayers, not always in the way we envision the answer, but according to His will. Say the following prayer out loud, sending your petition to Him.

Dear God,

Thank you for loving me unconditionally. Thank you for being intimately involved with every aspect of my life. Thank you for wanting to heal me. As I continue this journey of self-control, please give me insight and understanding concerning my eating disorder. Bring to my mind your word to give me the strength and courage and power to change. Be with me in a special way, as I desire to be healed and set free of this idol in my life.

Signed_____

Date _____

SET FREE BY THE TRUTH

> *You may need to reread this chapter, meditating again on the truth of God's word to free you from the stronghold of your eating habits.*

- **SEE** the stronghold as sin.

- **GIVE** the sin to God in confession.

- **FORGIVE** as Christ has forgiven you.

- **FORGET** the lies of Satan and the world telling you to overeat, starve, or vomit.

BE SET FREE by God's truth and His love for you, enabling you to be yourself.

> *We need to make a conscious decision in order to change. Our aim is to develop godly habits that will result in godly living.*

Behold what manner of love the Father has bestowed on us, that we should be called children of God! Therefore the world does not know us, because it did not know Him. 1 John 3:1

Review

This weeks memory verse:

- _____ *therefore in the liberty by _____ _____ has made us free, and* *do not be_____ again with a yoke of bondage.* _____ 5:_

- What have you learned about self-control?

- What have you learned about your strongholds pertaining to bulimia, anorexia, or over compulsive eating?

- What encouraged you about God's plans for eating to live and not living to eat?

• What do you need to do with your thoughts in order to be obedient to Christ in your personal situation with your eating habits?

• Does God look at the outward appearance or the inward heart?

• What challenged you about this chapter?

• In what specific way will you open your heart to let the healer set you free from any bondage your life?

C. Ignorant disobedience: you do not know what you are doing is sinful.

D. Willful disobedience: you know what you are doing is sinful and you continue to sin.

In the next chapter we will be taking a closer look at "Remembering to Forget" what is behind and look toward the higher calling in Christ Jesus.

SEE, GIVE, FORGIVE, FORGET, BE SET FREE

Love

*I*f I can speak eloquently and sing like an Angel, but don't love others, I sound like a sounding brass or prolonged clanging noise. If I'm very bright and considered brilliant, and can answer all the hardest Bible questions or understand cutting edge computer system's but don't love others, I am nothing.

love will stand in line and wait it's turn.

love is friendly and looks for the good in others.

love doesn't always demand their own way.

love doesn't envy another's better fortune.

love is polite, even when the other person is rude.

love doesn't get angry over the small things.

love doesn't remember reasons to keep a wrong to be hurt.

love doesn't delight when someone else fails, but delights in the truth.

love will always protect others, especially those who are made fun of or teased.

love always believes the best about others.

love hopes all things, endures all things.

ONLY THREE THINGS REALLY MATTER IN LIFE,
FAITH, HOPE, AND LOVE

BUT THE GREATEST OF THESE IS LOVE.

Chapter 7

Remembering to Forget

Forgetting those things which are behind and reaching forward to those things which are ahead.

Philippians 3:13

There are four main tools we will weave into the very fiber of our hearts day by day: **SEE, GIVE, FORGIVE, FORGET,** and **BE SET FREE**. Thinking about the past will never change the past. But you can change your future and Be Set FREE from your past. As you deal with your past and present hurts, you can either embrace the truth and let go of the burdens you carry, or carry your burdens and reject the truth and the freedom it brings. The choice is yours. Getting real with God is the first step you need to always take as you face deep, dark hurts that have chipped away at your peace for 1 year, 10 years, 20 years, and some 50 years. God's love is bigger then all of our hurts and fears. You will have many blessings in front of you as God's truth unfolds in your heart and Sets you Free.

Let's Day By Day Go over the Four Steps to Keep Our Hearts Clean

🌿 Tools To Become Set Free

* **Tool #1 "SEE ":** I must **SEE** the truth about what is in my heart, so I'm not defiled.

> *Looking carefully lest anyone fall short of the grace of God; lest any root of bitterness springing up cause trouble, and by this many become defiled. Hebrew 12:15.*

* **Tool #2 "GIVE":** I must **GIVE** the sin in repentance, knowing Christ is waiting to take it. (I must be sorry enough to change and choose to go God's way over my own way.)

> *For godly sorrow produces repentance leading to salvation, not to be regretted; but the sorrow of the world produces death. 2 Corinthians 7:10*

* **Tool #3 "FORGIVE":** I must **FORGIVE**, as I am forgiven by Christ. (Forgiving those that hurt, bruised, wronged, hurt, rejected, betrayed or harmed me whether unintentionally or deliberately.) Ask God to Forgive you for holding unforgiveness and know that He will.

> *Bearing with one another, and forgiving one another, if anyone has a complaint against another; even as Christ forgave you, so you also must do. Colossians 3:13*

* **Tool #4 "FORGET":** I must **FORGET** by remembering to no longer dwell on the hurt.

> *Brethren, I do not count myself to have apprehended; but one thing I do, forgetting those things which are behind and reaching forward to those things which are ahead. Philippians 3:13.*

🌿 **BECOME SET FREE:** Christ will open the shackles from my past hurts showing me the truth so I can become a cleansed vessel that is Healed and Set Free.

> *You shall know the truth, and the truth shall make you free. Therefore, if the Son makes you free, you shall be free indeed. John 8:32-36.*

SATAN IS DEFEATED AND THE SHACKLES ARE GONE AND YOU ARE FREE!

Week 9 Day 1

Bow your heart before the Lord in prayer before completing today's Bible study. Ask God to show you the lessons of " Remembering to Forget" the suffering and trials of the past

The Past is No Longer Reality

If God lives in our heart, why doesn't our life reflect that? Sometimes it's because the past can have quite a hold on our minds. When we dwell on past insults we become tired, depressed and bitter. The past teaches us about God, life and ourselves. We are to learn from what lies behind, but then we are to take those lessons and move ahead. We have to remember to forget.

After giving my sin of selfishness, pride, and unforgiveness to Christ, I began moving ahead to put my focus on Christ Jesus, not on my past. God led me to Philippians 3:13: Brethren, I do not count myself to have apprehended; but one thing I do, forgetting those things which are behind and reaching forward to those things which are ahead.

This is a big part of being Set Free - you must **SEE**- you must **GIVE**- you must **FORGIVE** - you must take the next step to **FORGET**! STOP mulling it over in your mind.

Learn to Forget. Do not dwell on past sin. There may be things in your past of which you are ashamed, which might haunt you, and which might cut the sinews of your strength. Remember, if you have handed them over to God in confession and faith, He has put them away and forgotten them. Reach forward to realize the beauty of Jesus in your life.

Forgetting is in the Present Tense

Forgetting relates to events that happened in the past. Note that the word forgetting is in the present tense. Forgetting is not an act done once and for all.

Like Paul, we must keep on forgetting those things that have hurt us or hold us back. Paul doesn't want to rest on his past accomplishments and neither should we. Paul doesn't want his past mistakes nor past hurts to keep him from moving on and neither should we. Don't let the past hold you back.

Again and again, I have told myself, "No, Tam, that is past. That is over. - That is no longer real. Don't dwell on it. Don't let it hold you back. - Forget that which would keep you from moving forward in faith and in your spiritual growth." I look to the past only to remember God's role in solving the problems and pains of yesterday. I remember His gracious provision for His presence, His faithfulness, His compassion, and His healing for me.

Looking to the past for lessons God has taught us will help us to remember the importance of getting real with God. We must **SEE, GIVE, FORGIVE,** and **FORGET** the pain and resentment, then be set free. What does the apostle Paul teach us about forgetting those elements of the past that would block our Christian growth and our progress toward Christ likeness?

God wants you and me to move on from the suffering of the past. He doesn't want the circumstances and situations of life to weigh us down. This results in bitterness and causes us to question Him and His goodness. With any suffering you've experienced in the past, either two minutes or twenty years ago, whether it resulted from someone's thoughtless comment, or unexplainable sinful acts against you, move on, and be **SET FREE**.

God's Remedy is the Same

We live in a fallen world and the innocent suffer when people sin. In other words, "Remember to Forget". The sin that was committed against you is no different or greater then the sin that's hidden in your heart towards those that hurt you.

Words to Remember

Fill in the blanks

Brethren, I do not _____ myself to have apprehended; but one_____ I do, forgetting those things which ___ behind and _____ forward to those things which ____ ahead, I press toward the goal for the _____ of the upward call of God in Christ Jesus. Philippians 3:13-14

1. Do you want to move from the past hurts?

2. According to Philippians 3:13-14 what are we to press toward?

For we ourselves were also once foolish, disobedient, deceived, serving various lusts and pleasures, living in malice and envy, hateful and hating one another. Titus 3:3

3. If hate and envy consume a life, what is happening to that life according to Titus 3:3?

Finally, brethren, whatever things are true, whatever things are noble, whatever things are just, whatever things are pure, whatever things are lovely, whatever things are of good report, if there is any virtue and if there is anything praiseworthy; meditate on these things. Philippians 4:8

4. What are we to meditate on as we look toward Christ?

For God has not given us a spirit of fear, but of power and of love and of a sound mind. 2 Timothy 1:7

5. What has God not given us?

Learning God's Truth

This week's tool and memory verse:

🌹 **FORGET:** I must _____ those things, which are _____. (Not dwelling on painful reminders, such as phrases, smell, places, songs, and comments, but putting my mind on the higher calling Christ Jesus has for me.)

Forgetting those things, which are behind, and reaching forward to those things, which are ahead, I press toward the goal for the prize of the upward call of God in Christ Jesus. Philippians 3:13-14

The Past Smell That Triggered Feelings of Terror and Distress

For the first ten years of my marriage I had changed the sheets on our bed almost daily. The smell of even slightly dirty sheets made me irritable and upset. I could not go to bed unless there were fresh clean sheets on it. I carried this behavior into the rest of my house as well. My husband felt I was a little compulsive about clean sheets, and I too knew this wasn't really right, but I did not understand fully why I was so compulsive about clean smelling sheets. I certainly didn't know how to change my compulsive behavior. As a child I could not walk past my abusive father's bedroom without the horrible smell of body odor. My father rarely bathed, and his bed sheets were a smelly reflection of his personal behaviors. Sometimes the smell would envelop the entire house. There were times that I just couldn't breathe; I was surrounded by violence, and the smells of violence. During the course of my Healed and Set Free Bible study I learned that the slightest smell of uncleanness reminded me of my abusive father, and this was robbing me of my peace. If my home was not clean (including the smell), then I felt unsafe, insecure. The smell triggered the feelings of terror and distress I felt while living with my father. I would clean my house with strong cleaners and burn candles just to keep those feelings of terror at bay. I learned this was Satan's way of keeping me in the shackles of fear!

I prayed a great deal asking Jesus if he would help me let go of my feelings associated with smells. I asked Jesus to help me see that I did not have to fear my father any longer, my home was not his home, and he was no longer there. I had to truly understand for the first time in my life that my abusive dad was my dad but that God is the Father in my home, and I did not have to fear Him. Praying and asking Jesus to heal me really helped me to get past the idea that everything had to come up smelling like roses in my home. I needed to put into practice a new way of behaving. I had to stop washing sheets and give myself a time to do them every week, not every day. It was hard at first because I would crawl into bed with my husband and imagine the smell was there just because I knew the sheets weren't fresh. Sometimes I concentrated on my husband's yummy smelling cologne to distract me, and sometimes I would just lay there praying for Jesus to calm my imagination and help me go to sleep without fear. After a while, I could crawl into bed and not even think about the sheets! I still love to burn candles and have a clean home, but its not because I'm wrapped up in the fear of that smell, but because I love to burn candles and have a clean home. Simple as that. I learned that Jesus, my healer, wanted to release those shackles for me and He did! Thank you, Jesus, for giving me freedom from the oppressiveness of smells that would have set me back without your healing powers!

Freed from shackles ~ Cheryl

SEE, GIVE, FORGIVE, FORGET, BE SET FREE

The Marriage Bed is Honorable Between a Husband and Wife

The memories from a hurtful past of sexual abuse, rape or sexual relationships outside of marriage can bring difficulty with sexual intimacy in a marriage thus damaging the married couples relationship. Satan has corrupted sex in the media on TV, movies, and magazines and has harmed children's lives through sexual abuse. We need to transform our minds from the defiled past where sex may be a painful subject. Instead we need to see the truth of God's pure undefiled design for sex in the marriage bed where married couples enjoy sexual fulfillment as God designed it to be—Holy and pure.

Marriage is honorable among all, and the bed undefiled; but fornicators and adulterers God will judge. Hebrews 13:4.

Honorable in the Greek is *timios*, which means valuable, of high costly price, most precious, dear, desirable, honored, esteemed, beloved.

Bed Undefiled in the Greek is *amiantos*, which means unsoiled, pure, unpolluted, unstained, undefiled by sin. Amiantos is only used 4 times in the New Testament. (Notice the holy beauty of its uses in these verses.)

1. Used of Jesus: For such a High Priest was fitting for us, who is holy, harmless, undefiled, separate from sinners, and has become higher that the heavens. Hebrews 7:26

2. Used of True Religion: Pure and undefiled religion before God and the Father is this: to visit orphans and widows in their trouble, and to keep oneself unspotted from the world. James 1:27

3. Used of our Heavenly Inheritance: To an inheritance incorruptible and undefiled and that does not fade away, reserved in heaven for you. 1 Peter 1:4

4. And last but not least it is used of the Holy and Beautiful Bed where Married couples enjoy sexual fulfillment as God designed it to be. Hebrews13:4

Let us search out and examine our ways, and turn back to the Lord; let us lift our hearts and hands to God in heaven. Lamentations 3:40-41

1. Is sexual intimacy in your marriage fulfilling for both of you?

2. How are you to look at your marriage bed?

3. Is your mind defiled or undefiled concerning sex in a marriage?

4. In your marriage is sexual intimacy in your mind pure or dirty?

Let us search out and examine our ways, and turn back to the Lord; let us lift our hearts and hands to God in heaven. Lamentations 3:40-41

5. When we realize that we have held on to negative thoughts and emotions rather than release them to God, what are we to do? What is our responsibility?

6. Do you want to forget about the past corruption of sex? Confess them before Christ and move forward.

7. What will you do when the sinful things of your past come to mind?

The Marriage Bed is Honorable/ Physically love him

Read 1 Corinthians 7:3-5. A fundamental principle for marriage is "rendering affection" to one's mate. The Song of Solomon details physical love in marriage, and Proverbs 5:19 says our husband is to be drunk with our sexual love.

Author Elizabeth George said, " I remember hearing God's view of physical love taught at a seminar I attended when I was a new Christian. I was so impressed (and convicted) I went straight home and announced to my husband that I was available to him physically at any and all times for the rest of our life together! That may have been a slight over-reaction, but I wanted to act on God's Word and my husband got the message."

What's Your Focus?

Let the only measure of your expectations for yourself be the resurrection power of Jesus Christ. You can then live a truly powerful life. Not because you are no longer weak, but because being weak, you count on His power to work in you. We can be Healed and Set Free to be the people God made us to be. Satan wants us to take our eyes off the blessing's God showers on us and put our focus on all the negative. That snake wants to rob you of your blessings.

When you are faced with past reminders of hurts such as a smell, a phrase, a place, or a song recognize that it's coming from the snake planning his angle to try to get you back in those shackles.

8. When you start thinking about sex as dirty within your marriage bed, what scripture can you memorize to keep you from believing this lie? Quickly go to prayer. Hold on to God's grace and remember. Philippians 3:13.

Drink water from your own cistern, and running water from your own well. Should your fountains be dispersed abroad, Streams of water in the streets? Let them be only your own, and not for strangers with you. Let your fountain be blessed, and rejoice with the wife of your youth. As a loving deer and a graceful doe, Let her breasts satisfy you at all times; and always be enraptured with her love. For why should you, my son, be enraptured by an immoral woman, and be embraced in the arms of a seductress? For the ways of man are before the eyes of the LORD, and He ponders all his paths.   Proverbs 5:15-18

9. How can your fountain or relationship be blessed?

10. Write down 4 things that make you rejoice over your spouse?

   1.

   2.

   3.

   4.

11. Have you decided to make your relationship with your husband your number one human relationship? If so, what actions show that you are choosing him over all others? If not, why are you hesitating? Take your hesitation to the Lord in prayer.

What can you and I do to show our husband's affectionate, indulgent friendship-love? Whisper a prayer for your husband as you consider these ways to show him you care!

Prepare for him daily

Preparing for your husband's homecoming each day, show him that he's a priority and communicate your heart of love to him.

Prepare the house - Take a few minutes before your husband is due home to quickly pick up. Have the children help by putting away their toys. The goal is not perfection, but instead an impression of order and neatness. I enjoy lighting scented candles, turning on relaxing Christian music and even having dinner on the stove so the man of the house arrives home to a peaceful refuge-which together communicates " we're glad you're home".

Prepare your greeting - You probably know approximately when your husband will get home from work each day. So warm his welcome as you wait and watch for him. Greet him with a hug and a kiss each day when he comes home. Also be sure to plan your words of greeting. Your greeting will be more fruitful if you do. "A good man ponders what to say"(Proverbs 15:28). The moment of your husband's homecoming is not the time to ask. "Where have your been?" " Why are you so late?" "Why didn't you call?" It's also not the time to start listing the trials of your day. So ask God to give you just the right words. Words that are positive and welcoming, words that focus on your husband and his frame of mind, rather than yours!

Prepare the children to greet their father too. Be sure the TV is off. Give younger children a snack if it helps eliminate whining and grumping while they wait for Daddy.

As women with a heart full of love for God and for the special husband He has given each of us, you and I are privileged to be able to prepare for our husbands arrival and to lavish our love on them. Do pour out God's love, which is poured out in your heart (Romans 5:5), when your husband walks through the door of his home! As Martin Luther said, " Let the wife make her husband glad to come home." Be sure he's not treated and greeted as the man who wrote the following words was!

THE HOMECOMING

You know, when I get home after work, the only one who acts as if she cares at all is my little dog. She really is glad to see me and lets me know it.... I always come in the back door because Doris is in the kitchen about then.... But she always looks up from whatever she is doing with the most startled look and say, " Oh, are you home already?"....

Somehow she makes me feel like "I've done the wrong thing, just by getting home. I used to try and say hello to the kids, but I don't do that anymore. Seems I would get in between them and the TV set at just the wrong minute.... So now, I just pick up little Suzy, my dog, stick her under my arm and go out in the yard. I act like I don't care. And maybe I shouldn't really-but I do. It gives me the feeling that all I am hanging around there for is just to pay the bills and keep the place up. You know, I believe that if the bills are taken care of and nothing broke, I bet I could be gone a whole week and nobody would even notice it.

I know that in some marriages the wife arrives home after her husband, and maybe that's true for you. If so, what can you do to prepare for your husbands?

Positively respond to him -- We've discussed picking a positive word of response-a word or phrase like "Sure!" " No problem!" "All right!" "Okay!"

Let me tell you about a true story I read, from a wife that gave a positive response.- Early one morning while she was drying her hair with a blower, Her husband asked if she could help him find something. Her first (and fleshly) thought was " Can't you hear I'm drying my hair?" A less selfish option -- and a better one- was to yell above the noise of the blower, " Sure! I'll be right there as soon as I finish drying my hair. "But God gave her the wisdom to do the least selfish-and best-thing: " Sure!" She said turning off the blower. Then she asked her husband, "Do you need me to do that right now, or is there time to finish drying my hair?" Even though she asked the question, she was ready to do whatever her husband said. She stopped to communicate with her husband, indicating her willingness to serve. Of course her husband let her finish her hair, but the point was she really desired to respond to him. Her simple but positive response meant no power struggle, no hurt feelings, no bitter words, no raised voices, and a much better start to her day and his.

Praise Him - Ladies, never pass up an opportunity to bless your husband in public. (And bless him to his face.) If you catch yourself speaking critically about your husband, quickly shut your mouth and do these two things:

- Search your heart. "Hatred stirs up strife, but love covers all sins"(Proverbs 10:12)... Love does not gossip.

- Seek a solution. If some serous area in your husband's life needs attention, follow a better path than putting him down. Instead devote yourself to prayer and if you need to speak up, do so after much preparation and with gracious, edifying, sweet speech (Ephesians 4:29). You may also need to speak to your Pastor but remember that your time with the Pastor is not for venting about your husband, but getting help for yourself so you can properly deal with the problem.

Blessing your husband in public --- and in private --- is one way to sow seeds of love for him in your heart.

Week 9 Day 2

Bow your heart before the Lord in prayer before completing today's Bible study. Ask Him to show you your outlook on what you SEE.

Changing your Outlook

The perspective is all about how we choose to SEE things. We look as much with our mind as with our eyes. We tend to see what we expect to see or want to see. Changing our perspective calls for a willingness to see things differently.

As one Christian woman says, " As I prayerfully prioritize the activities of my day, God grants me a vision of His will for all the days of my life and that day in particular. This prioritizing also gives me a passion for what I am trying to achieve with my life efforts. That passion has also been fueled by the following comments I first heard at one of our women's retreats 15 years ago (or longer). Since the day I first heard these statements, they have motivated me to follow after God's plan for my life with all my heart, soul, mind, and strength! I want to pass these women's statements on to you in hopes that they will help fuel your passion and vision for God and His calling to you. But first let me set the stage. A reporter interviewed four women and asked each of them what she thought about "the golden years," that period in life after middle age traditionally characterized by wisdom, contentment, and useful leisure. Hears their thoughts and fears:

Age 31: "Golden years? I have so much to do before then that I doubt I'll ever have them. I have to help my husband succeed. I want to raise our children decently to get them ready for a very tough world. And, of course, I want time for me, to find myself, to be my own person."

Age 44: "Only 20 years to go! I just hope we make it. If we can just get the kids through college and on their own, if we can just keep my husband's blood pressure under control and see me sanely through menopause...I'm just hoping we get there."

Age 55: "Doubtful. Sometimes I think our golden years will never come. My parents are still alive and need constant attention. Our daughter was divorced last year and lives with us again. Of course, she had a baby. And of course my husband and I feel responsible for both her and our grandson."

Age 63: "We're supposed to be on the brink, aren't we? Well, we're not. I'll be frank. We thought we were saving enough to live comfortably ever after, but we haven't. Inflation has eaten it up. Now my husband talks about deferring his retirement. If he does, so will I. Keeping a house much to big for us. We're both unhappy about the way things have turned out."

Sobering comments, aren't they? As you and I stand looking down the corridor of time, life can appear so hopeless, so pointless, and so futile! But what does God think? Let's look at a godly perspective from a woman to whom I sent a copy of what you've just read. Here's her inspiring response: " To treat each day as if it and it alone was our "golden day"- then what a beautiful string of golden days becoming golden years we would have to give back again to our Lord!"

Imagine being a woman who treats each day as if it and it alone were her golden day! When I thought about this, I said, " That's it!" Treating each day as if it and it alone were our golden day is the how of practicing priorities and it's also the why—the motivation and the perspective we need—for practicing them!

If you desire a good life, focus on having one good day, one quality day-today! After all, as someone has observed, "every day is a little life, and our whole life is but a single day repeated."

But what if yours was a way of failures? A day of merely trying to survive? A day of taking shortcuts? A day of neglecting things you wanted to focus on. We all have those days. Thanks be to God who enables us to forget the day that is done, to reach forward to the next morning, and to press on toward the goal again and again and again. (Philippians 3:13-14) In His power and by His grace, we keep following after God's heart - no matter what!

After all, every morning He gives you a fresh new day, His gift of fresh, unspoiled opportunity to live according to His priorities. Furthermore, by exercising the privilege of confession and because of Jesus' forgiveness, you have a clean start with the dawn. God's mercies are new every morning and His faithfulness is great (Lamentations 3:22-23). So every morning remember that your goal is simple: you want to have just one good day of living your priorities. Then keep focused on following God's plan for your life for just this one day.

When such a focused day is done, you'll probably be tired as you drop into bed. I know I am! But you'll also know an unmatchable peace in your heart. A peace that comes from resting in the Lord and doing things His way. A peace that comes from knowing that, because you lived out God's priorities for you, all is well under your roof. God's beauty and order reign there in the refuge you've created.

"For the Lord God is a sun and shield; the Lord will give grace and glory; no good thing will He withhold from those who walk uprightly. Psalm 84:11

1. Write four blessings you **SEE** from your time of healing.

    1.

    2.

    3.

    4.

Learning God's Word

This week's memory verse:
ℒ *Forgetting _____ things which ___ behind and reaching _____ to those things which are ahead, I press _____ the goal for the prize of the upward call of God in _____ Jesus. Philippians 3:13-14*

According to 2 Corinthians 2:5-8 *But if anyone has caused grief, he has not grieved me, but all of you to some extent; not to be too severe. This punishment which was inflicted by the majority is sufficient for such a man, so that, on the contrary, you ought rather to forgive and comfort him, lest perhaps such a one be swallowed up with too much sorrow. Therefore I urge you to reaffirm your love to him.*

2. When we remember all the hurt, what are we swallowed up with?

Forgiveness in Action

Bow your heart before the Lord in prayer. Ask Him to fill you with His peace and teach you to " Remember to Forget".

3. Spend some time in prayer. Ask God to help you begin to forget. If you say you have forgiven those who have hurt you, you are to put this forgiveness into action. Write on a sheet of paper the reasons why you have chosen to forgive those that hurt you.

_____

_____

_____

_____

_____

_____

_____

_____

_____

_____

_____

_____

_____

_____

_____

_____

_____

_____

_____

AUTHOR'S REFLECTION
He Stood There
Glaring

A few years ago we took a trip to our hometown and met up with the rest of the family at the fair. We just wanted to hang out, go on rides, eat fair food and enjoy the family. Then out of the blue I saw him. It was the brother of the guy that raped me. My heart started pounding. He walked a little closer, and I tried to keep my focus on the smile of my little girl who was excited about something. When I looked up there he was standing right next to my mom glaring at me! His wife had my mom's attention and their friendly conversation went on.

I was looking for a way to be as far from this guy as possible. I could tell by the look on his face, that he had already come to his own conclusions about me. I thought to myself, "If you only knew the true story, you wouldn't have that glare on your face." I couldn't believe it! I was in the process of completing the writing of *Healed and Set Free* and leading two separate classes through the study. BAM! An attack from the enemy. He was trying to drag me back into the past hurts from a different angle.

Flash Backs

I had given everything to God and had forgiven the guy who raped me; I started to hold a grudge against his brother whom I had not seen in seven years. As I looked at this guy glaring at me, hurtful emotions welled up within me. Flashbacks of that year of terror came flooding in. My heart started pounding and I became very withdrawn for about ten minutes. I needed to deal with my bad feelings toward this brother.

By faith, I chose to **GIVE** those feelings to God. For a moment I started to rehash the memories, but I stopped. I didn't let the enemy get a handle. Nor did I let him program those hurts down in me again. I wasn't going to allow the past to wreck my day. I had to get real with God right there at the State Fair. I used the four step principle of SEE, GIVE, FORGIVE, FORGET, AND BE SET FREE:

Healed and Set Free

I had to **SEE my own sin of "resentment"** toward this man that was judging me. I had to **GIVE** it over in the silence of my mind in repentance to Christ. I had to **FORGIVE** him for his judgmental attitude as Christ had forgiven me. I had to **FORGET** about the hurtful glare and look ahead towards Christ. **CHRIST SET ME FREE** and I enjoyed my day with a peaceful mind. We simply have to be willing to make the choice to set self aside and do what God desires in our lives.

Freedom to let go and let God

SEE, GIVE, FORGIVE, FORGET, BE SET FREE

4. What are we enabling Satan to do when we choose not to apply forgetting those things that are behind?

- *For the ways of man are before the eyes of the Lord, and He ponders all his paths. His own iniquities entrap the wicked man, and he is caught in the cords of his sin. Proverbs 5:21-22.*

- *Jesus answered them, "Most assuredly, I say to you, whoever commits sin is a slave of sin." John 8:34*

Let no corrupt word proceed out of your mouth, but what is good for necessary edification, that it may impart grace to the hearers. and do not grieve the Holy Spirit of God, by whom you were sealed for the day of redemption. Ephesians 4:29-30

5. What happens when we "rehash" negative thoughts about the past hurts?

6. Does it help us forget when we dwell on our past?

And those who are Christ's have crucified the flesh with its passions and desires. Galatians 5:24

7. What do we need to do daily with our sinful flesh?

8. What scriptures could you memorize to help you "REMEMBER to FORGET" if bad thoughts or emotions come in?

Now hope does not disappoint, because the love of God has been poured out in our hearts by the Holy Spirit who was given to us. Romans 5:5

9. Who gives you the love that you need to have toward others?

Learning God's Word

This week's memory tool and verse:

FORGET: ___ must _____ those things, which are behind. (Not _____ on painful reminder. Such as phrases, smell, places, songs, and comments, but putting my mind on the higher calling Christ Jesus has for me.

_____ those things, _____ are behind, and reaching forward to those things, which are _____, I press toward the goal for the prize of the upward call of God in Christ Jesus. Philippians 3:13-14

Let Go, Let God

As children bring their broken toys, with tears for us to mend,
I brought my broken dreams to God, because he was my friend.

But then instead of leaving Him in peace to work alone,
I hung around and tried to help with ways that were my own.

At last I snatched them back and cried, "How can you be so slow?"

"My child," He said, "**What could I do? You never did let go!**"

- Author unknown

Learning God's Word

This week's memory tool and verse:

FORGET: ___ must _____ those things, which are behind. (Not _____ on painful reminder. Such as phrases, smell, places, songs, and comments, but putting my mind on the higher calling Christ Jesus has for me.

_____ those things, _____ are behind, and reaching forward to those things, which are _____, I press toward the goal for the prize of the upward call of God in Christ Jesus. Philippians 3:13-14

Week 9 Day 3

> *Bow your heart before the Lord in prayer before completing today's Bible study. Ask Christ to show you what you have been SET FREE from.*

It's Time to Forget

Once you get real with God and let him bring peace to the heart that once had a war raging in it from all the hurts of the past, the emotions connected to that pain is no longer bitterness but forgiveness and compassion. Taking on the heart and attitude of our Lord and Savior Jesus Christ by forgiving allows us to fall back into His strong arms of grace and **FORGET**. We can move from the past and enjoy the abundant life God intended His Children to live.

The memories will never go away but the painful emotions do go away. When you embrace the truth and open up your heart and let the Healer Set you Free, your mind is transformed to BE SET FREE from the past hurts.

For I have satiated the weary soul and I have replenished every sorrowful soul.
Jeremiah 31:25

He heals the brokenhearted and binds up their wounds. Psalms 147:3

Making Christ Lord

Before you accepted Christ, you were a slave to sin. When you began to follow Christ, stepping out in faith and making Jesus Lord of your life, you became a slave to God. It sure is easy for priorities to get "out of whack," as one woman said! And making the choices to get back on track can sure be tough! But you and I must want to do God's will and therefore make the right choice even though they're hard choices! Is God speaking to you right now about how you are living your life? Is time with Him the first thing, you seek each new day? David cried out to God in the wilderness:

> *O God, You are my God;*
> *Early will I seek You;*
> *My soul thirsts for You;*
> *My flesh longs for You*
> *In a dry and thirsty land*
> *Where there is no water.*
> *(Psalm 63:1)*

1. Are you using the first fruits of your free time to be filled spiritually so that you can serve God and His people? And, finally, when you are with other people, are they refreshed by you, receiving out of the overflowing refreshment you find in the Lord?

And having been set free from sin, you became slaves of righteousness. But now having been set free from sin, and having become slaves of God, you have your fruit to holiness, and the end, everlasting life. I speak in human terms because of the weakness of your flesh. For just as you presented your members as slaves of uncleanness, and of lawlessness leading to more lawlessness, so now present your members as slaves of righteousness for holiness. For when you were slaves of sin, you were free in regard to righteousness. What fruit did you have then in the things of which you are now ashamed? For the end of those things is death. For the wages of sin is death, but the gift of God is eternal life in Christ Jesus our Lord. Romans 6:18-23

2. Read Romans 6:18-23. What do you gain from being slaves to God?

3. What effect did being a slave to sin have on your life, as shown in the following verses?

Jesus Christ, the faithful witness, the firstborn from the dead, and the ruler over the kings of the earth. To Him who loved us and washed us from our sins in His own blood, Revelation 1:5

4. From what have you been set free?

Then Jesus said to those Jews who believed Him, "If you abide in My word, you are My disciples indeed. And you shall know the truth, and the truth shall make you free." They answered Him, "We are Abraham's descendants, and have never been in bondage to anyone. How can you say, 'You will be made free'?" Jesus answered them, "Most assuredly, I say to you, whoever commits sin is a slave of sin. And a slave does not abide in the house forever, but a son abides forever. Therefore if the Son makes you free, you shall be free indeed." John 8:31-36

5. Who sets you free and how do you keep your freedom? Explain

6. Are there any areas in your life right now where you have been trying to improve yourself rather than simply laying down your will and your emotions in order to be His instrument in this world? Pray and ask Him to show you which areas need to be laid down according to His will in your life, (day by day and choice by choice).

Words to Remember

Fill in the blanks:

🌿 *Brethren, I do not count myself_____ have apprehended; but one _____ I do, forgetting _____ things which are behind and reaching forward to_____ things which are ahead I _____ toward the goal for the prize of the _____ call of God in Christ Jesus. Philippians 3:13-14*

Week 9 Day 4

> *Bow your heart before the Lord in prayer before completing today's Bible study. Ask God to help you, by the power of the Holy Spirit, give you a heart to reconcile within your heart.*

Jesus Reconciled all Things Through His Blood

There is no need to continue to hang onto the past. God wants you to walk in His forgiveness. He wants you to accept it as a gift. Are there any ways you have been punishing yourself? Wanting to punish yourself is saying to God that the sacrifice of His Son was not enough to cover your sins.

1. Is there anything else God could have done to cover your sins and the sins of those that have hurt you? If so, write down your thoughts.

2. Do you feel condemnation for your past? If so, what must you do to be free from condemnation?

3. Fill in the blanks to these verses.

There is therefore now _____, _____to those who are _____, _____, who do not walk _____ to the flesh, but _____ to the Spirit. For the law of the Spirit of life in _____, _____ has made me free _____ the law of ___ and _____. Romans 8:1-2

4. "Learning God's Truth" This weeks memory verse:

_____ those _____ _____ are _____ and _____ forward to those _____ which are ahead, _ press toward the goal for the prize of the upward call of God in Christ Jesus. _____ 3:__-__

The Devil, Your Flesh and The World

Three enemies prevent you from walking in forgiveness: the devil, your flesh and the world. Perhaps God's most beautiful gift to the believer is His provision for forgiveness and reconciliation.

It cost Him His Life

It cost Him His life but at His weakest point was His greatest victory.

It cost us our Pride

It only cost us our pride to humble ourselves in order to See if there is sin in our hearts.

For it pleased the Father that in Him all the fullness should dwell and by Him to reconcile all things to Himself, by Him, whether things on earth or things in heaven having made peace through the blood of His cross. Colossians. 1:19-20

Christians whose lives are transparent before the Father see themselves as sinners. They understand grace and praise God for it. One vital ingredient in our relationship with Jesus is our willingness to be honest with Him, to get real with God daily.

Now all things are of God, who has reconciled us to Himself through Jesus Christ, and has given us the ministry of reconciliation that is, that God was in Christ reconciling the world to Himself, not imputing their trespasses to them, and has committed to us the word of reconciliation. 2 Corinthians 5:18-19

5. Are you reconciled in your heart toward the person/people who hurt you? If, so how have you put this into action in your heart?

6. On a separate sheet of paper describe your attitude toward _____ when you first signed up for Healed and Set Free. What is your attitude today towards this person after the last seven weeks in Healed and Set Free?

Learning God's Word

This week's memory tool and verse:

⁀ FORGET: ___ must _____ those things, which are behind. (Not _____ on painful reminder. Such as phrases, smell, places, songs, and comments, but putting my mind on the higher calling Christ Jesus has for me.

_____ *those things,* _____ *are behind, and reaching forward to those things, which are _____, I press toward the goal for the prize of the upward call of God in Christ Jesus. Philippians 3:13-14*

7. Which areas are you struggling with in your mind?

8. What specific steps can you take this week to experience victory?

God Delights in Repairing our Hearts

We cannot work for our forgiveness but we can work for God because we have been forgiven. We can never physically demand for the one who has hurt us to be sorry. But we can allow God to repair our hearts. We can then help other people who need our support and encouragement to experience healing from the past.

- From the dictionary, restitution means ~~ restoring of a thing to its proper owner, repaired.

How much more shall the blood of Christ, who through the eternal Spirit offered Himself without spot to God, cleanse your conscience from dead works to serve the living God? And for this reason He is the Mediator of the new covenant, by means of death, for the redemption of the transgressions under the first covenant, that those who are called may receive the promise of the eternal inheritance. Hebrews 9:14-15

1. What is God's plan for you after you have cleansed your conscience before Him? Explain

2. What has God cleansed your conscience from?

3. What are some dead works that you are ready to forget? Explain.

4. Who are you to serve?

Share a situation where you had no love for another person and you had to be that open vessel so God could love them through you. What happened when you set your "self-life" aside?

_____

_____

_____

_____

_____

_____

_____

_____

_____

_____

_____

_____

_____

_____

_____

_____

_____

_____

_____

_____

_____

_____

_____

_____

Week 9 Day 5

> *Bow your heart before the Lord in prayer before completing today's Bible study. Ask Christ to work His unconditional love in your life.*

His Love at Work in Our Lives

He who loves father or mother more than Me is not worthy of Me. And he who loves son or daughter more than Me is not worthy of Me. And he who does not take his cross and follow after Me is not worthy of Me. He who finds his life will lose it, and he who loses his life for My sake will find it. Matthew 10:37-39

1. Do you love God enough that you are willing to die to your own justified hurts, fears and doubts so that His life can come forth through you?

2. YES or NO? Express your feelings…

Let this mind be in you which was also in Christ Jesus, who, being in the form of God, did not consider it robbery to be equal with God, but made Himself of no reputation, taking the form of a bondservant, and coming in the likeness of men. And being found in appearance as a man, He humbled Himself and became obedient to the point of death, even the death of the cross. Therefore God also has highly exalted Him and given Him the name, which is above every name, Philippians 2:5-9

3. Why do we need to set ourselves aside and become open vessels?

Learning God's Word

This week's memory verse:

🌹 _____ those _____ which are _____ and _____ forward __ those things which are _____, I _____ toward the _____ for the prize of the upward call of God in Christ Jesus. Philippians _:13-14

4. How can your life glorify God? Explain.

In this is love, not that we loved God, but that He loved us and sent His Son to be the propitiation for our sins. 1 John 4:10-12

5. How does God desire for His love to work in our lives?

Let nothing be done through selfish ambition or conceit, but in lowliness of mind let each esteem others better than himself. Let each of you look out not only for his own interests, but also for the interests of others. Philippians 2:3-4

6. What practical ways can we love others on a day to day basis?

7. Fill in the blanks. This week's memory verse:

ℒ _____ those _____ which are _____ and _____ forward __ those things which are _____, I _____ toward the _____ for the prize of the upward call of God in Christ Jesus. *Philippians _:13-14*

8. As you learn to move from the past, write down some of the results you see in yourself this week.

This week begin to take every thought captive. Be aware of negative emotions.

SEE, GIVE, FORGIVE, FORGET, BE SET FREE

A New Creation in Jesus

If you are in Christ, you are a new creation. Each of the following verses gives a description of who you are in Christ. Record from these verses who you are if you have accepted Christ and what each of these verses means to you personally.

- *But you are a chosen generation, a royal priesthood, a holy nation, His own special people, that you may proclaim the praises of Him who called you out of darkness into His marvelous light; 1 Peter 2:9*

- *Beloved, I beg you as sojourners and pilgrims, abstain from fleshly lusts which war against the soul, 1 Peter 2:11*

Letting the Past Hurts Work for Good

Our heavenly Father does indeed use our past. The great truth of Romans 8:28-29 is God's promise that any and all events in the past will be worked for good to make you more like Christ. He will redeem even the worst, the most painful, and the most perplexing aspects of your past, and use it all for more good. I have seen God redeem the suffering and terrible trials in many people's lives. In fact, some of the people I know who extend most freely God's gentleness, peace, and grace to those around them are people who know pain. God has used their experiences to make these people more Christ like, and He is truly glorified in their lives.

Healed From the Hard Times of the Past

The next time you catch yourself saying or thinking "if only", I encourage you to pause and ponder the fact of God's sovereignty, knowledge and presence in that past situation. Refuse to allow yourself to get bogged down thinking about something that is no longer real. Instead, draw near to God by thanking Him for His continual presence with you throughout time and for His promise to redeem the hard times of the past. Reflect back on your thankful list in chapter two.

God's grace and God's healing power are wide, deep and marvelous.

1. Write down the scriptures that accompany the first three tools to freedom.

"SEE ": (Asking God to expose the root cause of my sinful thought and actions. So I'm not defiled and I don't defile others.)

Hebrew 12:15

"GIVE": (I must be sorry enough to change and choose to go God's way over my own way.)

2 Corinthians 7:10

"FORGIVE": (I must forgive as Christ has forgiven me.)

Colossians 3:13

AUTHOR'S REFLECTION
I Got the ∿∿∿∿∿∿∿∿∿∿∿∿∿∿∿∿∿∿∿∿
Drift

I live in Idaho, the winters bring snow and more snow and the blowing winds cause large snowdrifts. One winter afternoon, I was heading out in my van to go to a few appointments in town. I only had a very narrow path to make my way out of the driveway. It had been cleared by the snowplow the day before, causing the snowdrifts to be piled up all around my driveway. As I was driving forward, I started thinking about a pole that was sticking up to mark our septic lid and I was wondering if the snow plow driver had knocked it over. My curiosity got the best of me. Continuing to drive forward, I quickly looked **behind** me to see if that pole was anywhere in sight, putting my attention on what was behind and taking my eyes off my narrow path of safety. The next thing I knew, I abruptly came to a stop smashing right into the side of the very snowdrift I was trying to avoid.

I was working the van back and forth trying to get it unstuck, and finally, one might say I got the drift. God wanted to teach me about more than just a little smash into a snowdrift. He spoke to my heart about the truth of what I had been doing for years.

I was always looking back in my mind and mulling over the past hurts, memories, and words hurled at me that bruised my feelings, physical attacks, betrayals, sexual abuse, past failures, and past wrongs that had hurt my life. I received a very clear picture. I was stuck in the past and could not continue to move forward because my focus was on what was behind. I was stuck in a snowdrift!

Looking behind and living in the past was robbing me of looking forward and living the life that was in front of me. God has set before us a straight and narrow path of truth to live by: Enter by the narrow gate; for wide is the gate and broad is the way that leads to destruction, and there are many who go in by it. Because narrow is the gate and difficult is the way which leads to life, and there are few who find it. Matthew 7:13-14

In your own power you cannot change the way you think. When **you are weak** and overwhelmed by life, you need to draw near to God and spend time **getting to know Him by getting to know His Word**. God is faithful to His Word. **His Word will transform** how you think and **His Word will strengthen** you.

SEEING what is left over in our hearts

Thinking about the past will never change the past. But you can change your future and BE SET FREE from your past.

Learn the truth and **SEE** what has you in shackles today, keeping you in bondage to your past. Hurt does not go away by itself. If you are denying the hurt, it will find ways to express itself anyway; forming roots of bitterness, hurting many that stand in its way and continuing to affect your life. You need to **SEE** what hurt still lingers in your heart from the past. It's time to get real with God about what is left over and growing in your heart because of your unacceptable past hurts.

You can attempt to bury your heartache and put on a smile and say everything is just fine. But on the inside your heart will still be filled with fear, shame, resentment, guilt, unforgiveness, self-centered desires, jealousy, and uncontrolled anger, all putting you right under the black cloud of depression. Emotional scars can affect other areas of your life such as your marriage, your children, your friendships, and your school or job performance. You may turn to the harmful behaviors of drug and alcohol abuse, deep depression, suicidal tendencies, eating disorders, outbursts of anger, and rebellion. You attempt to ease your pain, but you fail to heal your heart.

Review

Review this chapter on Remembering to Forget. Reflect on the truths you have learned.

- This weeks memory verse:

  _____ _____ _____ *which are_____ and reaching forward to those things which are ahead, I press toward ____ goal for the prize of the ____ ___ __ God in ____ _____.* Philippians 3:13-14

- I don't need to mull over my painful situation anymore because...

- Because the past is not reality, today is, I desire to focus on ...

- I'm ready to forget the way Satan has defiled sex because the truth about the marriage bed is...

- I'm ready to forget about_____ because God has instructed me to forget those things that are behind.

- What encouraged you about this chapter?

- What has challenged you?

- In what specific way will you apply God's truth to you life?

In the last chapter we will be taking a closer look at Healed and Set Free. God is the God of truth and only the truth will set you free.

"Stories of real people, real hurts, real healing, and a real SAVIOR"

Set Free From the Garbage That was in my Heart

I think my biggest struggle, as a mom has been guilt and fear, Since I have gone through **Healed and Set Free**, God has set me free from so much garbage. I told my daughter recently... " Honey, I am just figuring out this parenting thing, could you stay a couple more year and see me do it right?" We got a great laugh out of it all, but it is so true - I never knew that I feared so many things for my children and that was sin. I never really entrusted my children into the Lord's hands like I have done recently. I was always afraid that they would turn out like other family members... that they would not serve the Lord... that I would be embarrassed and shown to be an awful parent...etc. I daily take those thoughts captive and now realize there is NO perfect parent. God has a wonderful way, but we must entrust our lives to Him, and then take leadership roles as seriously. I have never seen a pastor lead his flock in strength when he had fear in his heart... I know now that same principle applies to leadership in the home. There is no perfect parent... only a perfect God.

New mom, ~ Minnesota

Tears That Flowed

Women started standing up and sharing how the Healed and Set Free Bible Study had changed their lives. We had our retreat this past week and friday night in between songs women stood up and gave their testimony's as the Lord led them. Women shared how the **Healed and Set Free** Bible Study had changed their lives. Tears flowed and women who are not accustom to praise and worship were praising God and weeping. God is using this ministry and healing lives, marriages, friendships and families. These women who felt there was no hope are now seeing that God has given them freedom through His word to walk in victory. God is creating within them a hunger for the Word.

Praise Reports From Women's Retreat

SEE, GIVE, FORGIVE, FORGET, BE SET FREE

We Are Pilgrim's Passing Through, This Place is Not Our Home

God Has Not Promised

Skies always blue

Flower strewn pathways all our lives through

God has not promised sun without rain

Joy without sorrow

Peace without pain

But God Has Promised

Strength for the day

Grace for the trails

Undying LOVE

Help from above

Unfailing sympathy

Rest for the labor, light for the way.

- Author unknown

Open Wounds

In the shadows of my hidden pain poured teardrops from my heart.
Flowing over open wounds that were ripping me apart.

I couldn't ever seem to shake the captivity from my past.
I stood within the darkened shadows from the turmoil that they'd cast.

So I took my heart to Jesus, I laid it at His throne.
I knew He was my only hope for it wasn't healing on it's own.

Lord, my heart's been wounded many times some scars have eased the pain,
but it's these OPEN WOUNDS that seem to cause the turmoil once again.

I can sense the roots of bitterness spreading throughout my life.
Anger is consuming me causing resentment, hurt, and strife.

I don't want my life to be this way, I need healing so I can live.
God tenderly held me close to Him and said "Child, you must forgive."

I found my tears came pouring forth "Lord that's so hard to do."
He handed me back my heart and said "And here's my gift to you."

Forgiveness will heal the very wounds that plague your inner soul.
You'll find your life worth living and your heart will then be whole.

I knew He was right as He took my sin and hurled it far from me.
My thoughts were cleansed, I was healed with a peace that SET ME FREE.

I also knew down deep inside He had given me a brand new start,
for as a reminder with His own blood He had autographed my heart.

Cei Cee

Chapter 8

Healed
and Set Free

*You shall know the truth
and the truth shall make
you free.*

John 8:31-32

There are four main tools we will weave into the very fiber of our hearts day by day: **SEE, GIVE, FORGIVE, FORGET,** and **BE SET FREE.** Thinking about the past will never change the past. But you can change your future and Be Set FREE from your past. As you deal with your past and present hurts, you can either embrace the truth and let go of the burdens you carry, or carry your burdens and reject the truth and the freedom it brings. The choice is yours. Getting real with God is the first step you need to always take as you face deep, dark hurts that have chipped away at your peace for 1 year, 10 years, 20 years, and some 50 years. God's love is bigger then all of our hurts and fears. You will have many blessings in front of you as God's truth unfolds in your heart and Sets you Free.

Let's Day By Day Go over the Four Steps to Keep Our Hearts Clean

🌹 Tools To Become Set Free

- **Tool #1 "SEE ":** I must **SEE** the truth about what is in my heart, so I'm not defiled.

    Looking carefully lest anyone fall short of the grace of God; lest any root of bitterness springing up cause trouble, and by this many become defiled. Hebrew 12:15.

- **Tool #2 "GIVE":** I must **GIVE** the sin in repentance, knowing Christ is waiting to take it. (I must be sorry enough to change and choose to go God's way over my own way.)

    For godly sorrow produces repentance leading to salvation, not to be regretted; but the sorrow of the world produces death. 2 Corinthians 7:10

- **Tool #3 "FORGIVE":** I must **FORGIVE**, as I am forgiven by Christ. (Forgiving those that hurt, bruised, wronged, hurt, rejected, betrayed or harmed me whether unintentionally or deliberately.) Ask God to Forgive you for holding unforgiveness and know that He will.

    Bearing with one another, and forgiving one another, if anyone has a complaint against another; even as Christ forgave you, so you also must do. Colossians 3:13

- **Tool #4 "FORGET":** I must **FORGET** by remembering to no longer dwell on the hurt.

    Brethren, I do not count myself to have apprehended; but one thing I do, forgetting those things which are behind and reaching forward to those things which are ahead. Philippians 3:13.

🌹 **BECOME SET FREE:** Christ will open the shackles from my past hurts showing me the truth so I can become a cleansed vessel that is Healed and Set Free.

   You shall know the truth, and the truth shall make you free. Therefore, if the Son makes you free, you shall be free indeed. John 8:32-36.

SATAN IS DEFEATED AND THE SHACKLES ARE GONE AND YOU ARE FREE!

Week 10 Day 1

Bow your heart before the Lord in prayer before completing today's Bible study. Thank God for the truth that has set you free.

In this "Healed and Set Free" chapter, we remove the secret root of sin, which kept us in bondage to the past. Once we pull out the roots of bitterness and unforgiveness we are Set Free to have a fresh beginning and to **FORGET** about the past hurts. Having accepted God's forgiveness, through His only Son that hung on that cruel cross of pain, we must never forget we are forgiven. We can forgive because Christ Jesus was forsaken; we are accepted because He was condemned. Stop and thank Christ for His amazing Love and ask Him how you can honor Him today in all you do.

We are Healed to step out from under the black cloud of depression, away from the shackles of guilt, anger, and shame. You shall know the truth, and the truth shall make you free. John 8:32.

We are Set Free to step into the joy of the Lord to live the life God intends for people to live, a life that glorifies Him. All Christians have eternal life, but very few Christians experience abundant Life. God wants us to have this kind of life here and now, even in the midst of our trails, disappointments, and failures. God is real, and yes, He does love us.

1. *Therefore* **strengthen** *the hands which hang down, and the feeble knees, and* **make straight** *paths for your feet, so that what is lame may not be dislocated, but rather be* **healed**. *Hebrew 12:12*

   • Dictionary definition for **Strengthen** ~~ renew, make strong, invigorate.

What has been strengthened, renewed, made strong and invigorated in your life during this time of healing? Quiet your heart before Your TRUE HEALER, pour out your heart to thank Him for what he has make straight and has healed.

Let's Day by Day Go Over the Four Steps to Keep Our Heart Clean

Learning God's Word

This week's memory tool and verse:

🌹 BE SET FREE: I must choose God's will over my own. (I will experience how Christ will open the shackles and experience freedom from having a junk drawer in my heart where records of wrongs are kept, choice by choice, and become an open vessel that's Healed and Set Free;)

Then Jesus said to those Jews who believed Him, "If you abide in My word, you are My disciples indeed, and you shall know the truth, and the truth shall make you free." John 8:31:32

Each of us is capable by the power of the Holy Spirit to lay down our own will, but not all are willing. It's our free choice to either **Embrace or Reject** the truth from the scriptures we learn. One day we will stand accountable for what we know.

2. When we Reject the will of God, the outcome of our daily life will be to put on a smile and say everything is alright, but our hearts will be filled with:

> Bitterness
>
> Resentment
>
> Pride
>
> Unforgiveness
>
> Self-centered desires
>
> Defensiveness
>
> Unhappiness
>
> Jealousy
>
> Anger

- When we Embrace the will of God, the outcome will be to deal with and acknowledge our true feelings, to get real with God, to get rid of the strongholds, and to follow the truth to have victory over the flesh Day by Day! Choice by choice!

- Jesus said, *"If you abide in my word, you are my disciples indeed." John 8:31.*

Learning God's Word

This week's memory tool and verse:

BE SET FREE: I must _____ God's will over my own. (I will experience how Christ will open the shackles and experience freedom from having a _____ in my heart where records of wrongs are kept, choice by choice, and become an open vessel that's Healed and Set Free;)

Then Jesus said to those Jews who believed Him, "If you abide in My word, you are My disciples indeed, and you shall know the truth, and the truth shall make you free." _____ 8:31:32

Walking in the Light

Walking in the light makes life so much easier and happier. When you walk in the light, you live to please only A Person, God. Examine your heart daily and Get real with God.

3. Ask yourself the question, " Who am I really seeking to please?" " Am I seeking to please God, or am I more concerned with being a friend to the world, pleasing other people or pleasing my own desires?" Explain your thoughts.

_____

_____

_____

_____

_____

_____

_____

_____

_____

_____

_____

_____

_____

_____

_____

_____

_____

_____

Let's Day by Day Go Over the Four Steps to Keep Our Heart Clean

Learning God's Word

This week's memory tool and verse:

BE SET FREE: I must _____ God's will over my own, (I will experience how Christ will open the shackles and experience freedom from having a _____ in my heart where records of wrongs are kept, choice by choice and become an open vessel that's Healed and Set Free;)

Then Jesus said to those Jews who believed Him, "If you abide in My word, you are My disciples indeed, and you shall know the truth, and the truth shall make you free. _____ 8:31:32

4. If you don't have a personal relationship with Jesus Christ or you're unsure, take a moment with the following:

- *For when we were still without strength, in due time Christ died for the ungodly. For scarcely for a righteous man will one die; yet perhaps for a good man someone would even dare to die. But God demonstrates His own love toward us, in that while we were still sinners, Christ died for us. Much more then, having now been justified by His blood, we shall be saved from wrath through Him. For if when we were enemies we were reconciled to God through the death of His Son, much more, having been reconciled, we shall be saved by His life. Romans 5:6-10*

- *"For God so loved the world that he gave His only begotten Son, that whosoever believes in Him shall not perish, but have eternal life, Jesus says in John 3:16.*

God loves us so much that He sent His Son to die for us on the cross that our sins would be washed away and His light would shine through us! All we have to do is believe in Him, and He will take residence in our hearts. The things of this world will pale in comparison to the brilliant Light of God's glory. There is nothing we can do or not do to earn the mercy of God. He gives it freely to any one who believes.

- *2 Corinthians 4:6 says, " For God...made his light shine in our hearts to give us the light of the knowledge of the glory of God in the face of Christ."*

- If you have never asked the Lord Jesus to come into your life, why don't you do it right now? It will be the best decision you will ever make. You can pray this prayer right now, silently and ask Jesus into your life and He will forgive you!!

"Lord Jesus,

I know I'm a sinner and I need Your forgiveness. I need the love, peace, and hope You offer me, so I turn from my own ways now. Come into my heart and fill me with Your Holy Spirit. Help me to follow You all the days of my life. Thank You that I am now going to Heaven.

In Jesus name, amen."

Don't waste the pain, use it— Let it drive you deeper into God!

When we are tempted to sin or go our own way, we are drawn away from the truth. It's important to recognize our negative thoughts and sinful emotions when they begin to get stirred up.

- *Keep sound wisdom and discretion; So they will be life to your soul And grace to your neck. Then you will walk safely in your way, And your foot will not stumble. When you lie down, you will not be afraid; Yes, you will lie down and your sleep will be sweet. Do not be afraid of sudden terror, Nor of trouble from the wicked when it comes; For the LORD will be your confidence, And will keep your foot from being caught. Do not withhold good from those to whom it is due, When it is in the power of your hand to do so. Proverbs 3:21-27*

Fill in the blanks: To know the tools to heal what becomes crippled from living in this fallen world.

- **SEE:** I must ____ what is really in my _____ and ask God to expose the root cause of my sinful thoughts and emotions.

- **GIVE:** I must _____ the sin in _____. I must be sorry enough to change and choose to go God's way over my own way.

- **FORGIVE:** I must _____,as I am _____ by Christ.

- **FORGET:** I must _____those things, which are behind and not dwell on painful reminders.

BE SET FREE: To choose God's will over my own. I will experience freedom from having a junk drawer in my heart where records of wrongs are kept, choice by choice, and become an open vessel that's Healed and Set Free!

Satan is Defeated and the Shackles are gone and YOU ARE FREE!

Words to Remember

Fill in the blanks:
Then our _____ was filled with laughter, and our _____ with singing. Then they _____ among the nations, "The Lord has done great things for _____." The Lord has done great things for ___, and we are glad. Psalm 126:2-3

Week 10 Day 2

> *Bow your heart before the Lord in prayer before completing today's Bible study. Thank God for the truth that has set you free.*

Our Hope

Brethren, I do not count myself to have apprehended; but one thing I do, forgetting those things which are behind and reaching forward to those things which are ahead, I press toward the goal for the prize of the upward call of God in Christ Jesus. Philippians 3:13-14

1. For all the tears that have been shed and the brokenness of a contrite heart that has been felt, what great hope is there to look forward to?

2. What are you reaching for today?

For whatever things were written before were written for our learning, that we through the patience and comfort of the Scriptures might have hope. Romans 15:4

3. In the future, when you are reminded of your painful experiences, where can you find hope and encouragement?

4. Why is it so important to ask God to expose the root cause of our thoughts and emotions?

5. Fill in the blanks

He _____ _____ _____ out of darkness, and brings the shadow of death _____ _____. Job 12:22

He uncovers deep things out of darkness, and brings the shadow of death to light. Job 12:22

6. What healing has been brought to light from the Healed and Set Free homework?

7. According to Paul's prayer found in Romans 15:13, what does God want to fill you with?

Let's Day by Day Go Over the Four Steps to Keep Our Heart Clean

A Heart That Encourages

"With every encounter, make it your aim that people are better off for having been in your presence. Try in every encounter to give something to the other person." What a great and simple way to positively influence the lives of other people- your husband, children, friends, parents, and strangers! Everyone needs edification and encouragement, and we are free to offer that when we have a heart filled by God and a heart Healed and Set Free from lingering hurts. Here are some hints for encouraging God's people.

☞ Take Time To Be Filled:

Ministry is stimulated when we take the time to develop our skills and overcome our weaknesses or past and that makes sense. After all, how much can a teacher teach, a counselor counsel, an administrator administrate? Only as far as each has grown! And each of us grows, each of us finds power and knowledge for overcoming personal weaknesses and for more effective ministry, in Jesus Christ.

☞ Memorize Scripture Of Encouragement

You can have the ministry of saltiness--the ministry of encouragement with everyone you meet. If you let your speech always be with grace, seasoned with salt (Colossians 4:6), you will never fail to minister to those you encounter. Your life and lips will offer refreshing encouragement to all who cross your path. Like our Messiah, you will be able to "speak a word in season to him who is weary" (Isaiah 50:4).

But, as we've seen before, we can't give away what we do not possess. So it's good to memorize some pertinent words of encouragement from the Bible to share with people in need. Knowing Scripture gives you " a word in season", something timely and appropriate to the situation.

☞ Make Phone Calls To Encourage

An easy way to encourage and make a heart glad is to reach out and touch someone by phone. I'm not talking about making lengthy calls. A simple, quick call can do much to gladden the heart of the recipient!

You and I can also reach out in this way to people recovering from illness or dealing with a crisis. The telephone offers us a very effective way to encourage others, and it takes very little effort. Most important to that ministry is a heart that cares!

☞ Write Notes Of Encouragement

Writing notes to those who need encouragement is another way to share a good word that makes the heart glad. (Proverbs 12:25). Whether I'm writing to the sick, those in leadership, or a recent hostess, telling myself "just three sentences!" gets me going. Sentence #1 conveys I miss you, I appreciate you, or I'm thinking of you. Sentence #2 lets readers know they are special to me and why. And Sentence #3 says I'm praying for them and includes a verse I'm praying for them. We can encourage others with a note in just three sentences.

🌿 **Ministry Opportunities**

If you take time to sit at Jesus feet and be filled by God's Spirit as you study the written Word, if you focus on overcoming internal obstacles to doing God's work, you will never lack for ministry. God's fullness in you will naturally overflow into the lives of others. I think immediately of two women including myself who increased their ministry potential when they overcame their shyness.

Evangelist Corrie Ten Boom had a problem with shyness. Corrie enrolled in a Dale Carnegie course so she could learn to talk to people. If she could talk to people, then she could witness to them about Jesus Christ! Developing herself led to greater ministry.

While my husband was on staff as the youth and college pastor at Calvary Chapel San Jose. The senior pastor's wife, Jean McClure asked me to administrate and MC a Sexual Purity Seminar. I was nervous but excited to accept the opportunity to serve God and take a step to overcome my shyness. As I stood before 500 teen girls and women God's grace poured over me and enabled me to serve Him in my weakness.

1. What would you consider to be a major weakness in your life, one that hinders you in the area of ministry to others? We looked at two women who suffered from shyness. What causes you to suffer and / or fail to minister to others? Name it and then list steps you can take this week to strengthen this weakness and move toward overcoming it altogether. Create a plan of action.

2. In what areas of your life have you found new hope springing forth from your past experience?

Learn to Reach Out

Again and again Jesus tells us to give-to give to everyone (Luke 6:30); to give hoping for nothing in return (verse 35); to give in the generous way God, who is kind to the unthankful and evil, gives (verse 35); and to care for others by giving (verse 38). You and I can learn to give in this way, to overflow with care for all others. Here are a few ideas:

*"**Develop a bountiful eye**"* - When I go into public, I intentionally look for wounded sheep- and, believe me, they are there! I've found women and teen girls in the church lobby crying, in the ladies bathroom, on benches sobbing. We can ask- questions like, "Can I do anything to help you? Can I get you something? Would you like to talk or pray?" People all around us need a tender word or more. (SEE why you and I must be **Healed and Set Free** from lingering hurts and selfish tendencies? That way we can give to others.)

Your presence and sometimes a single touch are worth a thousand words- When it comes to reaching out, remember this principle of ministry: your very presence is a source of comfort. You may not have the exact words to say or the perfect Scripture to share. But in many, if not most, situations your touch can bring comfort far greater than words.

Be a giver- Just as you and I learned with our husband and children, we can give the smile, the greeting, the warm question, the touch, the hug, and the name. (Always use the person's name!)

Be bold- Be bold and give to the people God places in your path. If, however, you find yourself avoiding a certain person, ask God to show you why. Sin in our heart, a heart meant to overflow with care for others, keeps us from being confident in our relationships. So find out what is going on or not going on in your heart that's hindering your ministry. Then go a step farther and decide what you will say the next time you see that person. Actively search for him or her and give the greeting you planned. With a heart clean before God, you should have nothing to hide, nothing to withhold. Learn to reach out to the people you meet up with every day.

Go to Give

Missionary and martyr Jim Elliot once said, "Wherever you are, **be all there**. Live to the hilt in every situation you believe to be the will of God." As Mrs. George says, " I keep these words in mind whenever I attend any church or ministry event, and I go expecting God to use me. Here's an overview of my approach and I encourage you to make it yours.

"***Be all there***- Before I go to an event, I pray that I will go to give - to reach out, to look out, to be direct, to withhold nothing. Then, as I go, I put my thought life on guard. While I'm at Bible study, I don't want to be thinking about what I'm gong to fix for dinner that night. During my pastor's message, I don't want to be planning my week. I don't want to be concerned about what happened before I got there or what will happen after the event. I want to be all there!

"***Divide and conquer***- Agree with your closest girlfriends, mother, or daughter not to visit the entire time. Instead share the commitment to divide and conquer. Remember that you came to give! Your closest friends have greater access to your life, plenty of one-on-one time with you in private, so why should they also have all your public time? They can talk to you later. One Christian woman and her friend have made a pact that, when they find themselves gravitating towards each other, one of them will announce, "Come on! Lets go touch some sheep!"

One more word about going to give. You'll find yourselves doing a lot of receiving.

3. Can you comfort others who hurt with what you have been comforted?

4. Write down four important truths you've learned from "Healed and Set Free"

    1.

    2.

    3.

    4.

Though I speak with the tongues of men and of angels, but have not love, I have become sounding brass or a clanging cymbal. And though I have the gift of prophecy, and understand all mysteries and all knowledge, and though I have all faith, so that I could remove mountains, but have not love, I am nothing. And though I bestow all my goods to feed the poor, and though I give my body to be burned, but have not love, it profits me nothing. Love suffers long and is kind; love does not envy; love does not parade itself, is not puffed up; does not behave rudely, does not seek its own, is not provoked, thinks no evil; does not rejoice in iniquity, but rejoices in the truth; bears all things, believes all things, hopes all things, endures all things. 1 Corinthians 13:1-7

Love holds no record of wrong, according to 1 Corinthians 13:1-7.

5. What do we become if we have no love in the eyes of our husband, children, others, and God?

6. Have you moved past the wrongs that were done to you? In what way are you pressing toward Jesus Christ?

Mom's Enduring Heart

Enduring to keep the focus on the high calling and the assignment we have been given as moms.

Children will rise up and call you blessed. Proverbs 31:28

This poem tells how a little girl learned to love life by watching the way her mother lived hers.

Mary's father left their marriage just before their 40th wedding anniversary, turning her mother's life upside down the last couple of years. "She prayed and worked hand-in-hand with God to put her life back together again," said Mary, one of six children.

When You Thought I Wasn't Looking

When you thought I wasn't looking
    You hung my first painting on the refrigerator
        And I wanted to paint another.

When you thought I wasn't looking
    You fed a stray cat
        And I thought it was good to be kind to animals.

When you thought I wasn't looking
    You baked a birthday cake just for me
        And I knew that little things were special things.

When you thought I wasn't looking
    You said a prayer
        And I believed there was a God that I could always talk to.

When you thought I wasn't looking
    You kissed me good-night
        And I felt loved.

When you thought I wasn't looking
    I saw tears come from your eyes
        And I learned that sometimes things hurt –
            But that it's alright to cry.

When you thought I wasn't looking
    You smiled
        And it made me want to look that pretty too.

When you thought I wasn't looking
    You cared
        And I wanted to be everything I could be.

When you thought I wasn't looking –
    I looked ...
        And wanted to say thanks
            For all those things you did
When you thought I wasn't looking.

Mary Rita Schilke Korzan
"This poem was inspired by my mother, Blanche Elizabeth Montgomery Schilke,
and dedicated to her June 14, 1980."

Week 10 Day 3

Bow your heart before the Lord in prayer before completing today's Bible study. Ask Him to let you SEE how you have grown in your trials from past hurts.

Tears to Joy

Once you have accepted God's forgiveness in your life, joy replaces shame and guilt. Forgiveness replaces resentment and bitterness.

1. After David accepted God's forgiveness how did he respond in the following Psalms?

   • *You will show me the path of life; In Your presence is fullness of joy; At Your right hand are pleasures forevermore. Psalm 16:11*

   • *You have turned for me my mourning into dancing; you have put off my sackcloth and clothed me with gladness, To the end that my glory may sing praise to You and not be silent. O Lord my God, I will give thanks to you forever. Psalm 30:11-12*

2. What burdens from the past have turned from mourning into dancing?

"Learning God's Truth"

3. Fill in the blanks for this weeks memory verse:

Then Jesus said to those Jews who _____ Him, "If you abide in ___ word, you are My disciples indeed, and you shall _____ the truth, and the truth _____ make you free. John 8:31:32

4. Knowing that you are set Free what are you thankful for? Reread Romans 1:21-22

Lord, I pray, help me move past the futile thoughts and help me keep my heart from being foolish and darkened by the hurts. Help me SEE what I can be thankful for each and every day. In Jesus' name, Amen.

5. Satan doesn't want us to SEE the blessing in our life. When you are thankful for the trails and hard times from the past, then you have truly been Set Free.

Can you SEE 5 things you are thankful for: Write them down

    1.

    2.

    3.

    4.

    5.

Offer a prayer of thankfulness to God for allowing the painful circumstances to lead you to His love, mercy, and forgiveness. God has made the way straight so the heart can be "Healed and Set Free."_____

"And because lawlessness will abound, the love of many will grow cold. Matthew 24:12

6. Jesus is coming back soon. Is your heart cold, lukewarm or hot for Jesus?

"We need to be on Our Guard not to Hurl Words that Wound."

One of Satan's greatest attacks is tempting God's people to hurt or wrong other Christians. Whether intentional or unintentional, the hurt is done and the bridges are burned. People are cut out of each others lives and difficulty and hurt surrounds their relationships, if one decides to hang on to the wrong. But if both put their pride aside and reconcile their differences, the bridge can be rebuilt with God's love, forgiveness, and trust.

Satan has come to kill, steal, and destroy. Yes, even Christian relationships. Christians, who gossip, criticize, and find fault will always maintain that chain reaction that Satan loves: getting others to have tongues that work overtime tearing down and discouraging fellow Christians.

No doubt you've had your share of words that wound. You know the betrayal and hurt of a broken heart or bruised feeling by others that have fallen into the trap of backbiting or fault finding. Maybe you're the one that has fallen into that trap. We never have to look very far at the things we do not like about people. But to look beyond the petty and get to the heart of a person, that is truly mature.

We should not be surprised by these attacks. Jesus is the only one who is perfect. He was misunderstood, rejected, disliked, hated, and abandoned. We will be also. Friendly fellow believers will trip and fall and end up landing on us, it could be happening right now. Will you burn bridges? Will you cut people out of your life?

Let's Day by Day Go Over the Four Steps to Keep Our Heart Clean

We need to love unconditionally, and to pray that God would give us a humble heart like the tax collector and say, "Be merciful to me, I am a sinner."

Be the one to say, "If I try to save my life (with pride) I will lose it, but if I lose my life in Christ (humble myself) I will find it." Let's tell the truth in love. Then concentrate on keeping our own heart right before God. We cannot do anything to keep another person's heart right, only our own.

AUTHOR'S REFLECTION
Wounding Words

Just recently I had to grab my four tools to set me Free from new hurts. **SEE, GIVE, FORGIVE, FORGET, BE SET FREE** because a fellow Christian was gossiping and criticizing me behind my back. Of course I was hurt and disappointed to hear about it, but I began to apply the four tools right away so a junk drawer would not get started. Then God led me to Matthew 5:44, *"But I say to you, love your enemies, bless those who curse you, do good to those who hate you, and pray for those who spitefully use you and persecute you."*

Praying Blessing on those who Curse me

Every day for two weeks, when I thought about the wounding words I would replace the hurtful words they said with what God's word says and prayed God would shower blessings on their life, their home, their hands, to bless whatever they were doing.

At first this was just the opposite of what I wanted to do. Before I knew it I was so filled up with God's love for this person who had hurled wounding words my way that the hurt was gone.

It is so wonderful to **BE SET FREE** and have a sincere heart of love for those who wrong you. It can only be done through God's grace and mercy.

- Try it for two weeks, pray that God would shower blessings on the lives of those that have hurt you. In return your heart will be blessed.

Matthew 5:44," But I say to you, love your enemies, bless those who curse you, do good to those who hate you, and pray for those who spitefully use you and persecute you."

You cannot think about yourself and others at the same time. As you and I settle our personal needs with God in private prayer, we can then rise up and focus all our attention outward -- away from self and on to others. You cannot hate the person you are praying for, Jesus instructed us to pray for our enemies (Matthew 5:44), and God changes our hearts as we do so. An end to self-centeredness, the dissolution of ill will, and an end to neglect- these results of praying for someone will inevitably heal and set us free from unforgivness. Remember to always leave others with a heart they were glad to be around.

    Praying blessings on those who curse me, Only through God's grace

SEE, GIVE, FORGIVE, FORGET, BE SET FREE

1 Peter 1:4-9 to an inheritance incorruptible and undefiled and that does not fade away, reserved in heaven for you, who are kept by the power of God through faith for salvation ready to be revealed in the last time. In this you greatly rejoice, though now for a little while, if need be, you have been grieved by various trials, that the genuineness of your faith, being much more precious than gold that perishes though it is tested by fire, may be found to praise, honor, and glory at the revelation of Jesus Christ, whom having not seen you love. Though now you do not see Him, yet believing, you rejoice with joy inexpressible and full of glory, receiving the end of your faith; the salvation of your souls.

1. Why were these strangers in a world filled with an inexpressible joy even during various trials in this fallen world?

2. In what four ways are you rejoicing with inexpressible joy through faith in Jesus concerning your trials from the past?

    1.

    2.

    3.

    4.

3. Describe the last time you felt an inexpressible joy.

Words to Remember:

4. Fill in the blanks.

Then our mouth was _____ with laughter, and our tongue with _____. Then they said among the nations, "The Lord has done _____ things for them. The Lord has done great_____ for us, and we are glad. Psalm 126:2-3

5. Write down the ways you have grown in your relationship with Christ Jesus our Lord during your healing time.

Then the Lord said to him, "Now you Pharisees make the outside of the cup and dish clean, but your inward part is full of greed and wickedness. Foolish ones! Did not He who made the outside make the inside also?" Luke 11:39-40

6. In your own words, what does it mean to only make the outside clean but the inward is dirty?

7. As you look toward the higher calling that Christ has for you what will you become? Read 2 Tim.2:21 A _____ _____ _____

Let's Day by Day Go Over the Four Steps to Keep Our Heart Clean

Week 10 Day 4

> *Bow your hart before the Lord in prayer before completing today's Bible study. Ask Him to shine His spotlight on what new direction or new outlook He wants you to have as He works all things together for good.*

A New Direction

In continuing to teach the **Healed and Set Free Bible Study**, I believe Tammy has the heart of God in getting this book to a hurting world. For the lessons found here can change a person's life. But if we use it as a one time study, the whole will not be solidified. For the glue which will hold all the parts together is continued use. Life goes on and the potential of this study, applied on a daily basis, will cause us to SEE, GIVE, FORGIVE, FORGET, and BE SET FREE for always.

In these pages she has also taught us the importance of prayer, Bible reading and study, sharing, and relationship. What a new concept, many would say, confessing our sins one to another and praying together. But what a joy and a privilege to have someone to help us keep from building stone walls in our hearts.

As iron sharpens iron, so a man sharpens the countenance of his friend. Proverbs 27:17. Therefore it has been my desire to encourage you in your daily Bible reading and quiet time before the Lord in prayer. And it is my prayer that you will find a dear friend: one who will hold you accountable for your walk with God, one who will pray for you on a daily basis, and one who would not think of breaking that confidence and trust.

🌹 Jonnie, Idaho

Let's Day By Day Go over the Four Step to Keep Our Heart Clean. As a person moves from tears to joy, their eyes are off their past, instead, they are seeking the face of the Lord and His direction through prayer, His Word and His plan for their life. They will earnestly search for the direction God wants them to take to turn hurts into healing, believing God will make all things work together for good including pain and heartache from past experience.

"But rise and stand on your feet; for I have appeared to you for this purpose, to make you a minister and a witness both of the things which you have seen and of the things which I will yet reveal to you. I will deliver you from the Jewish people, as well as from the Gentiles, to whom I now send you, to open their eyes, in order to turn them from darkness to light, and from the power of Satan to God, that they may receive forgiveness of sins and an inheritance among those who are sanctified by faith in Me." Acts 16-18

1. What did the Lord tell Paul he had planned for his life?

2. How was Paul using his past to work out the plans God had for him?

Learning God's Truth

This week's memory verse:

🌹 Then ____ _____ to those Jews ____ believed ____, "If you abide in My ____, you are My disciples ____, and you shall know the ____, and the truth shall ___ you free." John. 8:31:32

3. Compare your future with Paul's. How have your eyes been opened to your past? Having the eyes of your heart flooded with Light. *Ephesians 1:18: What darkness was in your heart that has been replaced with light?*

4. How can you use your past to glorify the Lord as Paul did and not give Satan power over you?

5. How can you help others that have painful pasts? Not to waste the pain but use it and let it drive them into a deeper walk with God!

AUTHOR'S REFLECTION
Let's Get On With Living In God's Love

There once was a time I felt my past had altered the plans God had for my life because of my troubled background of sexual abuse, rape, bulimia and anger. My past had affected other areas of my life, such as my marriage, children, and other relationships.

I really thought I would always be a critical, angry, out of control, screaming, yelling, rebellious Christian woman. I thought, that's just how I was and if Rick, my kids, and others didn't like it, well, too bad!

But that's not what I wanted to be. I really disliked the person I was. First I had to take the painful step to look at my own heart and get real with God. I had to SEE the root cause so I could deal with it. I needed to stop mulling over the hurt of the past, and center in on the truth that God had shown me. When my heart and mind were filled with the negative emotions of the past it would cause me to overreact to absolutely everything. Watch out for this! Catch that wrong thinking and choose to deal with them rather than entertain them. Thoughts such as how it used to be, how it could have been, and how could they have done that to me, pulls us down into the pit faster than anything else. Let's get on with real living.

Living in Gods Grace

SEE, GIVE, FORGIVE, FORGET, BE SET FREE

Seize the Day

"For I know the plans I have for you," says the Lord. "They are plans for good and not for disaster, to give you a future and a hope. In those days when you pray, I will listen. If you look for me in earnest, you will find me when you seek me. I will be found by you," says the Lord. Jeremiah 29:11-14

We easily find God in nature: The majesty of a rainbow after the thunderstorm. We quickly identify God's involvement in the big celebration of our live: the birth of a child, the new job, or the car crash that left the vehicle totaled but our children unscathed. God is there, and we thank Him for His provision.

And we even acknowledge God's presence in the mist of tragedy: the report from the pathology lab; or the heartache in a home filled with broken relationships. God is there, and we depend upon Him for strength.

But seeing God in these " big things" of life is easy. The more difficult task - yet a challenge just as rewarding- is seeing God in our everyday, mundane activities.

When we realize that God is in the ordinary, our daily grind suddenly has meaning and purpose. The household chores, whether the lawn or the laundry, become an opportunity to express love and care for the other members of the household. A walk to the mailbox brings a chance to greet the neighbor (who may be in desperate need of an encouraging word). The day at work presents the challenge of giving wholehearted effort, which will be pleasing to God.

Live your life with an overwhelming sense that God is present in the details all around you. There will be no boring moments. Life will take on new meaning when you begin to see God in your daily life.

To quote an old but effective phrase, *"Today is the first day of the rest of your life."* You can't do a thing to change yesterday, and only God knows for sure what is going to happen tomorrow. So today is the only day you have.

How do you seize the day? First build upon the knowledge you have that God has worked in your life in the past. Second, have faith that God has secured your future - no matter what happens. He has given you hope.

If you live in the context of these dynamic beliefs, then you will live in God's power today. When you know that God works through your circumstances, they will energize you.

So go out and make a difference in your world. Leave an impression on everything and everyone you touch because of what God has done for you.

🌹 Live life on purpose, not by accident.

🌹 Remember that there is a time for love and a place for love. Any time, any place.

🌹 What you think determines what you do.

🌹 Discover your spiritual gifts. Then, get involved in a ministry so you can use them.

🌹 Always go the extra mile...whether for a spouse, child, or friend.

🌹 Make it a goal to always make good on your promises, no matter how long it takes.

🌹 Display what you believe by how you behave.

🌹 Whenever you look back on your life, be positive.

🌹 If you seek God's wisdom over opportunity, opportunity will usually follow.

🌹 Change is a process, not an event.

☞ Follow the prompting of your heart rather than the desires of your flesh.

☞ Refuse to be lazy. Take control of your time.

☞ Have someone over on the spur of the moment.

☞ Enjoy each day as if it were your last.

☞ When you spend time with God, His Word, and other people, you are investing in eternity.

7. What plans does the Lord have for your life?

8. What three things will we do when we believe in our hearts that God has a future for us?

Therefore, if anyone is in Christ, he is a new creation; old things have passed away; behold, all things have become new. Now all things are of God, who has reconciled us to Himself through Jesus Christ, and has given us the ministry of reconciliation, that is, that God was in Christ reconciling the world to Himself, not imputing their trespasses to them, and has committed to us the word of reconciliation. 2 Corinthians 5:17-19

9. To what ministry has the Lord called you in your walk, at home, at work, at school, at church? Write down your thoughts.

_____

_____

_____

_____

_____

_____

_____

_____

_____

_____

Week 10 Day 5

> *Bow your heart before the Lord in prayer before completing today's Bible study. Thank Him for His comfort and Healing in your life through the truth of His word.*

A Fresh Beginning

1. Through all the pain, suffering, heartache and trials of looking directly at the truth of your past experience, what is one thing you have gained?

2. To summarize your feelings, finish these statements:

In the future when I am confronted with painful feelings, I will remember to get real with God by taking the Four steps: 1. SEE   2. _____   3. _____   4._____ to be SET FREE.

What if your child, friend, spouse or a family member begins to grow a root of bitterness from a small or big hurt in their life and they are weighed down **with a junk drawer in their heart**. What tools can you share with them to help them clean out that junk drawer?

3. Fill in the blanks: Blessed *be the God and Father of our Lord Jesus Christ, the Father of _____ and God of ___ _____, who _____ us in all our tribulation, that we may be able to _____ those who are in any trouble, with the _____ with which we ourselves are _____ by God. 2 Corinthians 1:3-4*

Grace Grants us Freedom from Sin and the Flesh

Grace grants us freedom from sin and the flesh, and it grants us freedom to love and to serve. We don't serve to earn favor with God or people. We will serve others in freedom, to the glory of God.

For you, dear friends have been called to live in freedom— not freedom to satisfy your sinful nature, but freedom to serve one another. Galatians 5:13

4. What are we called to live in?

Learning God's Truth

This week's memory verse:

🌹 _____ _____ said to _____ Jews who _____ Him, "If you _____ in My word, you are My disciples _____, and you shall know___ ___, and the_____ shall make you free John. 8:31:32

But God, who is rich in mercy, because of His great love with which He loved us, even when we were dead in trespasses, made us alive together with Christ (by grace you have been saved) and raised us up together, and made us sit together in the heavenly places in Christ Jesus, that in the ages to come He might show the exceeding riches of His grace in His kindness toward us in Christ Jesus. For by grace you have been saved through faith, and that not of yourselves; it is the gift of God, not of works, lest anyone should boast. For we are His workmanship, created in Christ Jesus for good works, which God prepared beforehand that we should walk in them. Ephesians 2:4-10

5. Grace enables us to have a new life in Christ. What does this verse indicate this new life is to include?

6. Read John 8:32 you shall know the truth and the truth shall make you free. Where do you find the truth?

A Letter from The Heart

Dear Tammy

While curling my hair this morning I came to realize why I took **Healed and Set Free** Bible study. It was to clean out the junk drawer in my heart and forgive my abusers. But it has also made me look at myself. I am a lot like my dad. When my parent's marriage wasn't so good, Dad would run to me. I was his comfort. I do the same thing, only I turn to other men. When things got bad between my husband and me, I'd kick him out and go find someone who would love me the way I was taught to love, "SEX".

Since I have been in this Bible study I don't need that any more. When my husband went to jail,. I did not want or need a man to be there for me this time. I am so thankful for this Bible Study! It has helped me **SEE** all the evil that I was doing in my life.

I know Jesus loves me and He has forgiven me. I have also been able to forgive myself. Tammy, thank you for this Bible Study!

🌹 A healed woman

SEE, GIVE, FORGIVE, FORGET, BE SET FREE

Learning God's Word

This week's memory verse:
🌹 *Then Jesus said to those Jews who believed Him, "If ___ abide in My word, ___ are My disciples indeed, ___ and ___ shall know the truth, and the truth shall make ___ free. John. 8:31:32*

Freedom

Freedom to love God with our entire mind is truly experiencing His love for us. From our own power we cannot change the way we think, but when we draw near to God and spend time getting to know Him by getting to know His Word, He uses the Truth to transform how we think. When we feel weak or overwhelmed by life, we can use Scriptures to give us strength. He can use the Truths we find in His Word to give us strength and to set us free to go on.

> I like to think of God's Holy Word as an instrument He uses in our life to **guide, comfort, correct, rebuke, and teach.** The passages we commit to memory are like a surgeon's sterilized tools carefully arranged on instrument trays and ready for His expert use. When there is a need in our life, God can pick up exactly the verse we need and cut right to our heart. He has done it for me, and I know He will do it for you.

We can also love God with our entire mind by the choices we make. We can choose to dwell on the negative, on our weakness and on our pain, or we can let those things turn us to God. Regardless of how life looks or feels, we can make the deliberate decision to yield to God's wisdom and His ways. We can choose, for instance, too:

- ❦ Believe the truths of the Bible rather than trust our emotions.
- ❦ Work on what is real rather than worry about what is unreal.
- ❦ Reach forward and press on rather than remaining a prisoner of the past.
- ❦ Act on what is revealed in Scripture rather than on what appears to be true in the world.
- ❦ By making these choices, we are choosing to love God with our entire mind. The result is what I call the right prospective, that peace and well being the Spirit gives when we think and act on the truths of the Bible.

AUTHOR'S REFLECTION
Lord, Help Me
Finish Well

I am not perfect by any means, many challenges still confront me. God has given me hope for the future. He desires for me to fight the good fight and finish well. I know I can talk to the Lord and be completely honest with Him, with no performances.

I can say, "Today I'm not feeling that I can trust. Help me, Lord, to have a heart to trust." "Today I'm really upset with my children, help me, Lord, to have patience and to love and train my children in your way."

A Real friend

The one thing I really have experienced with the Lord is that I can tell Him anything. He is not going to tell anyone else. He will comfort me and work with me to **SEE, GIVE, FORGIVE, FORGET, BE SET FREE.**

He will never stop loving me. That is a real friend! A friend can love you in spite of who you are. A friend can comfort you wherever you are. A friend can speak to you in honesty, but then encourage you to move to the next step.

God has shown me, by what He has done in my life and the lives of so many people I know, that I can really trust Him. Again and again in the face of pain, doubt and despair my God has proven himself trustworthy.

Trusting God with My Past, Present, and Future.

I think of my dear friend Kelly Vincent - who lost her beloved husband in an accident. She was four months pregnant with their first child. They were so in love. I wondered what she would do as a single parent, how she would go on without her husband. But what a privilege it has been to see the way God has provided for my sweet friend through the years. He has taken her step by step. She has learned to trust God for all her needs. He has taken her from being a widow that was going to take her own life to a new bride blessed with a wonderful godly husband. Her new husband Roger adopted her little girl. She speaks boldly of God's love and grace in her life.

I think of Joni Erickson Tada - who became a quadriplegic as a teenager but who speaks, writes, draws, and sings so eloquently about God's goodness.

I think of my husband Rick - who came from a broken home. His step-father was a convict who was in and out of prison. Rick followed right along in his example, in and out of trouble with the law.

God took a man who had no future, who stoled, lied, used drugs, partied, was in drunken fights, and led a lifestyle of sexual immorality, and forever changed him when he gave his life to Christ Jesus. Step by step, Rick learned the real meaning of life, the great fulfillment of serving His great Savior. He left his old lifestyle of emptiness in the past and reached toward the higher calling in Christ Jesus. He became a senior Pastor at the age of 25 and started two other Calvary Chapel churches before the age of 30, as well as a Christian school. He is truly a man after Gods own heart. His daily devotions and personal relationship with Christ are his first and most important desire. Everything else, being a husband, dad, leading our home, being a pastor over the Church and school, comes after his time with Christ Jesus. When you seek God first He gives you the strength and wisdom to face the rest.

I think of my own life - God took a teenage girl who distrusted men for good reason and healed that distrust by giving me a husband who is godly, protective, dependable, and loving.

God took a very angry, confused, broken woman and Set me Free so that I could, by God's grace, become a loving wife and loving mom to our two children.

God took a very shy little girl that was in a shell of shame from sexual abuse, assumed retarded in the second grade, healed me from my past, and allowed me to point women to the true Healer. (God's strength is made perfect in our weakness. 2 Corinthians 12:9). God is able to do much more then I could ever dream to make me what He wants me to be.

God has taken a shameful past that could have destroyed my life and marriage and has turned it around to offer others comfort with the same comfort God has given me, and has offered a fresh beginning to other hurting people through the writing of "Healed and Set Free."

God's Gift of Trust for the Future

God gives us all a gift of trust for our future. *He will work all things together for good for those who love Him and are called according to His purpose. (Romans 8:28).*

We can trust God with our future as these examples show. He is a God that can be trusted. Again and again in my own life He has given me exactly what I needed in order to grow spiritually and to heal me from my past and to be Set Free to move toward Him. Let's keep Jesus first in our daily lives.

God gives us all a gift of trust for our future. Satan can use trials and suffering to destroy us or we can let the trials and suffering drive us to Christ to become Christian people who survive in God's perfect love. May we have a heart to finish this race well, and to be steadfast in the will of God.

Review

Review the key points in Healed and Set Free. Reflect on the truth you have learned from this Study.

From Chapter 1 ~ Getting real with God

1. What comes first, SEE or FORGET? (When the hurt is so deep)

2. Christ Jesus, help me SEE what could be defiling my heart. Why do we need to See what is in our hearts?

3. **Tool #1 "SEE "**: I must _____ the truth about what is in my heart, so I'm not defiled.

   _____ *carefully lest anyone fall short of the grace of God; lest any _____ of bitterness springing up _____ trouble, and by this _____ become defiled. Hebrew 12:15.*

Chapter 2 ~ Knowing Gods Heart

4. *"My sheep hear My voice, and I know them, and they follow Me." John 10:27*
   What does God ask of you in order for God to provide the protection you need?

5. **Tool #2 :** I must **GIVE** the sin in repentance, knowing Christ is waiting to take it. (I must be sorry enough to change and choose to go God's way over my own way.)

   *For godly _____ produces repentance leading to salvation, not to be regretted; but the _____ of the world produces death.
   2 Corinthians 7:10*

Although they knew God, they did not glorify Him as God, nor were thankful, but became futile in their thoughts, and their foolish hearts were darkened. Professing to be wise, they became fools. Romans 1:21-22

6. Have your thoughts become unprofitable, unsuccessful, and futile? Ask God to show you 10 things for which you can be thankful. What is true today that you can see more clearly about your future? Don't let your heart become foolish and darkened by the past hurt.

Lord,

*I pray, help me move past the futile thoughts and help me keep my heart from being foolish and darkened by the hurts. Help me **SEE** what I need to give to Christ. In Jesus' name.*

SEE, GIVE, FORGIVE, FORGET, BE SET FREE

Chapter 3 ~ Letting Go Of Anger

My strongest testimony is my daily walk.

Two things were necessary for me to change this destructive behavior of Anger

🌹 **SEE**—why I was letting myself get so upset. Either I was not trusting God or I was keeping a record of wrongs towards another person.

🌹 **GIVE**—I had to give my struggle with "over the edge" anger to God in prayer everyday. I prayed for self-control. **Every time I lost control I would apologize and ask for forgiveness.** After humbling myself time and time again, I began to have self-control over my actions and destructive emotions. I found I had to practice self-control one day at a time. I still have stress and disappointments, and I will until the day I meet Jesus face to face. However I can now choose how to act or react to stress and disappointments. *For godly sorrow produces repentance to salvation, not to be regretted; but the sorrow of the world produces death. 2 Corinthians 7:10*

7. Do you find yourself practicing self-control when you're stressed out or angry?

8. If you go "over the edge" with anger and hurt someone, do you ask for forgiveness from that person for your actions towards them?

Chapter 4 ~ Forgiving the Unacceptable

Three enemies prevent you from walking in forgiveness: the devil, your flesh and the world. Perhaps God's most beautiful gift to the believer is His provision for forgiveness and reconciliation.

9. **Tool #3 :** Learn how **I must FORGIVE**, as I am forgiven by Christ. (Forgiving those that hurt, bruised, wronged, hurt, rejected, betrayed or harmed me whether unintentionally or deliberately.) Ask God to Forgive you for holding unforgiveness and know that He will.

   Bearing with one another, and forgiving _____, if anyone has a complaint against another; even as Christ forgave ____, so ____ also must do. Colossians 3:13

10. In Chapter 4, you learned the choices to follow the wrong answers or the right answers concerning hurts. Write down 2 wrong choices not to follow.

    _____ , _____

11. I have forgiven _____ for...

For God has not given us a spirit of fear, but of power and of love and of a sound mind. 2 Timothy 1:7

Chapter 5 ~ Conquering Depression

12. When I opened my heart to the Healer He set me free from...

A merry heart does good, like medicine, but a broken spirit dries the bones. Proverbs 17:22

This week lets put the perspective where it belongs. Let's be reminded that whatever happens doesn't have to get us down. Let's be quick to **SEE, GIVE, FORGIVE, FORGET, AND BE SET FREE** to laugh and enjoy life. The pain will then dissolve, frustrations vanish, and burdens roll away when we can make light of our own and other's shortcomings.

Chapter 6 ~ Living to Eat or Eating to live

SEE the Stronghold

- You can make the choice to change and enter into a self-controlled life with the help of God.

- Self-control is the ability from the Holy Spirit to say no to what is wrong and to say yes to what is right. Take each day one at a time. Face the truth about any weakness in your life. Ask for God's strength to apply self-control in this area.

13. Finish the statements that apply to you by inserting *self-control.*

- If I want to over eat at meals or during the day I can remember the fruit of the Spirit of_____ to stop eating once I'm full.

- If I want to vomit after meals I can remember the fruit of the Spirit of_____ not to vomit after meals.

- If I want to starve myself I can remember the fruit of the Spirit of_____ to eat when I'm hungry and not let the food control me.

Chapter 7 ~ Remember to Forget • FORGET

14. **Tool #4 :** I must **FORGET** by remembering to no longer dwell on the hurt.

Brethren, I do not count myself to have apprehended; but one thing I do, forgetting those things which are _____ and reaching forward to those things which are _____. Philippians 3:13.

Instead, like Paul, we must keep on forgetting those things that have hurt us, which hold us back. Paul doesn't want to rest on his past accomplishments and neither should we.

SEE, GIVE, FORGIVE, FORGET, BE SET FREE

Paul doesn't want his past mistakes nor past hurts to keep him from moving on and neither should we. Don't let the past hold you back.

Again and again, I have told myself, "No, Tam, that is past, that is over. That is no longer real. Don't dwell on it. Don't let it hold you back". "Forget that which would keep you from moving forward in faith and in your spiritual growth." I look to the past only to remember God's role in solving the problems and pains of yesterday. I remember His gracious provision for His presence, His faithfulness, His compassion, His healing for me.

Brethren, I do not count myself to have apprehended; but one thing I do, forgetting those things which are behind and reaching forward to those things which are ahead. Philippians 3:13

15. I now have hope that...

- When you are faced with past reminders of hurts such as a smell, a phrase, a place, or a song recognize that it's coming from the snake planning his angle to try to get you back in those shackles.

Quickly get real with God about what is in your heart. Then SEE ,GIVE, FORGIVE, FORGET and remember. Philippians 3:13.

16. Write out Philippians 3:13

Chapter 8 ~ Healed and Set Free

17. Healed and Set Free: Christ will open the shackles from my past hurts showing me the truth so I can become a cleansed vessel that is Healed and Set Free.

You shall know the _____, and the _____ shall make you free. Therefore, if the Son makes you free, you shall be free indeed. John 8:32-36.

18. One way I can help others to heal is...

Words to Remember

Fill in the blanks:
Then our mouth was _____ with laughter, and our tongue with _____. Then they said among the nations, "The Lord has done _____things for them." The Lord has done great_____ for us, and we are glad. Psalm 126:2-3

SEE, GIVE, FORGIVE, FORGET, BE SET FREE

Share your healing with others and with Calvary Chapel of Idaho Falls. We would love to hear all about how God has **Healed and Set you free**. Write down your personal story and mail it into Calvary Chapel of Idaho Falls, Idaho. (Ministry **Healed and Set Free**.)

An Invitation to Write:

_____

_____

_____

_____

_____

_____

_____

_____

_____

_____

_____

_____

_____

_____

_____

_____

_____

Postal: Calvary Chapel P.O. Box 52243 Idaho Falls, Idaho 83405
or E-mail: calvary@ida.net

He who has begun a good work in you will complete it until the day of Jesus Christ.
Philippians 1:6

Don't put this study on the shelf and forget it.
Constantly renew your thinking in order to:
SEE, GIVE, FORGIVE, FORGET, BE SET FREE
Pass it on:
Comfort others the way you have been comforted
in His word.

Forgiveness

Will you forgive me of the things both said and done?
There will be no tomorrow but before the setting sun,
let us break the bonds of bitterness and let's kill the fatted calf.
Let's forget the pain and anger, letting go of all the past.

Please forgive me.

Will you forgive me? And don't just say you do.
If our hearts are opened wide, our love He will renew.
For if I say I am in Him, then I must now forgive.

He died and suffered agony
so I will not forget
that there still remains redemption,
buying back that which is lost.
For the price of our forgiveness
came at the highest cost.

Let us break the bonds of bitterness
and let's kill the fatted calf.

Let's forget the pain and anger,
letting go of all the past.

Let there be joy and laughter
and let us now embrace.

Our voices sing in harmony,
our sorrow turned to Grace and Forgiveness.

-Dave Messenger

SEE, GIVE, FORGIVE, FORGET, BE SET FREE

Dear Fellow Laborer in Christ Jesus,

If you ever wonder how God can use you to make a difference, just look at those He used in the Bible and take heart. God used and uses people to make a difference. People! Not superhumans or geniuses. God has a plan and a purpose for every believer. You have been set aside for a very special ministry if you're getting ready to lead a Healed & Set Free Bible study. You will have many blessings in front of you as God's truth unfolds in the hearts of those in your group.

I may or may not know you personally, but I do know that if you are stepping out in faith and have a God-given desire to see others set free from chains of emotional scars, then you also are one who has been hurt deeply in some way. You know all about the shackles of the painful hurts. You also know how incredible it feels to be set free from those shackles. If you desire to lead a *Healed and Set Free Bible Study* in your church or in your home, it's exciting to open your arms to others so they can experience that same peace and freedom. As you reach out with God's love, you are making yourself available and opening your arms to others that are hurting, angry, and scared. Some may not be sure they will be accepted or loved by you, and some may not feel they can trust anyone with their deep, dark hurt that has chipped away at their peace.

If there is one clear lesson I can leave with you, if you remember anything from this letter, remember this: you will be walking on Satan's turf.

Many of those that you will meet with have been taken captive and have painful, heavy shackles that have been weighing them down for 10 years, 20 years, or some even 50 years. You are not going to a tea party where you can wear your high heels and a pretty, white dress. **You are going to war for those in your group. Get on your battle boots and the full armor of God.** It's time to battle in the Spirit. God is bigger than all of our hurts and fears.

PRAY! -To loose the bonds of wickedness.

PRAY! -To undo the heavy burdens from the past.

PRAY! -To let the oppressed go free.

PRAY!   *PRAY!*   *PRAY!*

"It's not by might, nor by power, but by My Spirit," says the Lord of hosts. Zechariah 4:6

He who is in you (Christ) is greater than he who is in the world (Satan.) 1 John 4:4

> *Prayer will unleash the power of God in the lives of the members of your group and will remind you that you are not responsible to set anyone free in your own strength. Jesus is the one who heals the brokenhearted and binds up their wounds. Psalm 147:3*

In closing, my prayers and heart are with you as you open your arms of God's love and truth to hurting people.

Set Free in Christ

Tammy Brown

If you would like more information about a Healed & Set Free Leader's guide, call; Calvary Chapel Idaho Falls 208-524-4747. This study guide will help you through the next ten weeks of the Healed & Set Free Bible study. Keep this guide readily available and read it each week to remind yourself of your role as a leader.

Notes

Chapter 1

Linda Cochrane, Forgiven and Set Free, Copyright 1986,1991,1996 Baker Books House Company. Used by permission from author

The Empty Chair (Author unknown)

Chapter 2

Bruce Bickel and Stan Jantz, God Is In The Small Stuff, Copyright 1998 Promise Press. Used by permission from author's.

Elizabeth George, A Woman After God's Own Heart, Copyrights 1997 Harvest House Publishers. Used by permission from author.

Linda Cochrane, Forgiven and Set Free, Copyright 1986,1991,1996 Baker Books House Company. Used by permission from author.

Dave Messenger, Broken Vessel, Copyright 1998 Used by permission.

Chapter 3

Elizabeth George, A Woman After God's Own Heart, Copyrights 1997 Harvest House Publishers. Used by permission from author.

Linda Cochrane, Forgiven and Set Free, Copyright 1986,1991,1996 Baker Books House Company. Used by permission from author.

Jonnie Landis, The Path, Copyright.© Used by permission from author.

Chapter 4

Zach Blickens, Chains I've Grown To Know, copyright 1998. Used by permission.

Linda Cochrane, Forgiven and Set Free, Copyright 1986,1991,1996 Baker Books House Company. Used by permission from author.

Self Preservation (Author unknown)

Chapter 5

Linda Cochrane, Forgiven and Set Free, Copyright 1986,1991,1996 Baker Books House Company. Used by permission from author.

Elizabeth George, A Woman After God's Own Heart, Copyrights 1997 Harvest House Publishers. Used by permission from author.

Understanding Your Emotions (Author unknown)

How You Spent Your Dash? (Author unknown)

Chapter 7

Bruce Bickel and Stan Jantz, God Is In The Small Stuff, Copyright 1998 Promise Press. Used by permission from author's.

Elizabeth George, Loving God With All Your Mind, Copyrights 1994 Harvest House Publishers. Used by permission by from author.

Elizabeth George, A Woman After God's Own Heart, Copyrights 1997 Harvest House Publishers. Used by permission from author.

Let Go, Let God (Author unknown)

Mary Korzan, When You Thought I Wasn't Looking, Copyright 1980 used by permission from author.

Chapter 8

Elizabeth George, A Woman After God's Own Heart, Copyrights 1997 Harvest House Publishers. Used by permission from author.

Bruce Bickel and Stan Jantz, God Is In The Small Stuff, Copyright 1998 Promise Press. Used by permission from author's.

Dave Messenger, Forgiveness, Copyright 1998. Used by permission.

Healed and Set Free... from lingering hurts

Women's Bible Study

By Tammy Brown

Also from Tammy Brown

Healed and Set Free... from lingering hurts

Teen Girl's Bible Study

By Tammy Brown

Healed and Set Free... from lingering hurts

Men's Bible Study

By Rick and Tammy Brown